ADVANCED LEVEL **Six-Way Paragraphs**

in the Content Areas

ADVANCED LEVEL

Six-Way Paragraphs
in the Content Areas

100 Passages for Developing
the Six Essential Categories of Comprehension in the
Humanities, Social Studies, Science, and Mathematics

**based on
the work of
W a l t e r
P a u k**

JAMESTOWN PUBLISHERS

a division of NTC/CONTEMPORARY PUBLISHING GROUP
Lincolnwood, Illinois USA

Readability

Passages 1–25: Level J
Passages 26–50: Level K
Passages 51–75: Level L
Passages 76–100: Level L+

ISBN: 0-8092-0373-1

Published by Jamestown Publishers,
a division of NTC/Contemporary Publishing Group, Inc.
4255 West Touhy Avenue, Lincolnwood (Chicago), Illinois 60712-1975 U.S.A.

10 11 12 QVR 14 13 12

Contents

To the Student

To succeed in the courses you take, one of the most important skills you can have is good reading ability. Depending on the content, different courses require different types of reading. For example, if material is easy for you or you have studied it before, you may read it quickly. If the material is new or difficult, you may need to read more slowly. In fact, you may need to read it several times. In all the courses you take, you will be able to use the reading skills featured in this book.

The passages in the book are readings in four general categories: the humanities, social studies, science, and mathematics. Each category has several subcategories. For example, social studies may include passages in areas such as history, geography, and anthropology. Mathematics may include consumer and computer topics and puzzles as well as basic mathematical facts. Humanities passages deal with literature, music, art, and architecture.

Certain subject areas may be unfamiliar to you. But this book does not require you to master many new facts. Instead, its purpose is to show you *how to read in the content areas*. You will learn techniques that textbook writers use to organize material. You will see how new information can be applied to things you already know. And you will learn about the six skills that can help you read just about anything.

The Six Types of Questions

In this book, the basic skills necessary for reading factual material are taught through the use of the following six types of questions: main idea, subject matter, supporting details, conclusion, clarifying devices, and vocabulary in context.

Main Idea. While reading anything it is a good idea to ask yourself, What point is the writer trying to make? Once you ask this question, your mind will be looking for an answer, and chances are that you will find one. But if you don't focus in this way, all things seem equal. Nothing stands out.

Try to find the main idea in the following humanities passage by asking, What point is the writer trying to make?

> Many brilliant people have been superstitious. Rousseau, the famous French philosopher, believed he had a ghost for a companion. William Blake, an English writer and painter, thought he was a brother to Socrates, who had died in 399 B.C.! And Sir Walter Scott would never go to Melrose Abbey when the full moon shone brightly.

A good answer here is, A lot of famous people from history have been superstitious. This passage is fairly easy to figure out because the first sentence is an excellent topic sentence.

The next example, from science, does not have a topic sentence. Nevertheless, the question What point is the writer trying to make? can still be answered. This time, think about the passage and come up with your own answer.

> The furry platypus, a native of Australia and Tasmania, looks like a mammal at first glance. Upon studying it more closely, however, one recognizes the birdlike characteristics that have puzzled scientists. For example, like some water birds, the platypus has webbed feet. It also has a leathery bill like a duck. That's how the animal got its name, the "duck-billed platypus." In addition, the semi-aquatic platypus lays eggs like a bird.

This passage may have required a bit more thought, and the correct answer is a summary type answer. Compare your answer with the following main idea statement: The furry platypus looks like a mammal but has several birdlike characteristics.

Subject Matter. This question looks easy and often is easy. But don't let that fool you into thinking it isn't important. The subject matter question can help you with the most important skill of all in reading and learning: concentration. With it, you comprehend and learn. Without it, you fail.

Here is the secret for gaining concentration: After reading the first few lines of something, ask yourself, What is the subject matter of this passage? Instantly, you will be thinking about the passage. You will be concentrating. If you don't ask this question, your eyes will move across the lines of print, yet your mind may be thinking of other things.

By asking this question as you read each passage in this book, you will master the skill so well that it will carry over to everything you read.

Let's see how this method works. Here is a short passage from science:

> Monarch butterflies are a common summer sight in the northern United States and Canada. These large orange and black insects brighten parks and gardens as they flit among the flowers. What makes monarchs particularly interesting is that they migrate—all the way to California or Mexico and back. They are thought to be the only insect that does this.

On finishing the first sentence your thought should have been something like, *Ah, a passage on monarch butterflies. Maybe I can learn something about how they migrate.* If it was, your head was in the right place. By focusing right away on the subject matter, you will be concentrating, you will be looking for something, your attitude will be superb, and, best of all, you will be understanding, learning, and remembering.

Supporting Details. In common usage, the word *detail* has taken on the meaning of "something relatively unimportant." But details are important. Details are the plaster, board, and brick of a building, while main ideas are the large, strong, steel or wooden beams. A solid, well-written passage must contain both.

The bulk of a factual passage is made up of details that support the main idea. The main idea is often buried among the details. You have to dig to distinguish between them. Here are some characteristics that can help you see the difference between supporting details and main ideas.

First, supporting details come in various forms, such as examples, explanations, descriptions, definitions, comparisons, contrasts, exceptions, analogies, similes, and metaphors.

Second, these various kinds of details are used to support the main idea. The words themselves—supporting details—spell out their job. So when you have trouble finding the main idea, take a passage apart sentence by sentence, asking, "Does this sentence support something, or is this the thing being supported?" In other words, you must not only separate the two but must also see how they help one another. The main idea can often be expressed in a single sentence. But a sentence cannot tell a complete story. The writer must use additional sentences to give a full picture.

The following social studies passage shows how important details are for providing a full picture of what the writer had in mind.

> Examination of the historical record doesn't support the notion that Cleopatra pursued men to any great extent. In fact, there is no evidence connecting her to any men other than, first, Julius Caesar, and then Mark Antony. Her relationship with Antony did not begin until four years after Caesar's death. Both unions were recognized in Egypt as marriages, and she was apparently a faithful and helpful wife to both men.

Here the main idea is in the first sentence. Having stated the main idea, the writer goes on to give example after example showing why it is true. These examples are supporting details.

Conclusion. As a reader moves through a passage, grasping the main idea and supporting details, it is natural for him or her to begin to guess an ending or conclusion. Some passages contain conclusions; others do not. It all depends on the writer's purpose. For example, some passages simply describe a process—how something is done. It is not always necessary to draw a conclusion from such a passage.

In some passages with conclusions, the writer states the conclusion. But in most passages in this book, the conclusion is merely implied. That is, the writer seems to have come to a conclusion but has not stated it. It is up to you to draw that conclusion.

In the following mathematics passage, the author strongly implies a conclusion but does not state it directly.

> Fermat's Last Theorem, hinted at by Pierre de Fermat in the 17th century, was the most significant unproved theorem in higher mathematics. It was not conclusively demonstrated to be true until 1994. At that time mathematician Andrew Wiles, who had spent years struggling with the problem, corrected his earlier 1993 proof, and his astonished colleagues certified his work as legitimate.

From the passage above, we can draw the conclusion that Andrew Wiles was both a brilliant and a persistent mathematician.

Sometimes a writer will ask you to draw a conclusion by applying what you have learned to a new situation, as in the following passage.

> In July 1918 the entire family of Czar Nicholas II of Russia was assassinated by Bolshevik revolutionaries in Siberia. Almost immediately, rumors began that the youngest daughter, 17-year-old Anastasia, had been spared, and pretenders began to proliferate: one, a woman named Anna Anderson, claimed to be Anastasia until her death in 1984. DNA testing has laid Anderson's story to rest. She was proven to be a fraud when the remains of all of Nicholas's children were found and identified at the assassination site.

If you were asked what this passage suggests about the value of DNA testing, you would have to generalize beyond the passage to pick the correct answer, "that there will be fewer false claims to thrones."

Looking for a conclusion puts you in the shoes of a detective. While reading, you have to think, *Where is the writer leading me? What conclusion will I be able to draw?* And, like a detective, you must try to guess the conclusion, changing the guess as you get more and more information.

Clarifying Devices. Clarifying devices are words, phrases, and techniques that a writer uses to make main ideas, subideas, and supporting details clear and interesting. By knowing some of these clarifying and controlling devices, you will be better able to recognize them in the passages you read. By recognizing them, you will be able to read with greater comprehension and speed.

Transitional or Signal Words. The largest single group of clarifying devices, and the most widely used, are transitional or signal words. For example, here are some signal words that you see all the time: *first, second, next, last,* and *finally.* A writer uses such words to keep ideas, steps in a process, or lists in order. Other transitional words include *however, in brief, in conclusion, above all, therefore, since, because,* and *consequently.* —————

When you see transitional words, consider what they mean. A transitional word like *or* tells you that another option, or choice, is coming. Words like *but* and *however* signal that a contrast, or change in point of view, will follow.

Organizational Patterns. Organizational patterns are also clarifying devices. One such pattern is the chronological pattern, in which events unfold in the order of time: one thing happens first, then another, and another, and so on. A time pattern orders events. The event may take place in five minutes or over a period of hundreds of years.

There are other organizational patterns as well. Writers may use spatial descriptions to tell what things look like. They may use lists of examples to make their point. In science writing, they may use scientific data. Seeing the organizational pattern will help you read the material more easily.

Textual Devices. Textbook writers in particular use patterns or particular text styles to make their ideas clear. Bulleted lists, subheads, and boldfaced or italicized words help to highlight important ideas in the text. Charts or diagrams help you to visualize concepts more easily than if they are just explained in words.

Literal Versus Figurative Language. Sometimes a writer's words do not mean exactly what they seem to on first reading. For example, a writer may say, "The great tragedy shattered the hero of the story." You may know *shattered* as meaning "breaking into pieces." The word is often applied to breakable objects, but here it is applied to a person's feelings. Being alert to such special meanings of words can help you better appreciate the writer's meaning.

Two literary devices that writers use to present ideas in interesting ways are similes (SIM-a-lees) and metaphors (MET-a-fors). Both are used to make comparisons that add color and power to ideas. An example of a simile is She has a mind like a computer. In this simile, a person's mind is compared to a computer. A simile always uses the words *like, as,* or *than* to make a comparison. The metaphor, on the other hand, makes a direct comparison: Her mind is a computer.

Vocabulary in Context. How accurate are you in using words you think you already know? Do you know that the word *exotic* means "a thing or person from a foreign country?" So, exotic flowers and exotic costumes are flowers and costumes from foreign countries. *Exotic* has been used incorrectly so often and for so long that it has developed a second meaning. Most people use *exotic* to mean "strikingly unusual, as in color or design."

Many people think that the words *imply* and *infer* mean the same thing. They do not. A writer may imply, or suggest, something. The reader then infers what the writer implied. In other words, to imply is to "suggest an idea." To infer is to "take meaning out."

It is easy to see what would happen to a passage if a reader skipped a word or two that he or she did not know and imposed fuzzy meanings on a few others. The result would inevitably be a gross misunderstanding of the writer's message. You will become a better reader if you learn the exact meanings and different shades of meaning of the words that are already familiar to you.

In this book, you should be able to figure out the meanings of many words from their context—that is, from the words and phrases around them. If this method does not work for you, however, you may consult a dictionary.

Answering the Main Idea Question

The main idea questions in this book are not the usual multiple-choice variety from which you must select the one correct statement. Rather, you are given three statements and are asked to select the statement that expresses the main idea of the passage, the statement that is too narrow, and the statement that is too broad. You have to work hard and actively to identify all three statements correctly. This new type of question teaches you to recognize the differences among statements that, at first, seem almost equal.

To help you handle these questions, let's go behind the scenes to see how the main idea questions in this book were constructed. The true main idea statement was always written first. It had to be neat, succinct, and positive. The main idea tells who or what the subject of the passage is. It also answers the question Does what? or Is what? Next, keeping the main idea statement in mind, the other two statements were written. They are variations of the main idea statement. The "too narrow" statement had to be in line with the main idea but express only part of it. Likewise, the "too broad" statement had to be in line with the main idea but be too general in scope.

Read the science passage below. Then, to learn how to answer the main idea questions, follow the instructions in the box. The answer to each part of the question has been filled in for you. The score for each answer has also been marked.

An Unusual Fish

Strange-looking creatures dwell in the deepest parts of the ocean, where no light ever reaches. One of the inhabitants of this dark, high-pressure underwater habitat is the anglerfish. It has several unusual features.

Since it is so dark in the depths of Davy Jones's Locker, it is very difficult for fish to spot possible prey or to find mates. The female anglerfish solves the hunting problem by means of a long tentacle of flesh, up to four inches long, which extends upward from the top of her body. This tentacle acts as a fishing pole of sorts: its end emits a glowing light that in the pitch darkness serves to attract smaller fish. At the appropriate moment, the female anglerfish quickly snaps up her prey.

Nature has apparently solved the anglerfish's problem of finding a mate by developing a relationship in which the male of the species acts as a parasite to the female. The much smaller male anglerfish attaches itself to a female early in its life by biting into her flesh. His mouth becomes firmly affixed to the female's skin, and soon they are even sharing the same bloodstream! After this stage has been reached, the male receives his nourishment through the connection to the female, and soon his own digestive organs and other major organs deteriorate. Only the reproductive organs remain intact.

Main Idea	1		Answer	Score
	Mark the *main idea*		M	15
	Mark the statement that is *too broad*		B	5
	Mark the statement that is *too narrow*		N	5

a. The anglerfish has special adaptations that help it live in the darkness of the ocean's depths.　　　　M　　15

[This statement gathers all the important points. It gives a correct picture of the main idea in a brief way: (1) anglerfish, (2) live in the darkness, (3) special adaptations.]

b. Strange-looking creatures live in the depths of the sea.　　　　B　　5

[This statement is too broad. It refers to strange-looking sea creatures, but it doesn't tell which ones or what they do.]

c. The female anglerfish has a special way of attracting other fish.　　　　N　　5

[This statement is correct, but it is too narrow. It refers to only one of the anglerfish's special adaptations.]

Getting the Most Out of This Book

The following steps could be called "tricks of the trade." Your teachers might call them "rules for learning." It doesn't matter what they are called. What does matter is that they work.

Think about the title. A famous language expert proposes the following "trick" to use when reading. "The first thing to do is to read the title. Then spend a few moments thinking about it."

Writers spend much time thinking up good titles. They try to pack a lot of meaning into them. It makes sense, then, for you to spend a few seconds trying to dig out some meaning. These few moments of thought will give you a head start on a passage.

Thinking about the title can help you in another way too. It helps you concentrate on a passage before you begin reading. Why does this happen? Thinking about the title fills your head with thoughts about the passage. There's no room for anything else to get in to break your concentration.

The Dot Step. Here is a method that will speed up your reading. It also builds comprehension at the same time.

Spend a few moments with the title. Then read quickly through the passage. Next, without looking back, answer the six questions by placing a dot in the box next to each answer of your choice. The dots will be your "unofficial" answers. For the main idea question (question 1) place your dot in the box next to the statement that you think is the main idea.

The dot system helps by making you think hard on your first, fast reading. The practice you gain by trying to grasp and remember ideas makes you a stronger reader.

The Checkmark Step. First, answer the main idea question. Follow the steps that are given above each set of statements for this question. Use a capital letter to mark your final answer to each part of the main idea question.

You have answered the other five questions with a dot. Now read the passage once more carefully. This time, mark your final answer to each question by placing a checkmark (√) in the box next to the answer of your choice. The answers with the checkmarks are the ones that will count toward your score.

The Diagnostic Chart. Now move your final answers to the Diagnostic Chart for the passage. These charts start on page 209.

Use the row of boxes beside Passage 1 for the answers to the first passage. Use the row of boxes beside Passage 2 for the answers to the second passage, and so on. Write the letter of your answer to the left of the dotted line in each block.

Correct your answers using the Answer Keys on pages 204–207. When scoring your answers, do not use an *x* for incorrect or a *c* for correct. Instead, use this method: If your choice is incorrect, write the letter of the correct answer to the right of the dotted line in the block.

Thus, the row of answers for each passage will show your incorrect answers. And it will also show the correct answers.

Your Total Comprehension Score. Go back to the passage you have just read. If you answered a question incorrectly, draw a line under the correct choice on the question page. Then write your score for each question on the line provided. Add the scores to get your total comprehension score. Enter that number in the box marked Total Score.

Graphing Your Progress. After you have found your total comprehension score, turn to the Progress Graphs that begin on page 214. Write your score in the box under the number of the passage. Then put an *x* along the line above the box to show your total comprehension score. Join the *x*'s as you go. This will plot a line showing your progress.

Taking Corrective Action. Your incorrect answers give you a way to teach yourself how to read better. Take the time to study these answers.

Go back to the questions. For each question you got wrong, read the correct answer (the one you have underlined) several times. With the correct answer in mind, go back to the passage itself. Read to see why the given answer is better. Try to see where you made your mistake. Try to figure out why you chose an incorrect answer.

The Steps in a Nutshell

Here's a quick review of the steps to follow. Following these steps is the way to get the most out of this book. Be sure you have read and understood everything in this To the Student section before you begin.

1. **Think about the title of the passage.** Try to get all the meaning the writer put into it.
2. **Read the passage quickly.**

3. **Answer the questions, using the dot system.** Use dots to mark your unofficial answers. Don't look back at the passage.

4. **Read the passage again—carefully.**

5. **Mark your final answers.** Put a checkmark (√) in the box to note your final answer. Use capital letters for each part of the main idea question.

6. **Mark your answers on the diagnostic chart.** Record your final answers on the diagnostic chart for the passage. Write your answers to the left of the dotted line in the answer blocks for the passage.

7. **Correct your answers.** Use the answer keys on pages 204–207. If an answer is not correct, write the correct answer in the right side of the block, beside your incorrect answer. Then go back to the question page. Place a line under the correct answer.

8. **Find your total comprehension score.** Find this by adding up the points you earned for each question. Enter the total in the box marked Total Score.

9. **Graph your progress.** Enter and plot your score on the progress graph for that passage.

10. **Take corrective action.** Read your wrong answers. Read the passage once more. Try to figure out why you were wrong.

To the Teacher

The Reading Passages

Each of the 100 passages included in this book is related to one of four general content areas: the humanities, social studies, science, or mathematics. Each of these areas has several subcategories; humanities, for example, includes passages that deal with literature, music, art, and architecture. The graphic accompanying the title of each piece identifies the general content area to which it belongs.

In addition, each piece had to meet the following two criteria: high interest level and appropriate readability level.

The high interest level was assured by choosing passages of mature content that would appeal to a wide range of readers. In essence, students read passages that will convey interesting information in a content area, whether that area is the student's chosen field of study or not.

The readability level of each passage was computed by applying Dr. Edward B. Fry's *Formula for Estimating Readability*, thus enabling the arrangement of passages according to grade levels within the book. *Six-Way Paragraphs in the Content Areas, Introductory Level* contains passages that range from reading level 4 to reading level 7, with 25 passages on each level. *Six-Way Paragraphs in the Content Areas, Middle Level* contains passages that range from reading level 7 to reading level 10, with 25 passages on each reading level. The passages in *Six-Way Paragraphs in the Content Areas, Advanced Level* range from reading level 10 to reading level 12+, with 25 passages on each reading level.

The Six Questions

This book is organized around six essential questions. The most important of these is the main idea question, which is actually a set of three statements. Students must first choose and label the statement that expresses the main idea of the passage; then they must label each of the other statements as being either too narrow or too broad to be the main idea.

In addition to the main idea question, there are five other questions. These questions are within the framework of the following five categories: subject matter, supporting details, conclusion, clarifying devices, and vocabulary in context.

By repeated practice with answering the questions within these six categories, students will develop an active, searching attitude about what they read. These six types of questions will help them become aware of what they are reading at the time they are actually seeing the words and phrases on a page. This type of thinking-while-reading sets the stage for higher comprehension and better retention.

The Diagnostic Chart

The Diagnostic Chart provides the most dignified form of guidance yet devised. With this chart, no one has to point out a student's weaknesses. The chart does that automatically, yielding the information directly and personally to the student, making self-teaching possible. The organization of the questions and the format for marking answers on the chart are what make it work so well.

The six questions for each passage are always in the same order. For example, the question designed to teach the skill of drawing conclusions is always the fourth question, and the main idea question is always first. Keeping the questions in order sets the stage for the smooth working of the chart.

The chart works automatically when students write the letter of their answer choices for each passage in the spaces provided. Even after completing only one passage, the chart will reveal the type or types of questions answered correctly, as well as the types answered incorrectly. As the answers for more passages are recorded, the chart will show the types of questions that are missed consistently. A pattern can be seen after three or more passages have been completed. For example, if a student answers question 4 (drawing conclusions) incorrectly for three out of four passages, the student's weakness in this area shows up automatically.

Once a weakness is revealed, have your students take the following steps: First, turn to the instructional pages in the beginning of the book and study the section in which the topic is discussed. Second, go back and reread the questions that were missed in that particular category. Then, with the correct answer to a question in mind, read the entire passage again, trying to see how the writer developed the answer to the question. Do this for each question that was missed. Third, when reading future passages, make an extra effort to correctly answer the questions in that particular category. Fourth, if the difficulty continues, arrange to see your teacher.

A D V A N C E D
L E V E L **Six-Way Paragraphs**
in the Content Areas

Each of the 100 passages included in this book is related to one of four general content areas: humanities, social studies, science, or mathematics. The graphic accompanying the title of each piece identifies the general content area to which it belongs.

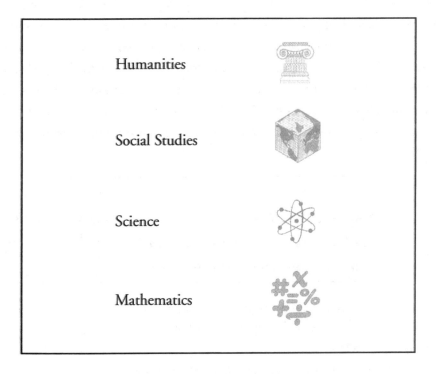

Humanities

Social Studies

Science

Mathematics

1 Not Quite as It Seems

The short story is a literary form that is not successful for all writers. Characters must be developed, a setting established, a story told, and an effective conclusion reached—all in a few pages. One of the masters of the short story was American writer William Sydney Porter, better known by his <u>pseudonym</u> O. Henry. O. Henry turned out hundreds of stories in the period from about 1895 until his death in 1910. Set in the city or in the country, dealing with people both young and old, the stories have one thing in common: nothing in them is exactly as it seems.

What gave most of O. Henry's stories their surprising twists was *situational irony*. This technique involves something happening that is the opposite of what is expected. One of O. Henry's most famous and most ironic stories is "The Gift of the Magi." Set in New York, as many of his stories are, it deals with a struggling young couple desperate to buy Christmas gifts for one another. She sells her long, beautiful hair in order to get money to buy him a chain for his precious gold watch—at the same time he is selling the watch in order to buy tortoiseshell combs that she has coveted to wear in her hair.

O. Henry found irony in all situations, not excepting those that related to his own life. While a young man living in Texas, a failed publishing venture led him to embezzle money, for which he ultimately spent three years in a penitentiary. O. Henry draws on that experience in another famous story, "A Retrieved Reformation." In it, a bank robber on the run is about to marry and go straight, until his breaking-in abilities are needed to save the life of a child. Stories like "After Twenty Years" and "The Ransom of Red Chief" also deal with lawbreakers who get their comeuppance in surprising ways.

Main Idea   1

	Answer	Score
Mark the *main idea*	M	15
Mark the statement that is *too broad*	B	5
Mark the statement that is *too narrow*	N	5

a. Situational irony is when something that occurs is opposite of what is expected. ☐ _____

b. O. Henry, a famous short story writer, made frequent use of irony. ☐ _____

c. O. Henry wrote many short stories. ☐ _____

2

Score 15 points for each correct answer.

Subject Matter   **2**   Another good title for this passage would be
- [ ] a. O. Henry and His Use of Irony.
- [ ] b. What Is Situational Irony?
- [ ] c. O. Henry's Life and Times.
- [ ] d. How You Can Learn to Write a Good
       Short Story.

_____

Supporting   **3**   O. Henry set his stories
Details
- [ ] a. only in cities like New York.
- [ ] b. primarily in the Wild West.
- [ ] c. in a wide variety of places.
- [ ] d. usually in places that were not recognizable.

_____

Conclusion   **4**   Based on information in the passage, you can
                             conclude that "After Twenty Years"
- [ ] a. tells about O. Henry's life in prison.
- [ ] b. uses situational irony.
- [ ] c. is set in New York.
- [ ] d. was written over a period of several months.

_____

Clarifying   **5**   The writer summarizes the plots of two stories in
Devices   order to
- [ ] a. amuse the reader.
- [ ] b. explain how all of O. Henry's stories are
       based on his own life.
- [ ] c. show how plots must be developed quickly.
- [ ] d. show how O. Henry uses irony.

_____

Vocabulary   **6**   A <u>pseudonym</u> is
in Context
- [ ] a. a real name.
- [ ] b. a false name.
- [ ] c. the name of a company.
- [ ] d. another word for "short story."

_____

Add your scores for questions 1–6. Enter the total here   **Total**
and on the graph on page 214.   **Score**   _____

2 Descended from Dinosaurs

What do ancient dinosaurs have in common with modern snakes, crocodiles, lizards, turtles, and the tuatara? They all are classified in the same formal category, the class *Reptilia,* or reptiles. Dinosaurs were only a small number of the reptiles that dominated the land, seas, and sky millions of years ago. Though dinosaurs are extinct, the reptiles of today descend from them and are reminders of the era known as the Age of Reptiles.

Only four main groups, or orders, of reptiles live on Earth today. These orders include species of alligators and crocodiles; turtles and tortoises; lizards and snakes; and a single species called the tuatara, a lizardlike animal from New Zealand. These animals at first appear to be very different, but they have many characteristics in common. All reptiles are cold-blooded—that is, they are unable to generate heat inside their own bodies. Reptiles are vertebrates, or animals with a bony skeleton that supports their bodies. They have thick, dry skin covered by scales or plates to protect them from predators and to prevent them from drying out. Finally, reptiles develop inside an egg that is protected by a leathery, waterproof shell.

Reptiles have adapted to habitats such as deserts, fresh water, oceans, swamps, plains, and cities. They also have adapted to most climates, although the tropics is their most popular habitat. Reptiles come in all sizes and shapes—the gecko looks like a lizard and averages only 0.7 inches in length; an adult leatherback sea turtle weighs in at about 2,000 pounds. Excluding snakes, all reptiles have four limbs, usually with claws, that are used for walking, climbing, and digging. Reptiles also have well-developed respiratory and circulatory systems for breathing air through lungs and providing cells with a constant supply of oxygen. Characteristics and adaptations like these have enabled reptiles to survive on Earth for hundreds of millions of years.

Main Idea	1		
		Answer	**Score**
	Mark the *main idea*	M	15
	Mark the statement that is *too broad*	B	5
	Mark the statement that is *too narrow*	N	5

a. Reptiles, descendants of ancient dinosaurs, have many traits in common. ☐ _____

b. Many animals are reptiles. ☐ _____

c. Reptiles are cold-blooded, meaning that they cannot generate their own body heat. ☐ _____

Subject Matter   **2**   Another good title for this passage would be
- [ ] a. The Small but Mighty Gecko.
- [ ] b. Characteristics of Vertebrates.
- [ ] c. *Reptilia,* a Class of Survivors.
- [ ] d. The Tropics: A Habitat for Reptiles.   _____

Supporting Details   **3**   A reptile has thick, dry skin
- [ ] a. because the tropical sun has damaged it.
- [ ] b. that always looks wet and slimy.
- [ ] c. from which the animal's age is determined.
- [ ] d. to protect the reptile and to keep it moist.   _____

Conclusion   **4**   Since a reptile cannot generate heat inside its body, it most likely
- [ ] a. buries itself during the summer.
- [ ] b. absorbs heat from its outside surroundings.
- [ ] c. frequently freezes to death.
- [ ] d. loves the cold weather.   _____

Clarifying Devices   **5**   To help the reader understand that reptiles vary greatly in size and shape, the author presents
- [ ] a. examples.
- [ ] b. scientific studies.
- [ ] c. vivid word pictures.
- [ ] d. similes and metaphors.   _____

Vocabulary in Context   **6**   In this passage adaptations means
- [ ] a. activities.
- [ ] b. adjustments.
- [ ] c. afflictions.
- [ ] d. attributes.   _____

Add your scores for questions 1–6. Enter the total here   **Total**
and on the graph on page 214.   **Score**   _____

5

3 Space Invaders

A normal conversation between strangers involves more than talk. It also involves the <u>dynamics</u> of space interaction. If one person gets too close, the other person will back up. If the first person invades the other's space again, the other person will back up again. The person who finds himself or herself backing up is trying to increase the distance of the comfort zone. The person closing in is trying to decrease that distance. Most likely neither person is fully aware of what is going on.

In the 1960s American anthropologist Edward T. Hall was a pioneer in the study of human behavioral use of space. His field of study became known as *proxemics*. Hall said that personal space for Americans can be defined as having four distinct zones: the intimate zone within 18 inches of your body for whispering and embracing; the personal zone of 18 inches to four feet, for talking with close friends; the social zone of four to 10 feet, for conversing with acquaintances; and the public zone of 10 to 25 feet, for interacting with strangers or talking to a group.

Historians say that our standards of personal space began with the Industrial Revolution in the 18th century. In cities such as London and New York, people of different social and economic classes were suddenly crammed together, so they unconsciously developed a commonly understood code of courtesy and space to restrict the area around them.

People exhibit nonverbal messages of discomfort when their zones are violated. Invaded people might tap their toes, pull at their hair, become completely rigid, or even become angry. As Hall noted in his landmark work, a comfortable conversation needs to include the parameters of human personal space.

Main Idea	1		
		Answer	**Score**
	Mark the *main idea*	M	15
	Mark the statement that is *too broad*	B	5
	Mark the statement that is *too narrow*	N	5

    a. People have a need for personal comfort zones. ☐ _____

    b. People exhibit nonverbal messages of discomfort. ☐ _____

    c. People engage in conversations. ☐ _____

Score 15 points for each correct answer.   **Score**

Subject Matter   **2**   This passage is mostly about
     ☐ a. what nonverbal communication is.
     ☐ b. human conversation.
     ☐ c. the life of Edward T. Hall.
     ☐ d. human behavioral use of space.   _____

Supporting   **3**   Edward T. Hall identified
Details
     ☐ a. interactions between strangers.
     ☐ b. angry people.
     ☐ c. four zones of personal space.
     ☐ d. the Industrial Revolution.   _____

Conclusion   **4**   If you and a close friend began talking when you
were eight feet apart, you would probably soon
     ☐ a. move closer together.
     ☐ b. move farther apart.
     ☐ c. begin talking more softly.
     ☐ d. ask another friend to join the conversation.   _____

Clarifying   **5**   The third paragraph provides
Devices
     ☐ a. a historical perspective on personal space.
     ☐ b. an economic reason for personal space.
     ☐ c. an overview of Edward T. Hall's field of study.
     ☐ d. a definition of personal space.   _____

Vocabulary   **6**   The word <u>dynamics</u> means
in Context
     ☐ a. difficulties.
     ☐ b. forces or influences that cause change.
     ☐ c. largeness.
     ☐ d. explosions so large they are beyond belief.   _____

Add your scores for questions 1–6. Enter the total here   Total
and on the graph on page 214.   Score   _____

4 Get Me to the Airport on Time

People overestimate and underestimate constantly. Whether you over- or under-estimate depends on whether you prefer to end up with a surplus or a <u>dearth</u>.

Liz Wolski is a restaurateur whose well-run cafe features a daily fish special. Liz feels that it is essential for fish to be extremely fresh. Unfortunately, she says, even well-refrigerated fresh fish often tastes "fishy" on the second day. Thus Liz habitually underestimates the number of customers who will order the fish special each day. She would rather disappoint some patrons than waste food and money. Also, she's confident that most customers will be willing to order something else.

Al Conway is a business executive whose position requires frequent travel. Al absolutely detests waiting at the airport for flights to leave. As a result, he always used to depart for the airport at the last possible moment. By cutting his time so close, he occasionally missed flights altogether. Conway's wife Mary (who often drives him to the airport) finally put her foot down and refused to take him under such stressful conditions. As a result, Al reluctantly pledged that in the future he would leave for the airport with plenty of time to spare.

Overestimating or underestimating can lead to wasted food or money, missed airline flights, or even disaster. (According to some, the designers of the *Titanic* purposefully underestimated the number of lifeboats needed to accommodate all passengers.) However, carefully considered over- or underestimating can help people function more effectively. The next time you're uncertain whether to overestimate or underestimate, use the following formula: *If I end up with too much _____, then A will happen; if I end up with too little of it, then B will happen. I would rather have A happen than B (or vice versa).*

Main Idea   1 ─────────────────────────────────

	Answer	Score
Mark the *main idea*	**M**	15
Mark the statement that is *too broad*	**B**	5
Mark the statement that is *too narrow*	**N**	5
a. Liz saves money by underestimating.	☐	___
b. Judicious estimating helps people function well.	☐	___
c. Most people estimate frequently.	☐	___

Score 15 points for each correct answer.   **Score**

Subject Matter   **2**   Another good title for this passage might be
                          ☐ a. Don't Overestimate!
                          ☐ b. Enough, Too Little, or Too Much?
                          ☐ c. Liz's Restaurant.
                          ☐ d. Fresh out of Fresh Fish.   _____

Supporting   **3**   Al underestimated the amount of time it would
Details   take to get to the airport because
                          ☐ a. he was not good at keeping track of time.
                          ☐ b. his wife always drove too slowly.
                          ☐ c. he hated to wait for flights to leave.
                          ☐ d. it took him a long time to pack.   _____

Conclusion   **4**   We can conclude from the passage that it would be
                          wise to overestimate when calculating the amount of
                          ☐ a. time needed to complete a project with a
                             strict deadline.
                          ☐ b. cash to withdraw from a local ATM.
                          ☐ c. perishable food to buy for a beach picnic.
                          ☐ d. time children will spend on chores.   _____

Clarifying   **5**   The second and third paragraphs are included to
Devices   ☐ a. provide contrast to the first paragraph.
                          ☐ b. relate a humorous anecdote.
                          ☐ c. explain the steps in a process.
                          ☐ d. provide examples.   _____

Vocabulary   **6**   Dearth means
in Context   ☐ a. fiasco.
                          ☐ b. excess.
                          ☐ c. lack.
                          ☐ d. murder.   _____

Add your scores for questions 1–6. Enter the total here   Total
and on the graph on page 214.   Score   _____

5 Famous Fiddles

A genuine Stradivarius violin can sell for millions of dollars. So can a genuine Guarneri "del Gesu." What makes these violins so expensive? Is one type of violin better than the other?

Antonio Stradivari (1644?–1737) and Bartolomeo Giuseppe Guarneri "del Gesu" (1698–1744) both grew up in violin-making traditions, and both were making instruments at about the same time. The violins made by each are known for their full, rich, mellow sounds and for their great ease of playing, though some violinists say a Guarneri is better for players who make a lot of demands on their instruments. A Stradivarius, they say, needs a gentler approach. Estimates are that about 500–600 Strads still exist, but only around 100 Guarneris; and there is general agreement that these instruments are far superior to any made today.

A great deal of analysis has been performed on these violins to determine why their sound is so excellent. Much of the study centers on the type and thickness of wood the instruments were made from and the varnishes used to finish them. Violin makers choose their wood—usually maple—carefully, with many believing that the best wood grows slowly, in high altitudes with cold, harsh weather. There is some speculation that the wood used in Stradivari's and Guarneri's time was superior in that it had taken 400–500 years to grow, during which time there had been a mini Ice Age.

The varnish used to finish a violin can influence the sound by affecting the stiffness of the wood. The best varnish has a thin consistency and is not applied too thickly. In the era in which these masters were working, there was a great <u>mystique</u> about varnishes, with apprentice violin makers sworn to secrecy about what type was used. Despite the chemical analysis that can be done on existing varnishes today, no one is quite sure what effect they had on the excellence of Stradivari's and Guarneri's violins.

Main Idea   1 —————————————————————————————————

	Answer	Score
Mark the *main idea*	M	15
Mark the statement that is *too broad*	B	5
Mark the statement that is *too narrow*	N	5

a. Wood and varnish play a role in a violin's sound. ☐ _____

b. Violins can be worth a lot of money. ☐ _____

c. The high quality of Stradivarius and Guarneri violins makes them valuable. ☐ _____

Score 15 points for each correct answer.　　　**Score**

Subject Matter　　**2**　This passage is mostly about
- ☐ a. the art of violin making.
- ☐ b. what makes a good violin varnish.
- ☐ c. Stradivari's and Guarneri's violins.
- ☐ d. how expensive rare violins have become.　　_____

Supporting Details　　**3**　The best wood for violins
- ☐ a. comes from river valleys.
- ☐ b. is a relatively soft wood like birch.
- ☐ c. grows in warm climates.
- ☐ d. grows slowly.　　_____

Conclusion　　**4**　Information in the passage suggests it is fair to conclude that
- ☐ a. Stradivari's and Guarneri's violins are valuable because of their varnish.
- ☐ b. no one is certain what makes these violins so good.
- ☐ c. the violins are valuable mainly because they are old.
- ☐ d. Stradivari and Guarneri competed constantly.　　_____

Clarifying Devices　　**5**　The second paragraph is developed mostly through
- ☐ a. comparison and contrast.
- ☐ b. description.
- ☐ c. persuasion.
- ☐ d. definition.　　_____

Vocabulary in Context　　**6**　<u>Mystique</u> means
- ☐ a. discussion.
- ☐ b. atmosphere of mystery.
- ☐ c. surprise.
- ☐ d. expense.　　_____

Add your scores for questions 1–6. Enter the total here and on the graph on page 214.　　Total Score　　_____

6 Seasons

Spring, summer, autumn, and winter bring changes in the weather, plant and animal life, and the length of days and nights. Seasonal changes such as these are due to three factors: the tilt of Earth's axis to one side; the rotation, or turn, of Earth on its axis every 24 hours; and the <u>revolution</u> of Earth around the sun once every year. Since Earth remains tilted in the same direction during its revolution of the sun, the angle at which the sun's rays hit Earth changes, causing us to experience the changing seasons.

In the summer the Northern Hemisphere where we live points toward the sun, allowing us to receive its more direct and powerful rays. Six months later, when Earth is halfway through its revolution around the sun, the Northern Hemisphere is tilted away from the sun, exposing us to the more angled, weak rays of winter. The seasons in one hemisphere are opposite those in the other hemisphere. However, one area of Earth—the equator—receives the most direct rays, so equatorial regions experience hot weather all year. In contrast, the polar regions, which always get indirect rays, experience continuous frigid weather.

In the Northern Hemisphere, we observe a gradual alteration in the angle of the sun during the year. About June 21, on the summer solstice, or the first day of summer the midday sun reaches its highest point in the sky and produces the year's mazimum daylight hours. About September 22, on the autumn equinox, the midday sun is lower in the sky. Because Earth's axis is tilted neither toward nor away from the sun, equal periods of daylight and darkness result. About December 21, on the winter solstice, or the first day of winter, the midday sun is at its lowest point in the sky and brings the year's fewest daylight hours. About March 21, on the vernal equinox, or the first day of spring, the midday sun is higher in the sky and daytime and nighttime hours are again equal.

Main Idea	1		
		Answer	**Score**
	Mark the *main idea*	M	15
	Mark the statement that is *too broad*	B	5
	Mark the statement that is *too narrow*	N	5
	a. Seasons bring many changes to Earth.	☐	_____
	b. A change of seasons results from Earth's motions and the tilt of its axis.	☐	_____
	c. Earth remains tilted in the same direction as it revolves around the sun.	☐	_____

Subject Matter   **2**   This passage is mainly concerned with
- ☐ a. how Earth rotates on its axis.
- ☐ b. why the various seasons occur.
- ☐ c. why each season is three months long.
- ☐ d. which parts of Earth are coldest.   _____

Supporting Details   **3**   The summer solstice results in
- ☐ a. the midday sun being at its lowest point.
- ☐ b. Earth's axis being tilted neither toward nor away from the sun.
- ☐ c. equal periods of daylight and darkness.
- ☐ d. the greatest number of daylight hours of any day during the year.   _____

Conclusion   **4**   When the Northern Hemisphere is experiencing summer, the Southern Hemisphere is experiencing
- ☐ a. winter.
- ☐ b. spring.
- ☐ c. summer.
- ☐ d. autumn.   _____

Clarifying Devices   **5**   The writer presents facts about equinoxes and solstices to explain
- ☐ a. why it is hot at the equator.
- ☐ b. the various lengths of day and night.
- ☐ c. why the midday sun is directly overhead.
- ☐ d. the date of the autumn equinox.   _____

Vocabulary in Context   **6**   In this passage <u>revolution</u> means
- ☐ a. great change.
- ☐ b. an uprising.
- ☐ c. standing still.
- ☐ d. circling.   _____

Add your scores for questions 1–6. Enter the total here and on the graph on page 214.   **Total Score**   _____

7 City Planning

City planners are the people who guide the development of cities and towns. They might advise local governments on ways to improve communities, or they might design entirely new communities. In South Florida, for example, city planners are working to improve existing communities. The population of the area is expected to increase from 5.5 million to 7.5 million by 2020. This growth is headed to the west, where there is still open land. But western growth creates a costly need for new roads and is a threat to the ecological system of the Florida Everglades. City planners are trying to <u>lure</u> people back into the older, developed eastern section of the region by funneling growth in that direction and away from the western section.

City planners also plan and develop new communities. These communities, called new cities or new towns, include both places to live and places to work. New cities, such as Brazil's capital Brasilia, a community founded in 1900, can be constructed far from existing cities. Such cities are designed with enough facilities and job opportunities for all their residents. Building completely new cities is very costly, however. Brasilia and Canberra, Australia, are two examples of the few new cities that have ever been completed.

New towns are different from new cities in that they are built within commuting distance of large cities. They may also be planned communities within a city. New towns provide jobs for many of their residents, but they also rely on neighboring cities for jobs. Two of the first new towns built in the United States were Columbia, Maryland, and Reston, Virginia. At the end of the 20th century an estimated 100 new towns were planned or under construction in the United States.

Main Idea	1		
		Answer	**Score**
	Mark the *main idea*	M	15
	Mark the statement that is *too broad*	B	5
	Mark the statement that is *too narrow*	N	5

    a. New communities include places to live and work. ☐ _____

    b. City planners improve old communities or design new ones. ☐ _____

    c. City planners are at work around the world. ☐ _____

Subject Matter   **2**   This passage is mostly about
☐ a. choosing a good city planner.
☐ b. the planning of Reston, Virginia.
☐ c. the planning of Brasilia and Canberra.
☐ d. the work of city planners.   _____

Supporting
Details   **3**   Brasilia, Brazil, is an example of
☐ a. an improved old city.
☐ b. a planned new city.
☐ c. a planned new town.
☐ d. a suburban development.   _____

Conclusion   **4**   You would most likely hire a city planner if you needed
☐ a. advice on which crops will grow best on your land.
☐ b. someone to plan a city election campaign.
☐ c. someone to design a new office building.
☐ d. someone to guide the development of a new suburb.   _____

Clarifying
Devices   **5**   The number 2.0 million indicates the predicted
☐ a. decrease in South Florida's population.
☐ b. increase in South Florida's population.
☐ c. number of city planners in the year 2020.
☐ d. number of towns to be planned by 2050.   _____

Vocabulary
in Context   **6**   In this passage <u>lure</u> means
☐ a. an item to use while fishing.
☐ b. lie to.
☐ c. attract.
☐ d. perform magic on.   _____

Add your scores for questions 1–6. Enter the total here and on the graph on page 214.   **Total
Score**   _____

8 Brother, Can You Spare $100,000?

Demetrius Dembowski has obtained a 30-year, fixed-rate home loan of $100,000 with an annual interest rate of 7.5 percent. Because the loan extends for such a lengthy period, the mortgage company calculates a monthly payment that ensures it will get most of its interest back first. Thus in the beginning months, Dembowski's principal payment—the amount he pays toward his actual loan—increases extremely slowly.

Payment Number	Total Monthly Payment	Principal Portion of Payment	Interest Portion of Payment	Current Balance
1	$699.21	$ 74.21	$625.00	$99,925.79
2	$699.21	$ 74.68	$624.54	$99,851.11
359	$699.21	$690.56	$ 8.66	$ 694.87
360	$699.21	$694.87	$ 4.34	$ 0.00

Let's analyze Demetrius's early payments. Imagine that on December 15 the Mauritanian Mortgage Corporation gives Demetrius $100,000, and on January 15 his initial payment is due. Throughout this first month, interest <u>accumulates</u> on the entire $100,000. On a yearly interest rate of 7.5%, Demetrius's monthly rate is 0.625%, or 7.5% divided by 12. Multiplying $100,000 by 0.625% yields $625, the portion of Demetrius's first monthly payment that is interest. So Demetrius now owes $100,625 ($100,000 + $625), and after his initial payment of $699.21, he still owes $99,925.79 ($100,625 − $699.21). His February interest payment will be .625% of $99,925.79.

By the time Dembowski makes his last few payments, his monthly interest payment has decreased considerably. His balance following his 359th payment is $694.87, and 0.625% of that is about $4.34, his final interest payment. What was the total amount of interest Demetrius paid? Multiplying 360 months by $699.21 equals $251,715.60, and subtracting $100,000 (the loan amount) leaves $151,715.60—over 1.5 times what he actually borrowed!

Main Idea   1 ——————————————————————————————

	Answer	Score
Mark the *main idea*	M	15
Mark the statement that is *too broad*	B	5
Mark the statement that is *too narrow*	N	5

a. Demetrius took out a home loan. ☐ ____

b. The final interest payment was $4.34. ☐ ____

c. The interest on a large, long-term loan decreases gradually over time. ☐ ____

Score 15 points for each correct answer.   **Score**

Subject Matter   2   This passage is mainly concerned with
                        ☐ a. Demetrius Dembowski.
                        ☐ b. the Mauritanian Mortgage Corporation.
                        ☐ c. how interest payments on a loan change.
                        ☐ d. calculating the number of payments
                               Demetrius made.   _____

Supporting   3   The monthly interest rate on Demetrius's loan was
Details   ☐ a. 7.5%.
                        ☐ b. 6.5%.
                        ☐ c. 0.625%.
                        ☐ d. $625.   _____

Conclusion   4   We can conclude that Demetrius's total monthly
                        payment was always
                        ☐ a. $699.21.
                        ☐ b. $100,000.
                        ☐ c. $360.
                        ☐ d. $151,715.60.   _____

Clarifying   5   The table in the passage helps the reader see
Devices   ☐ a. Demetrius's down payment before he took
                               out the loan.
                        ☐ b. Demetrius's first and last interest payments.
                        ☐ c. how much his interest payments increased.
                        ☐ d. at what point the interest and principal
                               payments were just about equal.   _____

Vocabulary   6   <u>Accumulates</u> means
in Context   ☐ a. fades away.
                        ☐ b. builds up.
                        ☐ c. gets used to.
                        ☐ d. decreases.   _____

Add your scores for questions 1–6. Enter the total here   **Total**
and on the graph on page 214.   **Score**   _____

9 What Is a Wat?

Is a wat an electrical charge capable of lighting up a huge space, or perhaps the beginning of a question in an <u>obscure</u> British dialect? No, a *wat* is something far different: it is, in fact, a structure designed for worship.

Most wats are Buddhist monasteries found in the Southeast Asian countries of Thailand and Cambodia. Wats include several types of buildings within a walled compound and have very distinctive architecture. Within each wat is a *bot,* or main temple, housing a statue of a sitting or reclining Buddha that may be 160 feet tall or even larger. (Other statues of Buddha, from huge to tiny and often coated with gold, may be found throughout a wat.) Additional characteristic structures include *prangs,* cylindrical columns with round tops resting on sculptured bases, and *chedis,* sharply pointed spires on top of buildings with bell-shaped bases; both structures are repositories for sacred objects. It is the chedis that are most noticeable, their distinctive form silhouetting the sky even in large cities like Bangkok.

Wats have been constructed for centuries, and the ruins of many ancient wats still exist. Within the former Thai capital of Ayutthaya, which was built in 1350, many crumbling wats still stand, their chedis and giant Buddhas visible from a distance. Despite their deteriorated condition, these wats are still frequently used for worship.

One of the wats best known to the Western world is Angkor Wat in Cambodia. Constructed in the 1100s by the Khmer people, it was not rediscovered until the 1860s. It is surrounded by a moat, and its many courtyards are filled with characteristic tall, conical towers. Angkor Wat is a Hindu rather than a Buddhist center of worship. It was constructed to honor the Hindu god Vishnu.

Main Idea 1 _____

	Answer	Score
Mark the *main idea*	M	15
Mark the statement that is *too broad*	B	5
Mark the statement that is *too narrow*	N	5

a. Wats are places of worship with certain characteristic buildings. ☐ ____

b. Wats are places of worship in Southeast Asia. ☐ ____

c. A chedi is a spire found on certain buildings in wats. ☐ ____

Score 15 points for each correct answer. **Score**

Subject Matter **2** This passage deals mostly with
- [ ] a. Angkor Wat.
- [ ] b. the characteristics of wats.
- [ ] c. a short history of wats.
- [ ] d. life in Thailand and Cambodia. _____

Supporting **3** Most wats are associated with
Details
- [ ] a. Buddhism.
- [ ] b. Catholicism.
- [ ] c. Hinduism.
- [ ] d. Confucianism. _____

Conclusion **4** Based on information in this passage, you can
conclude that Buddhism
- [ ] a. is not associated with wats.
- [ ] b. is an ancient religion.
- [ ] c. is a new religion.
- [ ] d. requires people to pray frequently. _____

Clarifying **5** The writer uses questions in the first paragraph to
Devices
- [ ] a. confuse the reader.
- [ ] b. define an architectural term.
- [ ] c. present the main idea of the passage.
- [ ] d. follow up on the question in the title. _____

Vocabulary **6** In this passage <u>obscure</u> means
in Context
- [ ] a. faraway.
- [ ] b. little known.
- [ ] c. dark.
- [ ] d. hidden. _____

Add your scores for questions 1–6. Enter the total here **Total**
and on the graph on page 214. **Score** _____

10 Blankets of Ice

You may already know that more than a million years ago glaciers, or vast blankets of moving ice, covered nearly one third of the earth, including northern parts of Europe, Asia, and North America. You also may know that tens of thousands of years ago, the glaciers started to melt, retreating to their current positions in the Antarctic and Greenland. You might even know that glaciers also exist in all the world's great mountain regions. But do you know that glaciers cover about 6 billion square miles of the earth and store about 75 percent of the earth's fresh water?

A glacier forms in a cold climate when a winter's snow does not completely melt during the following summer. Snow continues to accumulate and partially melt year after year. As the accumulated snow becomes heavier, the lower layer crushes under the weight and changes into ice. Over time the mass of ice thickens and moves. The ice is either pulled slowly downhill by gravity—as in the valley glaciers found in the Alps, on the Alaskan coast, and in the western United States—or forced outward in all directions by its own weight—as in the ice sheets and ice caps covering most of Greenland and Antarctica. During glaciation a glacier moves (usually about 3 feet per day). It picks up rock fragments that <u>gouge</u> and polish the land and carve out steep-sided valleys. During deglaciation a glacier recedes and often leaves large deposits of sand and gravel. This process of glaciation and deglaciation formed the Great Lakes in North America during the Ice Age.

Some scientists believe that ice ages similar to those of the past will occur, but they disagree on when this will happen. Other scientists think that global warming will occur instead, melting the glaciers and flooding many coastal areas as sea levels rise. No one knows for certain which event will occur, but neither bodes well for mankind.

Main Idea   1

	Answer	Score
Mark the *main idea*	M	15
Mark the statement that is *too broad*	B	5
Mark the statement that is *too narrow*	N	5

a. Glaciers, huge blankets of moving ice, are formed in very specific ways. ☐ _____

b. Long ago there were many glaciers. ☐ _____

c. Glaciation and deglaciation formed the Great Lakes. ☐ _____

Score 15 points for each correct answer.   **Score**

Subject Matter **2** This passage is mainly about
- [ ] a. the Ice Age.
- [ ] b. valley glaciers.
- [ ] c. ice sheets and ice caps.
- [ ] d. glaciers.

_____

Supporting Details **3** During glaciation a glacier
- [ ] a. covers the land.
- [ ] b. retreats.
- [ ] c. melts.
- [ ] d. floods coastal areas.

_____

Conclusion **4** If global warming occurs instead of another ice age,
- [ ] a. vast blankets of ice will cover the earth.
- [ ] b. glaciers in the Antarctic will increase in size.
- [ ] c. plant and animal life in many areas will be destroyed.
- [ ] d. a winter's snow may not completely melt during the following summer.

_____

Clarifying Devices **5** To help the reader understand how a glacier forms, the author
- [ ] a. gives a step-by-step explanation.
- [ ] b. presents a detailed example.
- [ ] c. makes a strong argument.
- [ ] d. cites careful measurements.

_____

Vocabulary in Context **6** In this passage <u>gouge</u> means
- [ ] a. trick or cheat.
- [ ] b. cut holes into.
- [ ] c. smooth out.
- [ ] d. raise the surface of.

_____

Add your scores for questions 1–6. Enter the total here and on the graph on page 214.

Total Score

_____

11 Archaeological Fact or Fiction?

The demolition of a downtown Miami, Florida, apartment building in 1998 uncovered an archaeological site. The site contained many artifacts and a unique circle of holes cut into limestone bedrock. The 38-foot circle formed by the holes appeared to have an east–west axis that <u>aligned</u> with the rising and setting of the sun on the equinox. The formation became known as the Miami Circle. Archaeologist Robert Carr speculated that the circle and its holes once supported the wall posts of a structure. Perhaps the structure was a temple or council house constructed between 500 and 700 years ago. Or was it?

Thousands of genuine artifacts found at the site helped to support Carr's theory. The artifacts are typical of the Tequesta Indians, who lived in the area before the Spanish arrived in the 1500s. There were potsherds, stone axes, and beads. Also found were a five-foot shark and a sea turtle. The shark and the sea turtle were buried with their heads to the west and tails to the east.

Historical preservationists said the Miami Circle was the only "cut-in-rock prehistoric structural footprint ever found in eastern North America." However, others questioned its authenticity. This was because embedded in the limestone circle was a 1950s septic tank. Jerald T. Milanich, curator in archaeology of the Florida Museum of Natural History, wanted to know if Carr's "pre-Columbian postholes" were actually part of a 1950s septic drain field. Before he would believe that the septic tank and the circle are just a coincidence, as Carr believed, Milanich wanted more evidence. He called for radiocarbon dating, soil samples, and examination of the tool marks on the inside of the holes. Said Milanich, "When faced with coincidences and mysteries, an archaeologist needs to eliminate alternative explanations."

Main Idea	1	Answer	Score
Mark the *main idea*		M	15
Mark the statement that is *too broad*		B	5
Mark the statement that is *too narrow*		N	5

a. An archaeological site found in Miami may not be genuine. ☐ ____

b. Archaeologists sometimes find unusual sites. ☐ ____

c. Potsherds seemed to suggest that Tequesta Indians had built the site. ☐ ____

Score 15 points for each correct answer.   Score

Subject Matter   **2**   This passage is mostly about
                                  ☐ a. the lifestyle of the Tequesta Indians.
                                  ☐ b. why buildings should not be demolished
                                  in Miami.
                                  ☐ c. the authenticity of an archaeological site
                                  in Miami.
                                  ☐ d. how archaeological sites are excavated.   _____

Supporting   **3**   The Tequesta Indians lived in the area
Details   ☐ a. before the 1500s.
                                  ☐ b. in the 1950s.
                                  ☐ c. after the 1990s.
                                  ☐ d. after the Spanish arrived.   _____

Conclusion   **4**   The information in this passage is
                                  ☐ a. only factual.
                                  ☐ b. only speculative.
                                  ☐ c. both factual and speculative.
                                  ☐ d. only one person's opinion.   _____

Clarifying   **5**   Potsherds, stone axes, and beads are examples of
Devices   ☐ a. luxury items.
                                  ☐ b. things found in the Caribbean.
                                  ☐ c. things found in the Miami River.
                                  ☐ d. artifacts found at the site.   _____

Vocabulary   **6**   The word <u>aligned</u> means
in Context   ☐ a. became allies with.
                                  ☐ b. lined up with.
                                  ☐ c. strong.
                                  ☐ d. deeply carved into the earth.   _____

Add your scores for questions 1–6. Enter the total here   Total
and on the graph on page 214.   Score   _____

12 The Golden Rectangle

One of the most commonly used geometric shapes is the rectangle—a four-sided figure with four right angles. If you start looking for rectangular shapes in the physical world, you'll find them almost everywhere, perhaps because people are attracted to the precision and order conveyed by this shape. One way to classify a rectangle is by the ratio of its length to its width; for example, a square is a rectangle in which the ratio of the length to the width is 1 to 1. A rectangle with the length-width ratio 20 to 1 would be very long and skinny; one with the ratio 1.1 to 1 would be almost square.

Are some rectangular shapes more commonly used than others? In mathematics, one particular rectangle has been distinguished by being named "golden." In a golden rectangle, the length (L) and the width (W) must satisfy the proportion $W/L = L/(W + L)$. In other words, the ratio of the width to the length must be the same as the ratio of the length to the width-length sum. If W equals 1, then solving the formula for L results in approximately 1.618. Golden rectangles— rectangles with a length-width ratio of 1.618 to 1—have been found in art, architecture, and mathematical writings for more than 4,000 years, with one especially <u>notable</u> example being the base of the Parthenon in Athens, Greece.

Do you have golden rectangles in your home or where you work? To find out, simply divide the length of any rectangle by its width; if the quotient equals about 1.6, then you have a golden rectangle. Performing this division on a 5-by-3 index card results in the quotient 1.666 and performing it on an 8-by-5 card gives the quotient 1.6, so both of these shapes are close to being golden rectangles. With a ruler and a calculator, you can check your computer monitor, television screen, and the other rectangular shapes in your home and probably find quite a few additional examples.

Main Idea	1		Answer	Score
	Mark the *main idea*		M	15
	Mark the statement that is *too broad*		B	5
	Mark the statement that is *too narrow*		N	5
	a. Many common objects are rectangular.		☐	___
	b. A 5-by-3 index card is almost a golden rectangle.		☐	___
	c. Golden rectangles have a particular length-width ratio.		☐	___

Score 15 points for each correct answer.   **Score**

Subject Matter   2   This passage is mainly about
- ☐ a. identifying shapes that contain right angles.
- ☐ b. describing the proportions of golden rectangles.
- ☐ c. learning the sizes of index cards.
- ☐ d. solving formulas about rectangles.   _____

Supporting Details   3   The ratio of the length to the width of a square shape is
- ☐ a. equal to that of a golden rectangle.
- ☐ b. 1 to 20.
- ☐ c. 20 to 1.
- ☐ d. 1 to 1.   _____

Conclusion   4   Golden rectangles are found frequently in art and architecture because
- ☐ a. their proportions are pleasing to the eye.
- ☐ b. people think they bring wealth or good luck.
- ☐ c. they can substitute for squares.
- ☐ d. they can be drawn without right angles.   _____

Clarifying Devices   5   To find out if a rectangle is "golden," the writer suggests
- ☐ a. using the formula $W/L = L/(W + L)$.
- ☐ b. measuring a shape and then using division.
- ☐ c. comparing it to the shape of the Parthenon.
- ☐ d. comparing it to the shape of a square.   _____

Vocabulary in Context   6   In this passage the word <u>notable</u> means
- ☐ a. recorded.
- ☐ b. well-proportioned.
- ☐ c. important or worthy of notice.
- ☐ d. beautiful.   _____

Add your scores for questions 1–6. Enter the total here and on the graph on page 214.   Total Score   _____

13 A New Kind of Play

In the late 19th and early 20th centuries two European playwrights produced works that closely examined the lives, characters, and motivations of middle-class citizens. They were the Russian Anton Chekhov and the Norwegian Henrik Ibsen.

Chekhov, the younger of the two, did not begin his career writing introspective drama; in fact, many of his earliest plays were short comic farces designed to please wide audiences. Additionally, Chekhov wrote many short stories, for which he is just as well known as his plays. But several carefully crafted dramas have helped to form his reputation as an innovative playwright. These include *Uncle Vanya, The Seagull, Three Sisters,* and *The Cherry Orchard,* all of which deal in some way with the tragedy of everyday living. In *Uncle Vanya,* for instance, the title character realizes his life's work has been useless but fails in his violent attempt to change things. In *Three Sisters,* the Prozorov sisters try unsuccessfully to leave their country home for the excitement of Moscow. Plays such as these were not well understood when first introduced.

In contrast to Chekhov, Ibsen was a dramatist throughout his entire career. Though he declined to live in Norway through most of his playwriting years, his major works were all produced there. In general, they created a furor because they looked beneath the facades of middle-class society. *A Doll's House* shows how a dutiful wife responds when she realizes that her husband considers her to be nothing more than a foolish child. *Ghosts* examines the effects of syphilis, as well as a family's hypocrisy, on a young man. And *Hedda Gabler* is a character study of a selfish, <u>amoral</u> woman. These and other plays established Ibsen's reputation as a writer who was unafraid to portray life as it really existed.

Main Idea	1		
		Answer	**Score**
	Mark the *main idea*	M	15
	Mark the statement that is *too broad*	B	5
	Mark the statement that is *too narrow*	N	5

a. Ibsen and Chekhov wrote plays about middle-class beliefs and values. ☐ _____

b. Many plays have been written about the middle class. ☐ _____

c. Plays like *A Doll's House* questioned typical views of women. ☐ _____

Score 15 points for each correct answer.   **Score**

Subject Matter   **2**   This passage deals mainly with
- ☐ a. 19th century theater.
- ☐ b. the works of Chekhov and Ibsen.
- ☐ c. how women were presented in plays.
- ☐ d. definitions of drama and farce.

                                                              _____

Supporting Details   **3**   In *Ghosts* a young man has
- ☐ a. a bossy mother.
- ☐ b. an impoverished father.
- ☐ c. an unsatisfying job.
- ☐ d. syphilis.

    _____

Conclusion   **4**   Theatergoers of Chekhov's and Ibsen's time were
- ☐ a. not comfortable with plays about women.
- ☐ b. not comfortable with plays about feelings and issues.
- ☐ c. adventurous and forward-looking.
- ☐ d. not happy with lighthearted comedies.

    _____

Clarifying Devices   **5**   The writer deals with each playwright by
- ☐ a. summarizing major events in his life.
- ☐ b. discussing some of his major works.
- ☐ c. comparing his work with the other playwright's.
- ☐ d. listing all of his dramas.

    _____

Vocabulary in Context   **6**   <u>Amoral</u> means
- ☐ a. not caring about right or wrong.
- ☐ b. very good and proper.
- ☐ c. the main point or theme of a story.
- ☐ d. struggling to follow the rules.

    _____

Add your scores for questions 1–6. Enter the total here   **Total**
and on the graph on page 214.   **Score**   _____

14 In or Out of the Water?

Frogs and toads, salamanders and newts, and the little-known caecilian are amphibians, a word derived from the Greek *amphibios,* meaning "double life." The name is a good one to describe these animals that live part of their lives in water and part on land.

Structurally the groups of amphibians are very different. Frogs and toads, for example, are tailless. They have short, thick bodies, two short forelegs, and two long, powerful hind legs. Salamanders and newts have long tails, lizard-shaped bodies, and two pairs of equal-sized limbs. Caecilians may have short, pointed tails.

Although amphibians are structurally diverse, they have many similar characteristics. All amphibians are vertebrates, or animals with backbones that give the body shape and provide for movement. Amphibians have a circulatory system consisting of blood vessels and a three-chambered heart that moves the blood to and from all parts of the body. Amphibians also possess a well-developed nervous system that lets them receive and react to messages from their surroundings. Amphibians are cold-blooded, meaning that their body temperature changes with their surroundings. Amphibians also have a thin, moist skin with no surface scales, hair, or feathers.

Reproduction usually occurs in water, where female amphibians lay eggs with a jelly coating but no protective shell. Male amphibians fertilize the eggs by spreading sperm directly over them in the water. A characteristic of most amphibians is the metamorphosis, or series of body changes, that they undergo. After hatching from eggs, most young amphibians continue to live in water, taking in oxygen from the water as it flows over their gills. As amphibians change into adults, however, most develop lungs and reside on land at least part of the time. Those adult amphibians that live on land can also <u>respire</u> through their skin if they return to the water.

Main Idea	1		
		Answer	**Score**
Mark the *main idea*		M	15
Mark the statement that is *too broad*		B	5
Mark the statement that is *too narrow*		N	5

a. Amphibians have thin, moist skins with no surface scales, hair, or feathers. ☐ _____

b. Amphibians are a type of animal. ☐ _____

c. Amphibians are structurally diverse but have a number of similar characteristics. ☐ _____

Subject Matter   2   This passage focuses primarily on
☐ a. caecilians.
☐ b. frogs and toads.
☐ c. salamanders and newts.
☐ d. qualities of amphibians.   _____

Supporting Details   3   During metamorphosis, most amphibians
☐ a. develop backbones.
☐ b. form a circulatory system.
☐ c. replace gills with lungs.
☐ d. reproduce by laying eggs with a jelly coating.   _____

Conclusion   4   The last sentence of this passage suggests that amphibians are
☐ a. unable to stand change.
☐ b. adaptable.
☐ c. large.
☐ d. noisy at certain times in their lives.   _____

Clarifying Devices   5   The word *Although* at the beginning of the third paragraph signals
☐ a. a contrast.
☐ b. a similarity.
☐ c. an additional piece of information.
☐ d. a choice.   _____

Vocabulary in Context   6   The word respire means to
☐ a. grow.
☐ b. reproduce.
☐ c. swim.
☐ d. breathe.   _____

Add your scores for questions 1–6. Enter the total here and on the graph on page 214.   **Total Score**   _____

15 A Deadly Game of Hide and Seek

For six years Mexico had been locked in a bloody revolution, with each state controlled by a different <u>warlord</u>. Americans had more than a billion dollars invested in Mexican property and industry. So, to protect American interests, the United States stepped in, and President Woodrow Wilson supported Venustiano Carranza as the head of Mexico in hopes of stabilizing the Mexican government.

Francisco "Pancho" Villa, warlord of Northern Mexico, was outraged. The way Villa saw it, Wilson could not possibly have made a worse choice than Villa's rival, Carranza. In retaliation, Villa led his rebel army northward in 1916. His targets were his own Mexican government and the United States with its meddling president. Villa and his *Villistas* attacked the little border town of Columbus, New Mexico, to show Wilson and Carranza that they'd double-crossed the wrong man.

President Wilson ordered General John Pershing to cross the border into Mexico with some 6,600 cavalrymen. Their orders were to capture the bandit Villa dead or alive. All through the summer and fall of 1916, Pershing's forces wandered aimlessly through the Mexican state of Chihuahua, while Villa's army grew. Rumors reported that Villa's forces were as strong as 18,000 men.

When Pershing failed even to sight the elusive Villa, a joint Mexican-American Commission negotiated an agreement allowing both sides to back away peacefully. On February 5, 1917, the last members of the Pershing Expedition left Mexico for good. The cost to the United States: about 100 casualties and some $130 million spent in the pursuit of an outlaw whom U.S. troops could not bring to justice. But Villa did stop his raids on the U.S. side of the border.

Main Idea	1		Answer	Score
	Mark the *main idea*		M	15
	Mark the statement that is *too broad*		B	5
	Mark the statement that is *too narrow*		N	5

a. American presidents have attempted to influence Mexican politics. ☐ _____

b. Pancho Villa led troops into the United States. ☐ _____

c. Pancho Villa attacked the United States in revenge for U.S. meddling. ☐ _____

Score 15 points for each correct answer.   **Score**

Subject Matter   2   Another good title for this passage would be
         ☐ a. A New President for Mexico.
         ☐ b. General Pershing Wins a Battle.
         ☐ c. Pancho Villa and the U.S. President.
         ☐ d. Famous Mexican Leaders.   _____

Supporting   3   As Pershing's troops wandered in Mexico,
Details   ☐ a. Pancho Villa was brought to justice.
         ☐ b. Pancho Villa's army decreased in number.
         ☐ c. Villa was killed by his own men.
         ☐ d. Pancho Villa's army increased in number.   _____

Conclusion   4   In dealing with Pancho Villa, the United States
         ☐ a. got nothing for all its efforts.
         ☐ b. was the clearcut winner.
         ☐ c. apparently did frighten Villa somewhat.
         ☐ d. agreed to name Villa leader of Mexico.   _____

Clarifying   5   Information in this passage is generally presented
Devices   ☐ a. from earliest to latest.
         ☐ b. in order of importance.
         ☐ c. in spatial order.
         ☐ d. from latest to earliest.   _____

Vocabulary   6   The word <u>warlord</u> means a
in Context   ☐ a. guardian.
         ☐ b. military ruler.
         ☐ c. follower.
         ☐ d. wizard.   _____

Add your scores for questions 1–6. Enter the total here   **Total**
and on the graph on page 214.   **Score**   _____

16 Double or Nothing

Begin with a sheet of newspaper and cut it in half to get two pieces; then stack up the pieces and cut in half again to get four pieces. Continue this process until you can't cut the stack of paper anymore. How many times do you think you'll be able to repeat the process of doubling the number of pieces of paper? The doubling pattern that results from an activity of this type may surprise you in how quickly the numbers increase. In this example—where the <u>initial</u> number is a single piece of paper—the resulting pattern is 1, 2, 4, 8, 16, 32, 64, and so on, with each number equaling twice that of the preceding number and the total quantity doubling at each step.

Doubling patterns are also called exponential patterns because they can be represented by mathematical expressions such as 2^x. (The x, an exponent, indicates how many times a number should be used as a multiplying factor.) For example, let x equal each number in the sequence 1, 2, 3, and so forth. Substituting each number in the expression 2^x (2^1, 2^2 . . .) results in the same doubling pattern that develops in the newspaper cutting experiment: 2, 4, 8, 16, etc. Doubling patterns are among the simplest of the exponential relationships, so they are often used to introduce the concept of exponents in math classes and textbooks. Exponential relationships have numerous practical uses; in particular, the growth of populations is predicted using equations of this type.

The simple doubling pattern is the basis for many folktales and math puzzles. One folktale has a clever hero asking for a single grain of wheat on the first square of a chess board, then continually doubling the number until the 64-square board is full. A clever negotiator might agree to do a job for one penny on day one and then double the money each day until the job is done. A little experimentation with a calculator will show that such an agreement would result in more than 10 million dollars for a 30-day job!

Main Idea   1 ──────────────────────────────────────

	Answer	Score
Mark the *main idea*	M	15
Mark the statement that is *too broad*	B	5
Mark the statement that is *too narrow*	N	5

a. Number patterns have many uses. ☐ _____

b. One doubling pattern is 1, 2, 4, 8, etc. ☐ _____

c. In a doubling pattern, each number is twice that of the previous one. ☐ _____

Subject Matter   **2**   This passage is mostly concerned with
- ☐ a. describing population growth.
- ☐ b. multiplying numbers.
- ☐ c. explaining and showing uses for doubling patterns.
- ☐ d. showing how many folktales use math.   _____

Supporting
Details   **3**   The mathematical expression 2^x represents
- ☐ a. a doubling pattern.
- ☐ b. a halving pattern.
- ☐ c. cutting a newspaper in pieces.
- ☐ d. $2 \times 2 \times 2 \times 2 \times 2$.   _____

Conclusion   **4**   In the doubling pattern 3, 6, 12, 24, etc., the next
number would be
- ☐ a. 28.
- ☐ b. 36.
- ☐ c. 48.
- ☐ d. 64.   _____

Clarifying
Devices   **5**   The first paragraph describes cutting a newspaper
sheet in pieces in order to
- ☐ a. show how useful doubling patterns can be.
- ☐ b. show how to follow simple directions.
- ☐ c. make the reader laugh.
- ☐ d. demonstrate how a doubling pattern actually works.   _____

Vocabulary
in Context   **6**   In this passage <u>initial</u> means
- ☐ a. a letter representing a person's name.
- ☐ b. from the beginning of time.
- ☐ c. short and to the point.
- ☐ d. first.   _____

Add your scores for questions 1–6. Enter the total here   Total
and on the graph on page 214.   Score   _____

17 To Focus or Not to Focus

The late years of the 19th century saw a new, very artistic style of photography become dominant. This style, now known as Pictorialism, had its origins in Europe but quickly became popular in the United States. A primary intention of Pictorialist photographers was to make their work look like paintings. To do this they used processes—either chemically induced or caused by natural elements such as fog and snow—to give their photos a soft focus. Retouching to achieve a desired effect was also common. Many of these photos are difficult to distinguish from paintings.

As with many other artistic styles or movements, there soon was a reaction against this type of photography. Two leaders of the new movement were Americans Edward Weston and Ansel Adams. They believed that photographs should show things as they are, in the light that is naturally available. In 1932, along with several of their <u>contemporaries,</u> they formed Group f/64. This name refers to the smallest opening on the lens of a large-format camera and the one that gives the greatest clearness and definition to images. According to their group manifesto, the photos of Group f/64 members would emphasize "simple and direct presentation through purely photographic methods." They rejected techniques used in any other art form.

The beliefs of this group did not mean, however, that they did not regard photography as art. Quite the contrary. Weston took hundreds of photos of mundane objects such as peppers and shells, but he found in them a new and sometimes startling sensuality. Adams photographed Western landscapes, particularly in Yosemite National Park, that are masterpieces of light, shadow, and contrast. Art in photography didn't disappear, but it did evolve into something that uniquely fit the medium.

Main Idea	1		
		Answer	**Score**
Mark the *main idea*		M	15
Mark the statement that is *too broad*		B	5
Mark the statement that is *too narrow*		N	5
a. Photographic style changed from blurry to sharply focused.		☐	____
b. Styles in the arts are known to periodically change.		☐	____
c. Weston and Adams took artistic photographs.		☐	____

Score 15 points for each correct answer. Score

Subject Matter 2 Another good title for this passage would be
☐ a. Weston and Adams.
☐ b. How Soft-Focus Photos Are Made.
☐ c. Photographing the American West.
☐ d. Changing Styles in Photography. _____

Supporting Details 3 The group founded by Adams and Weston was called
☐ a. Pictorialists.
☐ b. Hard Edgists.
☐ c. Group f/64.
☐ d. Photographers for Change. _____

Conclusion 4 The change called for by Adams's and Weston's group addressed mainly
☐ a. style and technique.
☐ b. subject matter.
☐ c. color.
☐ d. type of camera used. _____

Clarifying Devices 5 The word *however* in the first sentence of the final paragraph signals
☐ a. an example.
☐ b. a contrast.
☐ c. a description.
☐ d. an argument. _____

Vocabulary in Context 6 In this passage <u>contemporaries</u> means
☐ a. modern and up-to-date items.
☐ b. styles of furniture.
☐ c. persons of similar age and interest.
☐ d. items not expected to last long. _____

Add your scores for questions 1–6. Enter the total here and on the graph on page 214. Total Score _____

18 Peering into the Sky

Astronomy is the study of the planets, stars, and other objects in space. About 400 years ago, the Dutch lensmaker Hans Lippershey held a glass lens at arm's length and looked at it through another lens held in front of his eye. He discovered that the two lenses made distant objects become brighter and magnified. This discovery led to the first optical telescope. An optical telescope uses visible light rays to produce images of distant objects. Optical telescopes with lenses are called refracting telescopes. As light passes through air and then through the lenses of a refracting telescope, the light refracts, or bends. These bent light rays create a problem in that they cause tiny "rainbows" to appear around the produced images. Another problem is that over time heavy lenses sag, which further <u>distorts</u> images created by them.

In 1668 Isaac Newton developed an optical telescope with mirrors, called a reflecting telescope. In a reflecting telescope, light rays coming from a distant object reflect off mirrors and create a focused image of the object. Because the image is focused, the reflecting telescope is the main optical telescope used by astronomers. Visible light, however, is only one way in which astronomers learn about space. Objects in space also send invisible rays toward Earth. Different types of telescopes detect such invisible rays as radio, infrared, ultraviolet, gamma, and x-rays.

A drawback of optical and other types of telescopes based on Earth is that rays from space pass through Earth's atmosphere before they reach the telescopes. Smog, clouds, winds, and precipitation in Earth's atmosphere filter out and refract some of these rays. The images and signals that reach telescopes on Earth often appear shifting and blurry. To obtain more accurate images, scientists employ rockets, satellites, and other spacecraft to carry telescopes high above Earth's atmosphere.

Main Idea	1		
		Answer	**Score**
Mark the *main idea*		M	15
Mark the statement that is *too broad*		B	5
Mark the statement that is *too narrow*		N	5

a. There are several types of telescopes.	☐	____
b. Light bends in a refracting telescope.	☐	____
c. Optical and other types of telescopes have both advantages and disadvantages.	☐	____

Score 15 points for each correct answer.   **Score**

Subject Matter   2   This passage is mainly about
☐ a. rays sent by objects in space toward Earth.
☐ b. different types of telescopes.
☐ c. "rainbows" produced by refracted light rays.
☐ d. differences between visible light rays and invisible rays.   _____

Supporting Details   3   Reflecting telescopes use
☐ a. satellites.
☐ b. radio waves.
☐ c. x-rays.
☐ d. mirrors.   _____

Conclusion   4   Earth-orbiting telescopes provide more accurate information than earthbound telescopes because
☐ a. rays from space are not distorted in Earth's atmosphere.
☐ b. earth-orbiting telescopes are more powerful.
☐ c. invisible rays are stronger than visible rays.
☐ d. earth-orbiting telescopes contain better mirrors.   _____

Clarifying Devices   5   In the first paragraph, "rainbows" is put in quotation marks to show that
☐ a. these are the exact words of a speaker.
☐ b. this is an unusual spelling of a word.
☐ c. the items being described aren't really rainbows.
☐ d. the images show up only after a storm.   _____

Vocabulary in Context   6   In this passage <u>distorts</u> means to make
☐ a. unclear.
☐ b. clear.
☐ c. larger.
☐ d. smaller.   _____

Add your scores for questions 1–6. Enter the total here and on the graph on page 214.   **Total Score**   _____

19 Can the Earth Feed Its People?

In 1950 the world population's reached almost 2.5 billion, and predictions were that by the year 2000 there would be more than 5 billion people. Some experts were convinced that the world was on the verge of widespread <u>famine</u>,

One reaction to the problem was the green revolution of the 1960s. This effort multiplied agricultural yields in poor countries by introducing new high-yield grains. India, for example, doubled its wheat crop in just six years. The food supply increased faster than demand, and the price of staple foods fell. One result of the green revolution was that global food production today remains sufficient to provide every person with an adequate diet. Yet the problem of hunger remains—about 20 percent of the developing world's population is undernourished.

The immediate cause of world hunger has less to do with food production than with food distribution. For example, millions of acres in Africa, Asia, and Latin America once supported subsistence farming. Now the lands are used to raise crops such as coffee, tea, chocolate, bananas, and beef for export. The subsistence farmers have been relocated to urban areas, where there is often no employment, or to areas unsuited for farming. Small farmers and poor countries did not benefit from the green revolution because they could not afford the expensive seeds and chemicals that make agriculture productive. Despite falling food prices, hundreds of millions of people cannot afford a balanced diet. It is estimated that in the United States alone 30 million people—mostly elderly, children, and the working poor—are hungry. The answer to the question seems to be that yes, the world can provide enough food, but it is up to people to find a way to distribute the food so that everyone has an adequate food supply.

Main Idea 1		
	Answer	**Score**
Mark the *main idea*	M	15
Mark the statement that is *too broad*	B	5
Mark the statement that is *too narrow*	N	5

a. The green revolution increased agricultural yields in poor countries. ☐ _____

b. Hunger is a world problem. ☐ _____

c. World food production has increased, but people are still hungry. ☐ _____

Subject Matter   **2**   This passage is mainly about
- ☐ a. the history of world hunger.
- ☐ b. world hunger in the 1950s and 1960s.
- ☐ c. one nation's story.
- ☐ d. problems of and solutions to world hunger.   _____

Supporting Details   **3**   The percent of the developing world population that continues to be undernourished is
- ☐ a. 2.5 billion.
- ☐ b. 20 percent.
- ☐ c. 30 million.
- ☐ d. 6 percent.   _____

Conclusion   **4**   One reason for the early concern about worldwide hunger was
- ☐ a. the green revolution.
- ☐ b. rapid worldwide population growth.
- ☐ c. farmers unwilling to plant every year.
- ☐ d. people not wanting to eat healthful foods.   _____

Clarifying Devices   **5**   The third paragraph is mainly developed through
- ☐ a. examples.
- ☐ b. comparison and contrast.
- ☐ c. a persuasive argument.
- ☐ d. a description.   _____

Vocabulary in Context   **6**   The word <u>famine</u> means
- ☐ a. population explosion.
- ☐ b. excessive enthusiasm.
- ☐ c. danger.
- ☐ d. a lack of food.   _____

Add your scores for questions 1–6. Enter the total here and on the graph on page 214.   Total Score   _____

20 Can We Get Rid of Some Zeros?

What's the largest number you can think of? For most people, a number in the trillions is about the largest quantity they will ever encounter. One trillion is 1 followed by 12 zeroes, or, written out in numerals, a trillion is 1,000,000,000,000. Because numbers this large are awkward to write out, they are usually abbreviated in some manner. Often a decimal and a word form are used: 3.2 trillion means 3.2 times one trillion, or 3,200,000,000,000.

You might assume that everyday people could never do calculations with numbers this large; after all, an ordinary calculator displays only eight digits. You could not even enter 3.2 trillion into such a device. Even using a calculator with a 12-digit display, a person doing calculations in the trillions would quickly run out of display space. It would seem that people working with numbers this large would need expensive computers for their work.

However, there are methods for doing computations with huge numbers that employ pocket-sized calculators and even paper-and-pencil techniques. The key to manipulating numbers of this sort involves writing them in a form called scientific notation. Scientific notation eliminates the need for writing out all the numerals in very large numbers and, what is even more useful, it provides a way to do computations with these quantities. In scientific notation 3.2 trillion is written as 3.2×10^{12}, with the exponent 12 representing the 12 zeros in one trillion. Multiplying numbers in scientific notation requires adding exponents. If 3.5 million people each got a tax refund of $2,000, the computation would be 3.5×10^6 times 2.0×10^3, which equals 7×10^9. For anyone who works with really enormous quantities frequently, the effort required to learn scientific notation is more than offset by the ease and accuracy this form of numeral writing can provide.

Main Idea	1		
		Answer	Score
Mark the *main idea*		M	15
Mark the statement that is *too broad*		B	5
Mark the statement that is *too narrow*		N	5

a. A trillion is 1 followed by 12 zeroes. ☐ ____

b. Exponents have many uses in math. ☐ ____

c. Scientific notation is a short way of writing very large numbers. ☐ ____

Score 15 points for each correct answer. Score

Subject Matter 2 This passage is mostly concerned with
- [ ] a. explaining what exponents are.
- [ ] b. the names for very large numbers.
- [ ] c. why scientific notation is needed.
- [ ] d. being accurate when using calculators. _____

Supporting Details 3 Multiplying of very large numbers is usually done
- [ ] a. on an eight-digit calculator.
- [ ] b. on an twelve-digit calculator.
- [ ] c. on a very large computer.
- [ ] d. with scientific notation. _____

Conclusion 4 Which of these professions would most likely involve using scientific notation for numbers?
- [ ] a. treasurer of a local block club
- [ ] b. law enforcement
- [ ] c. building construction
- [ ] d. astronomy _____

Clarifying Devices 5 The writer shows that numbers in scientific notation can be multiplied by
- [ ] a. demonstrating how to multiply two large numbers.
- [ ] b. explaining the steps on a calculator.
- [ ] c. writing long numbers in shorter forms.
- [ ] d. explaining how many zeroes are in a trillion. _____

Vocabulary in Context 6 In this passage everyday means
- [ ] a. done frequently.
- [ ] b. ordinary.
- [ ] c. poorly educated.
- [ ] d. routine. _____

Add your scores for questions 1–6. Enter the total here and on the graph on page 214. Total Score _____

21 A Little Book of Poetry

When Walt Whitman first published his thin volume of poetry *Leaves of Grass* in 1855, it was severely criticized by many prominent writers of the day. One called it "a gathering of muck"; many found it crude. In fact, Whitman had to print the work himself because no publishing house wanted to take it on. And yet today many consider *Leaves of Grass* to be the most influential poetry collection in American literature. Why was Whitman's work so roundly rejected at one point, only to be revered not too many years later?

What Whitman had done in writing the 12 untitled poems in his book was to go against most of the poetic <u>conventions</u> of the day. There were no American poets, for example, writing unrhymed lines with irregular meter or no meter as Whitman did. There were no poets writing extremely long lines, occasionally interspersed with very short ones, as Whitman did. There were few poets writing sympathetically about everyday American life, using the language of ordinary people. And there were no respected poets who dared to include some of the frank imagery that Whitman used.

Despite the generally negative response, Whitman kept writing. He put out several more editions of *Leaves of Grass,* adding new poems and revising the existing ones. And gradually critical opinion changed. The long, flowing lines of free verse that Whitman produced were recognized as revolutionary. By opening up poetry from the constraints of rhythm, rhyme, and delicate subject matter, Whitman had a great influence on poets of his own time and especially on those who followed him. Today he is widely regarded as the father of modern American poetry.

Main Idea	1		
		Answer	**Score**
	Mark the *main idea*	**M**	15
	Mark the statement that is *too broad*	**B**	5
	Mark the statement that is *too narrow*	**N**	5

a. Whitman's poems were criticized for both style and subject matter. ☐ _____

b. *Leaves of Grass* was first despised, then revered. ☐ _____

c. Poetry began to change in the 1800s. ☐ _____

Score 15 points for each correct answer. **Score**

Subject Matter **2** Another good title for this passage would be
- ☐ a. Walt Whitman's Master Work.
- ☐ b. Poetry in the 1800s.
- ☐ c. Using Rhyme and Rhythm.
- ☐ d. A Description of Free Verse.

_____

Supporting Details **3** *Leaves of Grass* was published
- ☐ a. only once.
- ☐ b. in 1854.
- ☐ c. in several different editions.
- ☐ d. by Walt Whitman's father.

_____

Conclusion **4** The early response to *Leaves of Grass* suggests that
- ☐ a. most people appreciate new writing styles.
- ☐ b. people distrust anything that is different.
- ☐ c. Whitman would have done better using a regular publisher.
- ☐ d. praise will often come if one is patient.

_____

Clarifying Devices **5** The second and third paragraphs in the passage
- ☐ a. briefly summarize Whitman's life and work.
- ☐ b. quote from some of Whitman's most famous poems.
- ☐ c. answer the question at the end of the first paragraph.
- ☐ d. are intended to convince the reader of Whitman's bravery in publishing his poems.

_____

Vocabulary in Context **6** In this passage <u>conventions</u> means
- ☐ a. large business gatherings.
- ☐ b. customs or practices.
- ☐ c. surprises.
- ☐ d. collections of writings.

_____

Add your scores for questions 1–6. Enter the total here and on the graph on page 214. **Total Score**

_____

22 The Earth's Blankets

You may watch those fluffy white formations floating across the sky for fun, but scientists watch them in hopes of accurately forecasting and eventually controlling or modifying the weather. Clouds are one visible element of a day's weather. They are formed when the sun heats the earth, which then radiates thermal energy to the air in its atmosphere. Since warm air is less dense than cool air, the heated air creates "thermal updrafts" that rise up and away from the earth. The temperature in the atmosphere's lower layer decreases with <u>altitude</u>, so as the warm air rises, it cools, and the water vapor in it condenses into tiny droplets of water or particles of ice, depending on the altitude. These liquid or ice particles are visible as cloud.

Clouds affect the earth's weather and climate in that, acting as sort of a blanket between the sun and the earth, they shield sunlight from reaching and warming the earth and block the amount of infrared radiation, or radiating heat, escaping from the earth into outer space. Thus, weather observers know that a cloudy day will be cooler than a clear day and that a cloudy night will be warmer than a clear night.

Scientist have divided clouds into three main classes—cirrus, cumulus, and stratus. *Cirrus,* a Latin word meaning "curl," describes white, wispy clouds stretching across the sky at high altitudes. *Cumulus,* a Latin word meaning "heap," characterizes piles of flat-based, cottonlike clouds at low altitudes. *Stratus,* derived from a Latin word meaning "spread out," identifies layers of flat, gray clouds spreading across the sky at low altitudes. Scientist use these three classes to specify the numerous combinations of clouds that exist. Masses of gray and white clouds rolling across the sky are stratocumulus. The Latin word *nimbus,* meaning "rain cloud," is added to a precipitating cloud. Cumulonimbus describes cumulus clouds producing thunderstorms.

Main Idea	1			Answer	Score
		Mark the *main idea*		M	15
		Mark the statement that is *too broad*		B	5
		Mark the statement that is *too narrow*		N	5

a.	Cloudy days are cooler than sunny ones.	☐ _____
b.	Clouds are fluffy white formations floating across the sky.	☐ _____
c.	Clouds, which affect the earth's weather, come in three main classes.	☐ _____

Score 15 points for each correct answer.   **Score**

Subject Matter   **2**   This passage is mainly about
    ☐ a. the importance and classification of clouds.
    ☐ b. how thermal updrafts produce weather.
    ☐ c. precipitation and why it occurs.
    ☐ d. why condensation occurs in the atmosphere.   _____

Supporting   **3**   Clouds are
Details   ☐ a. a weather forecaster's nightmare.
    ☐ b. infrared radiation escaping the atmosphere.
    ☐ c. visible liquid or ice particles in the air.
    ☐ d. a source of thermal energy.   _____

Conclusion   **4**   We can conclude that a cloudy night will be
warmer than a clear night because
    ☐ a. clouds trap the earth's heat in the area
         between the ground and the clouds.
    ☐ b. infrared radiation escapes into outer space.
    ☐ c. there will be few or no stars visible.
    ☐ d. clouds prevent much of the sun's heat from
         reaching the earth.   _____

Clarifying   **5**   The Latin definitions in the third paragraph are
Devices   intended to help you
    ☐ a. spell the names of clouds correctly.
    ☐ b. visualize the various types of clouds.
    ☐ c. see that there are only three types of clouds.
    ☐ d. memorize the names of clouds.   _____

Vocabulary   **6**   <u>Altitude</u> means
in Context   ☐ a. width.
    ☐ b. height.
    ☐ c. depth.
    ☐ d. circumference.   _____

Add your scores for questions 1–6. Enter the total here   Total
and on the graph on page 214.   Score   _____

23 The Family

The structure of a family takes different forms around the world and even in the same society. The family's form changes as it adapts to changing social and economic influences. Until recently, the most common form in North America was the nuclear family, consisting of a married couple with their minor children. The nuclear family is an independent unit. It must be prepared to fend for itself. Individual family members strongly depend on one another. There is little help from outside the family in emergencies. Elderly relatives of a nuclear family are cared for only if it is possible for the family to do so. In North America, the elderly often do not live with the family; they live in retirement communities and nursing homes.

There are many parallels between the nuclear family in industrial societies, such as North America, and of families in societies such as that of the Inuits, who live in harsh environments, The nuclear family structure is well adapted to a life of <u>mobility</u>. In harsh conditions, mobility allows the family to hunt for food. For North Americans, the hunt for jobs and improved social status also requires mobility.

The nuclear family was not always the North American standard. In a more agrarian time, the small nuclear family was usually part of a larger extended family. This might have included grandparents, mother and father, brothers and sisters, uncles, aunts, and cousins. In North America today, there is a dramatic rise in the number of single-parent households. Twice as many households in the United States are headed by divorced, separated, or never-married individuals as are comprised of nuclear families. The structure of the family, not just in North America, but throughout the world, continues to change as it adapts to changing conditions.

Main Idea	1	Answer	Score
	Mark the *main idea*	M	15
	Mark the statement that is *too broad*	B	5
	Mark the statement that is *too narrow*	N	5

a. North American family forms are influenced by the conditions people live under. ☐ _____

b. The nuclear family form was once the most common in North America. ☐ _____

c. Families take different forms. ☐ _____

Score 15 points for each correct answer.   **Score**

Subject Matter **2** Another good title for this passage would be
☐ a. What Makes a Family?
☐ b. The Life of the Inuits.
☐ c. Living with Hardship.
☐ d. The Failure of the Nuclear Family.   _____

Supporting Details **3** A nuclear family is defined as
☐ a. a married couple with their minor children.
☐ b. a single father with minor children.
☐ c. parents, grandparents, and children.
☐ d. parents, children, and aunts and uncles.   _____

Conclusion **4** The information in this passage would most likely be found in
☐ a. an anthropology textbook.
☐ b. a biology textbook.
☐ c. a mathematics textbook.
☐ d. a geography textbook.   _____

Clarifying Devices **5** The information in the first paragraph is presented mainly through
☐ a. listing statistics.
☐ b. telling a story.
☐ c. pointing out similarities.
☐ d. pointing out differences.   _____

Vocabulary in Context **6** The word <u>mobility</u> means
☐ a. money.
☐ b. readiness to move.
☐ c. organization.
☐ d. skill.   _____

Add your scores for questions 1–6. Enter the total here and on the graph on page 214.   **Total Score**   _____

24 Birthday Twins

When was the last time you met someone who has the same birthday as you do, someone born on the same day who might be called your "birthday twin"? Since there are 365 different days in every year except leap year, common sense would suggest that encountering a birthday twin is a pretty rare occurrence. You might guess that you'd need to meet 365 people to be certain of finding just one person born on the same day that you were. In this situation, common sense would lead you <u>astray</u>. You do not need a group of 365 people to be reasonably certain of finding a pair of birthday twins—in fact, the size of the group needed is considerably smaller.

Finding the chances of two people in a group sharing the same birthday is a well-known problem in the area of mathematics called *probability*. To compute probabilities of this type, mathematicians make use of the concept of *complementary probabilities*. This states that the probability of an event happening plus the probability of the event not happening must equal 1. Think of 5 balls in a vase. If there are only 2 white balls, the probability of drawing a white ball is 2 chances out of 5, or the fraction $\frac{2}{5}$. The probability of *not* drawing a white ball is 3 chances out of 5, or $\frac{3}{5}$, and $\frac{2}{5}$ plus $\frac{3}{5}$ equals 1. For some complicated types of probability problems, it is easier to first find the chance of something *not* happening and then subtract that quantity from 1.

Using computational techniques that apply complementary probabilities, you would discover that the chances of two people in a group of just 30 persons sharing the same birthday is over 70 percent. To have an even chance, a chance of 50 percent, of finding two birthday twins, all you actually need is a group of 24 people. The next time you attend a meeting or a party with more than 24 people, you might test this mathematical fact. Chances are good that two people in the group will be birthday twins.

Main Idea	1		
		Answer	**Score**
	Mark the *main idea*	M	15
	Mark the statement that is *too broad*	B	5
	Mark the statement that is *too narrow*	N	5

a. The probability of two people sharing a birthday is higher than you might think. ☐ _____

b. People may share the same birthday. ☐ _____

c. Complementary probabilities add up to 1. ☐ _____

Score 15 points for each correct answer.   **Score**

Subject Matter   2   This passage is mainly about
                           ☐ a. how common sense helps with probabilities.
                           ☐ b. adding up numbers to get 1.
                           ☐ c. drawing or not drawing balls of a given color.
                           ☐ d. the chances of two people in a group having
                               the same birthday.   _____

Supporting   3   The probabilities $\frac{2}{3}$ and $\frac{3}{3}$ are complementary
Details   because
                           ☐ a. they show that something is very likely
                               to happen.
                           ☐ b. when you subtract them, you get $\frac{1}{3}$.
                           ☐ c. they add up to 1.
                           ☐ d. they are both numbers less than 1.   _____

Conclusion   4   In a group of 100 people, the chances of two
                           people sharing the same birthday are
                           ☐ a. very low.
                           ☐ b. about even.
                           ☐ c. very high.
                           ☐ d. certain.   _____

Clarifying   5   The example of the white balls in the vase is used to
Devices   ☐ a. show how to subtract fractions.
                           ☐ b. explain complementary probabilities.
                           ☐ c. demonstrate the uses of percents.
                           ☐ d. help solve the birthday problem.   _____

Vocabulary   6   In this passage <u>astray</u> means
in Context   ☐ a. into error.
                           ☐ b. into a dangerous situation.
                           ☐ c. far away.
                           ☐ d. toward a goal.   _____

**Add your scores for questions 1–6. Enter the total here   Total
and on the graph on page 214.   Score**   _____

25 Nigerian Bronzes

Like many other societies, African cultural groups in Nigeria created a variety of beautiful artifacts. But two sites in particular are known for the remarkable sculptures, plaques, and jewelry that the residents created in bronze.

One site in the southwest section of the country called Ife, was an important political and religious center for the Yoruba people. From the 12th century to the 15th century beautiful bronze figurines were made in Ife, many of them related to the local royalty. There are, in particular, castings of the heads of kings and queens that are so realistic they seem almost lifelike. These sculptures were created at a time when there was nothing similar being made anywhere in Europe. In fact, nothing similar would be created there until several hundred years later.

The other important Nigerian site was Benin. This city, about 100 miles southeast of Ife, was the center of the Edo-speaking people. Bronzework here flourished a bit later than in Ife, the civilization having reached its height in the late 15th century. The influence of Ife sculpture can be seen in some of the artifacts found in Benin, but there are also many original works. A whole series of three-dimensional panels depicting local rulers and customs were forged. These were attached to the palace of the oba, or king. Also found at Benin were many beautiful bracelets, one full figure of a horn player, and remarkable animal figures, including a pair of exquisitely carved leopards.

Benin work also includes many sculptures of Portuguese sailors, who began exploring the region in about 1486. Contact with Europeans, however, had an ultimately tragic effect. In 1897 British soldiers looted Benin, burned it to the ground, and stole its artistic treasures. These treasures can now be found in museums throughout the world.

Main Idea	1		
		Answer	**Score**
	Mark the *main idea*	M	15
	Mark the statement that is *too broad*	B	5
	Mark the statement that is *too narrow*	N	5

a. Bronzework from two Nigerian cities was remarkably well crafted. ☐ _____

b. Heads of rulers were created in Ife. ☐ _____

c. Many societies have created beautiful artifacts. ☐ _____

Subject Matter   **2**   This passage is mostly about
☐ a. bronzework from Ife and Benin.
☐ b. plaques depicting the lives of kings.
☐ c. why bronze art thrived in Africa.
☐ d. what Europeans did to African art.   _____

Supporting Details   **3**   The art from Ife was primarily
☐ a. bracelets.
☐ b. figures of animals.
☐ c. panels or plaques.
☐ d. sculpted heads.   _____

Conclusion   **4**   The final paragraph suggests that Europeans
☐ a. wanted to destroy Benin art.
☐ b. knew that Benin art was quite valuable.
☐ c. wanted to help the artists of Benin.
☐ d. wanted European artists to copy what Benin artists did.   _____

Clarifying Devices   **5**   The last two sentences of the second paragraph are intended to show
☐ a. why Benin art resembled that of Ife.
☐ b. that European artists were very forward looking.
☐ c. how unique Ife art was.
☐ d. that no one understood the value of bronze.   _____

Vocabulary in Context   **6**   Depicting means
☐ a. picturing.
☐ b. confusing.
☐ c. criticizing.
☐ d. denying.   _____

Add your scores for questions 1–6. Enter the total here and on the graph on page 214.   **Total Score**   _____

26 To Soar Like a Bird

Designs are underway for a double-decker superjet capable of transporting up to 1,000 passengers and containing such convenience facilities as a health club, a medical treatment center, shops, sleeping compartments, and elevators. How is it possible for such a monstrous airliner to take flight, let alone stay airborne? The idea becomes believable when you understand the relationship between moving fluids and pressure. Bernoulli's law states that as a fluid, such as a gas or a liquid, travels faster, the pressure exerted by the fluid decreases. This explains the lift, or upward force, that allows airplanes to fly even though they are heavier than air, which is a gas.

Lift is created by airfoils, or wings, that are rounded in the front, thick in the middle, with a more rounded upper surface than lower surface, and narrowed in the back. The curved upper surface provides a greater distance for air to flow across than does the flatter lower surface. The greater distance across the wing's upper surface causes the air above the wing to flow faster than the air beneath. The air pressure of the slower-flowing air beneath the wing is greater than that of the faster-flowing air above it. The greater air pressure beneath the wing exerts an upward force, and lift results. The greater an airplane's thrust, or forward-moving force, the faster the airplane moves and the greater the lift. When the lift becomes greater than the weight of the plane, the airplane overcomes gravity and rises. In level flight, the lift force on an airplane's wings is equal to the weight of the airplane.

Airplane manufacturers may be capable of designing superjets that can attain and maintain lift. Have they contemplated, though, how to efficiently deplane 1,000 impatient passengers and <u>process</u> them through a crowded airport? Even worse, have they anticipated the lines of expectant passengers waiting at the baggage claim?

Main Idea   1

	Answer	Score
Mark the *main idea*	M	15
Mark the statement that is *too broad*	B	5
Mark the statement that is *too narrow*	N	5

a. There are forces that allow planes to fly even though they are heavier than air. ☐ _____

b. Flight is a complicated process. ☐ _____

c. Airfoils are rounded in the front, curved in the middle, and narrowed in the back. ☐ _____

Subject Matter   **2**   Another good title for this passage would be
- [ ] a. Bernoulli and His Law.
- [ ] b. Getting a Lift from Moving Air.
- [ ] c. The Friendly Skies Have It All.
- [ ] d. Flying Across Continents.

_____

Supporting   **3**   To understand flight, you must understand
Details   the relationship between
- [ ] a. moving fluids and pressure.
- [ ] b. air and force.
- [ ] c. speed and gravity.
- [ ] d. surfaces and tension.

_____

Conclusion   **4**   Bernoulli's law was probably established
- [ ] a. before the Wright brothers flew in 1903.
- [ ] b. just after the Wright brothers flew.
- [ ] c. just before the flight of the first passenger jet in 1958.
- [ ] d. just after the flight of the first passenger jet.

_____

Clarifying   **5**   To make the point that a superjet in the skies may
Devices   not be so super on the ground, the author
- [ ] a. presents the conveniences of the superjet.
- [ ] b. explains the purpose of airfoils.
- [ ] c. discusses the superjet's effects on airports.
- [ ] d. defines lift in terms of air and pressure.

_____

Vocabulary   **6**   In this passage <u>process</u> means
in Context
- [ ] a. advance in an orderly manner.
- [ ] b. a gradual change.
- [ ] c. a natural phenomenon.
- [ ] d. expect unreasonable delays.

_____

Add your scores for questions 1–6. Enter the total here   Total
and on the graph on page 215.   Score

_____

27 Alexandria's Sunken City

By the mid-fifth century A.D., the royal palaces and buildings within the Great Harbor of Alexandria, Egypt, had been destroyed by earthquakes and tidal waves. Over time the harbor floor dropped more than 20 feet. The ruined buildings of the Great Harbor sank beneath the water. Today archaeologist-divers, architects, photographers, geologists, and Egyptologists piece together information about the city that lies on the floor of the harbor.

The water in the harbor is between 6 and 30 feet deep. This shallow depth allows archaeologists to use the latest technology to map the harbor's archaeological features. They use a plumb bob suspended from a buoy to trace the outlines of the fallen columns, capitals, statues, and stone blocks, and the remains of streets littering the seabed of the modern harbor,. The buoy, at the surface of the water, has two waterproof Global Positioning System (GPS) receivers. One receives signals from satellites passing overhead. The other receives signals from an onshore beacon. The GPS data is transmitted to two research vessels anchored in the harbor, where it is entered into a database. The database is used to <u>generate</u> a map of the location of the archaeological remains.

The mapping of Alexandria's eastern harbor was substantially completed in 1997. Then the archaeologist-divers began excavations. The architectural and sculptural pieces were cleaned, identified, drawn, and photographed. Each find was given an inventory number, and its height, orientation, and location were recorded. The work is not complete, but plans are being considered to someday create an underwater archaeological park where visitors can explore Alexandria's ancient Great Harbor from glass-bottomed boats.

Main Idea	1		
		Answer	**Score**
	Mark the *main idea*	M	15
	Mark the statement that is *too broad*	B	5
	Mark the statement that is *too narrow*	N	5

a.	Underwater archaeology has helped to reveal Alexandria's Great Harbor.	☐	_____
b.	An ancient underwater city exists in Alexandria, Egypt.	☐	_____
c.	Satellites help archaeologists map Alexandria's Great Harbor.	☐	_____

Subject Matter   **2**   This passage primarily focuses on
☐ a. a history of Alexandria.
☐ b. the excavation of Alexandria.
☐ c. the excavation of Alexandria's harbor.
☐ d. creating archaeological parks.   _____

Supporting
Details   **3**   The Great Harbor was destroyed by
☐ a. tourists.
☐ b. archaeologists.
☐ c. earthquakes and tidal waves.
☐ d. shallow water.   _____

Conclusion   **4**   The underwater excavation of the Great Harbor
has been
☐ a. effortless.
☐ b. complicated.
☐ c. useless.
☐ d. simple.   _____

Clarifying
Devices   **5**   The second paragraph of this passage
☐ a. narrates a story.
☐ b. explains a process.
☐ c. describes a site.
☐ d. argues in favor of archaeology.   _____

Vocabulary
in Context   **6**   In this passage <u>generate</u> means to
☐ a. create electric power.
☐ b. describe.
☐ c. bring into existence.
☐ d. remove from the ground.   _____

Add your scores for questions 1–6. Enter the total here   **Total**
and on the graph on page 215.   **Score**   _____

28 Geometry on the Floor

When you move or rearrange the furniture in a room, two yardsticks and a pad of quarter-inch graph paper can prevent a tremendous amount of sweat and frustration, perhaps even an injured back! The yardsticks and graph paper are simple and inexpensive tools you can utilize to create a floor plan similar to the simplified sample shown in the illustration below.

When using the yardsticks to measure dimensions of rooms, lay the two measuring instruments end-to-end to measure six feet; move the first yardstick to get nine feet; and so forth. You'll discover that the two-stick method is more convenient than struggling with a very long tape measure, and it is a method easily <u>implemented</u> alone, whereas using a tape measure generally requires an additional person.

Use one square on the graph paper to stand for one square foot; then measure all distances and dimensions of furniture to the nearest half foot—that's close enough for most purposes and will make it easier to represent them on the floor plan. One mistake frequently made in planning room arrangements is to forget that a door takes up wall space when it is open. To avoid this mistake, use quarter-circle marks like the two shown in the sample floor plan to indicate the path of an opening door. If you look at the top width of the sample, you'll notice that three of the feet along this dimension are used when the door is open, thus leaving only five usable feet of space along this wall.

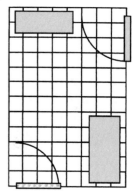

Main Idea   1

	Answer	Score
Mark the *main idea*	M	15
Mark the statement that is *too broad*	B	5
Mark the statement that is *too narrow*	N	5

a. Rooms can be drawn to proportion. ☐ _____

b. Drawing floor plans is simple to do and provides useful information. ☐ _____

c. Quarter-circles mark the openings of doors on floor plans. ☐ _____

Subject Matter   **2**   This passage is mostly concerned with
- ☐ a. preventing back injuries when rearranging furniture.
- ☐ b. tips for making floor plans for rooms.
- ☐ c. geometric figures used in interior decorating.
- ☐ d. explaining uses of graph paper.   _____

Supporting Details   **3**   The floor plan included with this passage
- ☐ a. shows a room with only one door.
- ☐ b. includes all window openings.
- ☐ c. is for a room measuring 12 feet by 12 feet.
- ☐ d. uses one square to stand for one square foot.   _____

Conclusion   **4**   The two gray rectangles in the sample floor plan most likely show
- ☐ a. bookcases or cabinets.
- ☐ b. chairs or end tables.
- ☐ c. rugs.
- ☐ d. measuring sticks.   _____

Clarifying Devices   **5**   The writer explains how to use two yardsticks to measure a room dimension by
- ☐ a. recommending the use of a tape measure.
- ☐ b. giving an example.
- ☐ c. describing the procedure to use.
- ☐ d. showing a diagram.   _____

Vocabulary in Context   **6**   In this passage the word <u>implemented</u> means
- ☐ a. understood.
- ☐ b. carried out.
- ☐ c. supplied with measuring tools.
- ☐ d. practiced.   _____

Add your scores for questions 1–6. Enter the total here and on the graph on page 215.   **Total Score**   _____

29 Asian-American Themes

It can be risky to generalize about the literature of any culture or group. For almost any statement that is made, exceptions can be found. Nevertheless, literary analysis is all about generalizations. Here are some that are made about Asian-American literature.

All Asian-American writers can be placed into one of two groups, those who emigrated to the United States and those who were born here but of immigrant families. They represent a broad and diverse range of countries, from Japan and the Philippines in the east to Iran and Turkey in the west.

Some of the topics that first-generation writers deal with are common to all immigrant peoples: the difficult journey to a new land, a loneliness for home, and an uncertainty about the new culture. So you might find tales of a Vietnamese immigrant's horrific departure after the fall of Saigon or the struggles against prejudice described in a book like Carlos Bulosan's autobiographical *America Is in the Heart.*

Family values can be a source of much rich literature. All Asian-American groups carried certain customs and practices with them, and sometimes these were looked on with surprise by their new countrymen. They certainly were a cause of misunderstanding and sometimes <u>contention</u> between immigrants and their American-born children. Books like Jade Snow Wong's *Fifth Chinese Daughter* make this clear.

More, perhaps, than some other groups, Asian Americans have been fascinated with language: how it sets them apart from others, the importance of mastering American English. In an essay called "Mother Tongue," for example, writer Amy Tan discusses how her mother's less-than-perfect English influenced her own life and her views of herself.

Main Idea	1		Answer	Score
	Mark the *main idea*		M	15
	Mark the statement that is *too broad*		B	5
	Mark the statement that is *too narrow*		N	5

a. Many immigrants write about their experiences. ☐ _____

b. Asian-American literature covers both expected and not so expected topics. ☐ _____

c. General conflict is a typical theme in Asian-American writing. ☐ _____

Score 15 points for each correct answer.   **Score**

Subject Matter   **2**   This passage mostly focuses on
☐ a. an overview of Asian-American literature.
☐ b. a detailed summary of Asian-American literature.
☐ c. the works of Carlos Bulosan and Amy Tan.
☐ d. why most Asian Americans write in their mother tongue.   _____

Supporting Details   **3**   Asian-American writers come from
☐ a. only the Near East.
☐ b. only the Far East.
☐ c. only countries where Chinese is spoken.
☐ d. all across Asia.   _____

Conclusion   **4**   Unlike writers from other immigrant groups, Asian Americans often write about
☐ a. families.
☐ b. loneliness for the country of origin.
☐ c. prejudice and discrimination.
☐ d. language issues.   _____

Clarifying Devices   **5**   The term *first-generation writers* refers to writers
☐ a. who are immigrants.
☐ b. who are children of immigrants.
☐ c. who are grandchildren of immigrants.
☐ d. of mixed parentage.   _____

Vocabulary in Context   **6**   In this passage <u>contention</u> means
☐ a. arguments.
☐ b. a meeting of many people.
☐ c. a family gathering.
☐ d. a new idea or product.   _____

Add your scores for questions 1–6. Enter the total here and on the graph on page 215.   **Total Score**   _____

30 Physical, Chemical, or Nuclear?

You know that matter is anything that has mass and occupies space. You may not know that matter contains energy that can be converted from one form to another, such as from solar energy to electric energy, and that matter gains or releases energy as it changes form. These transformations occur in physical, chemical, and nuclear changes.

A physical change is an alteration in the form of matter but not in its <u>composition</u>. A change of state, such as from a solid to a liquid or a gas, is a physical change. For example, water forms ice in its solid state and steam in its gaseous state, but the composition of the particles in each state remains the same—water molecules. During a physical change, matter *sometimes gains or releases energy,* usually as heat.

In a chemical change, one type of matter is converted into another. For example, when iron comes into contact with oxygen and water in air, the iron changes into rust. The atoms of the iron and oxygen and of the water molecules rearrange themselves and produce a new matter—rust. The composition of rust is chemically different from the original substances. During a chemical change, matter *always gains or releases energy.*

In a nuclear change, the nucleus of an element's atom is altered, thus producing a different element. In one type of nuclear change, fission, a single large nucleus splits into smaller nuclei. For example, the nucleus of a uranium atom may divide into two nuclei—a nucleus of the element barium and a nucleus of the element krypton. During a nuclear change, matter *always releases energy*—and a considerable amount. A quantity of uranium about the size of a golf ball produces as much energy as one million kilograms of coal. Scientists utilize these qualities of matter to improve existing energy sources and to search for new energy sources to provide power for commonly used items.

Main Idea	1		
		Answer	Score
	Mark the *main idea*	M	15
	Mark the statement that is *too broad*	B	5
	Mark the statement that is *too narrow*	N	5

a. During a nuclear change, matter always releases energy. ☐ ____

b. Changes to matter occur during many processes. ☐ ____

c. Matter is transformed during physical, chemical, and nuclear changes. ☐ ____

Score 15 points for each correct answer.   **Score**

Subject Matter   **2**   Another good title for this passage would be
- ☐ a. Matter: Create Energy by Changing It.
- ☐ b. Steam: It's Such a Gas.
- ☐ c. Changes of State: It's Physical.
- ☐ d. Fission: We're Just Splitting Atoms.   _____

Supporting Details   **3**   In a chemical change, the original matter is altered so that the new substance that is formed is
- ☐ a. of the same composition as the original.
- ☐ b. only a change of state.
- ☐ c. chemically different from the original.
- ☐ d. split into two or more nuclei.   _____

Conclusion   **4**   You can conclude from this passage that scientists searching for improved energy sources are most likely to explore
- ☐ a. composition changes.
- ☐ b. nuclear changes.
- ☐ c. physical changes.
- ☐ d. chemical changes.   _____

Clarifying Devices   **5**   To help the reader compare what happens to energy in the three types of changes, the writer
- ☐ a. italicizes key phrases.
- ☐ b. underlines key terms.
- ☐ c. states scientific facts.
- ☐ d. quantifies amounts.   _____

Vocabulary in Context   **6**   In this passage composition refers to
- ☐ a. an essay.
- ☐ b. a piece of written music.
- ☐ c. the makeup of a substance.
- ☐ d. an arrangement.   _____

Add your scores for questions 1–6. Enter the total here and on the graph on page 215.   **Total Score**   _____

31 Please Continue

In 1963 Stanley Milgram, a psychologist at Yale University, conducted a study focusing on the conflict between obedience to authority and personal conscience. This was nearly two decades after the World War II Nuremberg war criminal trials in which the defense of those accused of genocide was based on "obedience." The accused said they were just following the orders of their superiors.

In Milgram's experiment, so-called "teachers," who were the unknowing subjects of the experiment, were to administer an increasingly stronger electric shock to "learners." The <u>fictitious</u> story given to these "teachers" was that the experiment was exploring the effects of punishment on learning behavior. Unknown to the "teacher," the "learner" was really an actor pretending to be uncomfortable as the shocks increased. The teacher was to read a list of two word pairs and ask the learner to say them back. If the learner answered correctly, they moved on to the next word pair. If the answer was incorrect, the teacher was to shock the learner. Shocks began at 15 volts and went up to 450 volts.

At times, worried teachers questioned the experimenter, asking who was taking responsibility for harming the learner. The experimenter replied that he assumed full responsibility. At this, the teachers seemed able to continue. When teachers asked if they should continue increasing the shocks, the experimenter verbally encouraged them.

To Milgram's surprise and the surprise of his colleagues, 65 percent of the teachers obeyed orders to punish the learner to the very end of the 450-volt scale, and no teachers stopped before reaching 300 volts. One of Milgram's conclusions was that ordinary people, simply doing their jobs, can become agents in a destructive process.

Main Idea	1		
		Answer	**Score**
Mark the *main idea*		M	15
Mark the statement that is *too broad*		B	5
Mark the statement that is *too narrow*		N	5

a. Milgram's experiment tested obedience to authority. ☐ _____

b. Experimenters said they took full responsibility for harm to learners. ☐ _____

c. Psychological experiments can prove or disprove theories. ☐ _____

Subject Matter   **2**   This passage mainly focuses on
☐ a. the life of Stanley Milgram.
☐ b. a definition of social psychology.
☐ c. a summary of a psychological experiment.
☐ d. a history of the Nuremberg trials.   _____

Supporting Details   **3**   The "learner" in Milgram's experimenter was really
☐ a. a war criminal.
☐ b. Stanley Milgram.
☐ c. an experimenter.
☐ d. an actor.   _____

Conclusion   **4**   Most of the "teachers" in the experiment decided
☐ a. it was all right to inflict pain if someone else told them it was.
☐ b. 450 volts of electricity was a large jolt.
☐ c. that they liked to cause pain.
☐ d. that they resented being told what to do.   _____

Clarifying Devices   **5**   The quotation marks around the words *learner* and *teacher* in this passage mean that
☐ a. the real meaning of these words is not what is meant here.
☐ b. this is quoted material.
☐ c. these are titles.
☐ d. these are special, technical words.   _____

Vocabulary in Context   **6**   In this passage <u>fictitious</u> means
☐ a. not true; made up.
☐ b. elaborate and complicated.
☐ c. assumed in order to deceive.
☐ d. experimental.   _____

Add your scores for questions 1–6. Enter the total here and on the graph on page 215.   **Total Score**   _____

32 Good for Nothing?

Are there any practical purposes for the number zero, or could we function just as well without it? Zero describes the absence of something, and while on scales such as those used for temperature zero has a defined meaning, in general it doesn't seem to be as useful as many other numbers.

If you concur with the notion that the number zero is not particularly valuable, you probably have not considered the most important use for this number, a use that you see every day and most likely take for granted. The number, or more precisely, the digit zero makes our positional system of numbers possible. Without zero, the numerals for three hundred two and for thirty-two would be indistinguishable from each other—and from many other numbers as well. The use of zero keeps the digits in their correct places, so that the place value of each digit is immediately apparent. You know at a glance that the 3 in 302 has a value of 3 hundreds and not 3 thousands or 3 tenths or some other quantity. The place of each digit shows its value, and zeros keep the digits in the correct places.

So, what is so remarkable? you may be thinking. *Aren't all number systems positional with some kind of place value system?* The truth is that not all number systems are of this nature, and that most very early number systems were not positional. Roman numerals, which are still used today for a few applications, are positional but do not include a symbol for zero. Egyptian numerals included no zero and had no positional values. One early number system that did include zero was that employed by the Maya in Central America. For the most part, however, the use of a symbol for zero was a relatively late introduction in methods used to record quantities.

Main Idea	1		
		Answer	Score
	Mark the *main idea*	M	15
	Mark the statement that is *too broad*	B	5
	Mark the statement that is *too narrow*	N	5
	a. All number systems vary somewhat.	☐	___
	b. The zero in 302 separates the digits in the hundreds and ones places.	☐	___
	c. Zero is needed to make our number-writing system work.	☐	___

Score 15 points for each correct answer.   **Score**

Subject Matter **2** Another good title for this passage would be

    ☐ a. What Is Place Value?

    ☐ b. Using Digits to Write Numbers.

    ☐ c. Number Systems Throughout History.

    ☐ d. The Importance of Zero.   _____

Supporting **3** The digit 3 in the number 302 has a value of three
Details

    ☐ a. ones.

    ☐ b. tens.

    ☐ c. hundreds.

    ☐ d. hundredths.   _____

Conclusion **4** In a positional number system, the value of a symbol

    ☐ a. is always greater than zero.

    ☐ b. is sometimes equal to zero.

    ☐ c. indicates a large number.

    ☐ d. changes depending on its position.   _____

Clarifying **5** The writer shows that zero is needed
Devices

    ☐ a. in every type of number system.

    ☐ b. to compare numbers.

    ☐ c. to make a number system positional.

    ☐ d. because the Maya used it.   _____

Vocabulary **6** In this passage <u>apparent</u> means
in Context

    ☐ a. wearable.

    ☐ b. complicated.

    ☐ c. understood.

    ☐ d. written in numbers.   _____

Add your scores for questions 1–6. Enter the total here   **Total**
and on the graph on page 215.   **Score**   _____

33 To Whom Are You Speaking?

In many poems the writer seems merely to be reflecting on one small event or occurrence and trying to convey its significance. Poems like these, because of their personal nature, sometimes do not seem to have much concrete meaning. But in other poems, called dramatic monologues, the writer creates a character who speaks directly, either to the reader or to a silent listener. This character relates an incident or presents biographical information and in so doing reveals something of his or her personality.

One creator of dramatic monologues was American poet Edgar Lee Masters. In his *Spoon River Anthology*, published in 1915, he has 244 characters, all speaking from the graveyard in which they are buried, tell something of their life and times. There is Cooney Potter, who worked his family from "dawn to dusk" in his feverish desire to possess more—yet who dies before his 60th birthday. There is Lucinda Matlock, who with her husband raised 12 children, died at 96, and has no patience with younger generations who complain about life's hardships. Some of Masters's characters gossip about people; others are kind and charitable. Reading just a few of these dramatic monologues gives a sharp picture of life in the fictional town of Spoon River.

Another, more subtle master of the dramatic monologue was 19th-century British writer Robert Browning. The poem "My Last Duchess" reveals something of his craft. The narrator seems to be telling about his late wife, but as he describes how she wilted under his harshness, he actually conveys what a cruel, indifferent individual he is. In another poem, "Porphyria's Lover," the narrator describes in perfectly normal tones how he commits a <u>heinous</u> murder. The total effect leads the reader to infer that this narrator is, in fact, quite mad. In these and other dramatic monologues the narrator presents many facts, but it is up to the reader to decide how to interpret them.

Main Idea 1

	Answer	Score
Mark the *main idea*	M	15
Mark the statement that is *too broad*	B	5
Mark the statement that is *too narrow*	N	5

a. Dramatic monologues are interesting. ☐ _____

b. Narrators of dramatic monologues often reveal themselves in their tales. ☐ _____

c. Browning's dramatic monologues are more subtle than Masters's. ☐ _____

Score 15 points for each correct answer.   **Score**

Subject Matter   **2**   This passage deals primarily with
- ☐ a. the poems of Edgar Lee Masters.
- ☐ b. examples of dramatic monologues.
- ☐ c. who originated the dramatic monologue.
- ☐ d. how dramatic monologues and dramas differ.   _____

Supporting Details   **3**   Lucinda Matlock was
- ☐ a. a duchess.
- ☐ b. a woman murdered in a Browning poem.
- ☐ c. the wife of Cooney Potter.
- ☐ d. a long-lived woman of Spoon River.   _____

Conclusion   **4**   It is fair to conclude from this passage that
- ☐ a. Browning's poems are harder to understand than Masters's.
- ☐ b. Masters's poems are harder to understand than Browning's.
- ☐ c. dramatic monologues were invented in 1900.
- ☐ d. dramatic monologues are mostly about men.   _____

Clarifying Devices   **5**   The writer introduces the topic in the first paragraph through
- ☐ a. comparison with another type of poem.
- ☐ b. mentioning Browning and Masters.
- ☐ c. giving the plot of one dramatic monologue.
- ☐ d. telling why some dramatic monologues are more subtle than others.   _____

Vocabulary in Context   **6**   <u>Heinous</u> means
- ☐ a. surprising but expected.
- ☐ b. quickly done and hidden.
- ☐ c. shocking and terrible.
- ☐ d. noisy and bloody.   _____

Add your scores for questions 1–6. Enter the total here and on the graph on page 215.   Total Score   _____

34 Falling from the Skies

Technological advancements in the 20th century have made people healthier and more comfortable than ever before. Automobiles, telephones, and computers are everyday conveniences for many people. Oil-refining techniques and nuclear energy provide power for vehicles and communities. Drug therapies and medical technology improve and prolong life. Fertilizers and pesticides produce more fertile harvests. Plastics strengthen materials and fabrics. Satellites and shuttles explore distant regions in space. The <u>downside</u> to these developments, however, lies in how they affect the earth's environment.

The production processes for many of these advances require the burning of fossil fuels such as coal and oil. The combustion of these resources releases sulfur dioxide and nitrogen oxide gases, which react with oxygen and water in the atmosphere. The result is sulfuric and nitric acids that are carried to earth with rain, hail, and snow. This acid rain, or acid precipitation, falls on buildings and mountains, seeps into soil, and mixes into groundwater as well as into the waters of oceans, lakes, and rivers. Too much acid kills fish and other water-dwelling organisms. It breaks down soil nutrients and prevents plant growth. It even corrodes metals and dissolves the limestone and concrete of buildings and other structures.

Scientists fear that acid rain will destroy life's basic necessities—air, water, food, and shelter. We must take action to stop acid rain now! Let's start by burning only low-sulfur oil and coal and installing scrubbers in smokestacks to reduce oxides released into the air, and let's equip trucks with pollution-control devices to remove sulfur gases from exhaust. Big business and government argue that such measures are too expensive, but won't delaying be costly in other ways for future generations?

Main Idea   1 ───────────────────────────────────

	Answer	Score
Mark the *main idea*	M	15
Mark the statement that is *too broad*	B	5
Mark the statement that is *too narrow*	N	5

a. Acid rain, a result of technological development, is destroying many parts of our environment. ☐ ____

b. Too much acid kills fish and other water-dwelling organisms. ☐ ____

c. Acid rain is very destructive. ☐

Subject Matter   **2**   The passage focuses mainly on
    ☐ a. technological development in the future.
    ☐ b. the long-term effects of acid rain.
    ☐ c. how to develop low-nitrogen fertilizers.
    ☐ d. big business and government decisions.   _____

Supporting   **3**   Sulfuric acid forms as a result of
Details   ☐ a. fossil fuels such as coal releasing energy.
    ☐ b. low-sulfur oil and coal being installed in
       smokestacks.
    ☐ c. rain, hail, and snow falling.
    ☐ d. sulfur dioxide combining with water and
       oxygen.   _____

Conclusion   **4**   The writer of this passage
    ☐ a. thinks it costs too much to get rid of acid rain.
    ☐ b. blames ordinary citizens for acid rain.
    ☐ c. believes acid rain has no effect on children.
    ☐ d. has strong feelings about acid rain.   _____

Clarifying   **5**   The writer discusses technological advances to
Devices   help the reader understand that such developments
    ☐ a. have had both good and bad results.
    ☐ b. make life easier for people.
    ☐ c. have produced much wealth for big business.
    ☐ d. are good for the earth's atmosphere.   _____

Vocabulary   **6**   In this passage <u>downside</u> means
in Context   ☐ a. underneath part.
    ☐ b. a lowering of gears.
    ☐ c. a heavy rain.
    ☐ d. bad part.   _____

Add your scores for questions 1–6. Enter the total here   **Total**
and on the graph on page 215.   **Score**   _____

35 The Mystery of the Ancient Ones

The mystery of the prehistoric Native American culture known as the Anasazi begins with their very name, because no evidence exists telling what these people called themselves. *Anasazi* is a Navajo word meaning "ancient ones," but most Navajo <u>aver</u> that the word means "ancient enemies" while some translate the word to mean "ancient ancestors." The Hopi word for these early people is *Hisatsinom,* which means "those-who-came-before." And they did come before, having lived in the Southwest United States from before A.D. 1 to A.D. 1275.

The deep canyons, rock palisades, high mesas, and open desert of the Four Corners area, where Colorado, Utah, Arizona, and New Mexico converge, were home to this remarkable group of people. The dramatic remains of tens of thousands of Anasazi rock and mud dwellings document their building techniques. They constructed masonry homes that varied from simple underground pit structures to large, multistoried villages. We know that the population grew and clustered in small villages. We suspect that climatic changes and conflict with neighboring groups caused occasional shifts in settlement.

The Anasazi were highly skilled potters. Beautifully decorated bowls, ladles, and mugs have been discovered in Anasazi ruins, The Anasazi also produced fine baskets, ornaments, woven goods, and tools and had a trade network extending to central Mexico. We also know that they hunted game, gathered wild plants, and grew corn, beans, and squash.

But archaeologists still puzzle over the unsolved riddles of the Anasazi. Why, by A.D. 1300, had they abandoned the Four Corners area and, an even greater question, where did they go? Only time and further archaeological research can solve this mystery of the ancient ones.

Main Idea	1	Answer	Score
	Mark the *main idea*	M	15
	Mark the statement that is *too broad*	B	5
	Mark the statement that is *too narrow*	N	5

a. The Anasazi had a rich culture, but it is not known why it died out. ☐ _____

b. The Anasazi were a prehistoric culture. ☐ _____

c. The Anasazi built and traded. ☐ _____

Subject Matter   **2** This passage focuses mostly on
- [ ] a. the Four Corners area.
- [ ] b. what we know and don't know about the Anasazi.
- [ ] c. Anasazi buildings.
- [ ] d. what the word *Anasazi* means.   _____

Supporting Details   **3** The Anasazi disappeared before
- [ ] a. A.D. 1.
- [ ] b. A.D. 1300.
- [ ] c. A.D. 1750.
- [ ] d. A.D. 1900.   _____

Conclusion   **4** The things the Anasazi most likely traded were
- [ ] a. sheep.
- [ ] b. building materials.
- [ ] c. beads and skins.
- [ ] d. pottery, baskets, and woven goods.   _____

Clarifying Devices   **5** The term *Four Corners* is explained by
- [ ] a. describing its mountains.
- [ ] b. telling where it is.
- [ ] c. narrating a story about it.
- [ ] d. summarizing its history.   _____

Vocabulary in Context   **6** <u>Aver</u> means to
- [ ] a. assert to be true.
- [ ] b. avoid.
- [ ] c. provide a written history of.
- [ ] d. construct.   _____

Add your scores for questions 1–6. Enter the total here and on the graph on page 215.   **Total Score**   _____

36 Two Types of Spirals

The grooves on an old-fashioned phonograph record and the shape of our galaxy—what can these two things possibly have in common? The title of this passage suggests the answer—that both a record and the Milky Way are examples of spirals. Spirals are also found in the shapes of shells, in the growth patterns of plants and trees, and in some spider webs.

You might think that the mathematics needed to describe these fascinating shapes is complicated, with many difficult formulas, but that is not the case. The two principal types of spirals, one tight and the other loose and loopy, can be simply explained using arithmetic and geometric number sequences.

In an arithmetic sequence, numbers are separated by a common difference—in the sequence 3, 6, 9, 12, that difference is 3. In a geometric sequence, such as 1, 2, 4, 8, the numbers are all multiplied by the same number, in this case 2. To draw a tight spiral as in a phonograph record, make a larger version of the polar coordinate grid at the right and plot a point every 10 degrees. The first point would be at the center, the second 3 units (or circles) away from it, the third 6 units away, and so on. For a galaxy spiral, again <u>plot</u> a point every 10 degrees, but use a geometric sequence, placing the points 1, 2, 4, 8, etc., units from the center.

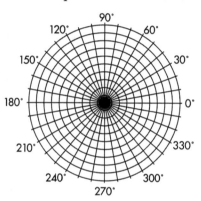

Main Idea   1

	Answer	Score
Mark the _main idea_	**M**	15
Mark the statement that is _too broad_	**B**	5
Mark the statement that is _too narrow_	**N**	5

a. Spirals can be found in nature and drawn using mathematics. ☐ _____

b. Mathematicians study many different complex curved shapes. ☐ _____

c. Spirals may be tight or loose and loopy. ☐ _____

Score 15 points for each correct answer. Score

Subject Matter 2 This passage is primarily concerned with
☐ a. explaining a polar coordinate grid.
☐ b. describing shapes of galaxies.
☐ c. describing how to create two types of spirals.
☐ d. measuring spirals in degrees. _____

Supporting 3 The spiraling galaxy that includes our solar
Details system is called
☐ a. Archimedean.
☐ b. geometric.
☐ c. polar.
☐ d. the Milky Way. _____

Conclusion 4 Compared with a phonograph-record-shaped
spiral, a spiral in a galaxy shape would look
☐ a. looser.
☐ b. tighter.
☐ c. smaller.
☐ d. the same. _____

Clarifying 5 The author includes the polar coordinate grid
Devices ☐ a. to show a spiral drawn on it.
☐ b. so you would know how to draw it if you
wanted to create your own spirals.
☐ c. to show the shape of a phonograph record.
☐ d. to prove there are only two types of spirals. _____

Vocabulary 6 In this passage the word <u>plot</u> means
in Context ☐ a. locate on a graph or grid.
☐ b. a piece of land.
☐ c. the events in a story.
☐ d. scheme. _____

Add your scores for questions 1–6. Enter the total here Total
and on the graph on page 212. Score _____

37 Which House Is the Bauhaus?

Most cities of even medium size have skyscrapers that look like glass boxes. Made with steel frames and huge glass windows, lacking any ornamentation, today these buildings strike some people as boring. When they began to be constructed in large numbers, however, in the 1950s, they represented a revolution in architecture.

These skyscrapers are constructed in what is known as the "international style," which some have called the first new truly new architectural achievement since the Gothic cathedral. A group called the Bauhaus originally developed the style in Germany in the 1920s. Besides stressing the importance of allowing abundant light into buildings, this group also believed that the construction itself was an important element of architecture. The visible steel frames of international style skyscrapers stand as testament to the belief that no element of a structure should be hidden.

One of the founders of the international school was Walter Gropius, who designed the building in Germany in which the Bauhaus group worked. When World War II began, he escaped to the United States, along with his colleague Ludwig Mies van der Rohe. It was Mies who popularized the glass-walled building in America. His architectural belief was "Less is more," and his clean-lined high-rise structures, often raised a story or two from the ground on narrow columns, look as if they float in the air. One of van der Rohe's first skyscraper projects was a pair of apartment buildings in Chicago in 1951. One of his best known structures, designed with colleague Philip Johnson, is the tinted-glass-covered, marble-walled Seagram Building in New York City, a beautiful and distinctive building.

The problem with the international style is that it looks <u>deceptively</u> easy to achieve. In the hands of a mediocre architect, the result is often a dull, monotonous structure.

Main Idea	1	Answer	Score
	Mark the *main idea*	M	15
	Mark the statement that is *too broad*	B	5
	Mark the statement that is *too narrow*	N	5

a. A new architectural style developed in the 20th century. ☐ ____

b. The international style favors clean lines and wide expanses of glass. ☐ ____

c. Mies believed that "Less is more." ☐ ____

Score 15 points for each correct answer.   **Score**

Subject Matter   **2**   Another good title for this passage would be
- ☐ a. Who Is Walter Gropius?
- ☐ b. The Purpose of Ornamentation on Buildings.
- ☐ c. The Earliest Skyscrapers in America.
- ☐ d. The "Glass Box" Style of Architecture.

                                                              _____

Supporting Details   **3**   The Seagram Building
- ☐ a. is located in Chicago.
- ☐ b. was designed by Walter Gropius.
- ☐ c. is one of van der Rohe's most famous buildings.
- ☐ d. was the first mostly glass skyscraper.

                                                              _____

Conclusion   **4**   It is fair to conclude that the international style
- ☐ a. is not as popular as it once was.
- ☐ b. is disliked because it did not originate in America .
- ☐ c. represents shoddy workmanship.
- ☐ d. began in the 1950s.

                                                              _____

Clarifying Devices   **5**   The final paragraph is intended to
- ☐ a. summarize Mies's work.
- ☐ b. be a comment on the international style.
- ☐ c. define *dull* and *monotonous*.
- ☐ d. tell a brief story.

                                                              _____

Vocabulary in Context   **6**   In this passage <u>deceptively</u> means
- ☐ a. untruthfully.
- ☐ b. misleadingly.
- ☐ c. unfortunately.
- ☐ d. unnecessarily.

                                                              _____

Add your scores for questions 1–6. Enter the total here and on the graph on page 215.   **Total Score**   _____

38 Achieving Cardiovascular Fitness

Heart attacks, strokes, and other cardiovascular diseases are the leading cause of death in the developed world. These diseases include disorders of the blood vessels that pump and carry blood throughout the body. In a disorder called *atherosclerosis,* for instance, the aorta or other major blood vessels become clogged with fatty deposits of cholesterol. As cholesterol builds up, the walls of the vessels harden and thicken. The narrowed passages in the vessels slow the flow of blood cells—and the oxygen they carry—to the heart, brain, and other muscles. When the heart is deprived of oxygen-rich blood, a heart attack occurs. If oxygen-rich blood doesn't reach the brain, a stroke results. Such cardiovascular diseases are likely in people who are overweight or smoke cigarettes. Other risk factors include high blood pressure, heart disease, and high cholesterol. With regular exercise, however, a person can reduce these risk factors.

Aerobic exercise, such as jogging, walking, skating, and swimming, helps people to become cardiovascularly fit. An aerobic workout must be vigorous so that the heart, lungs, blood vessels, and skeletal muscles constantly use energy. During aerobic activities, the muscle cells undergo aerobic metabolism. In this process, oxygen combines with a fuel source (fats or carbohydrates) to release energy and produce carbon dioxide and water. The muscle cells use the energy to <u>contract</u>, which creates a force that produces movement. The aerobic reaction only occurs if the circulatory and pulmonary systems provide a constant supply of oxygen and fuel to the muscle cells and remove carbon dioxide from them. Most people can achieve cardiovascular fitness by raising their heart and breathing rates for 25 to 30 minutes about every other day. Those people will have the energy to do easily all the things they want to do.

Main Idea	1				
				Answer	**Score**
		Mark the *main idea*		M	15
		Mark the statement that is *too broad*		B	5
		Mark the statement that is *too narrow*		N	5

a. Cardiovascular diseases cause many deaths. ☐ _____

b. Cardiovascular diseases are dangerous, but aerobic exercise can prevent them. ☐ _____

c. Atherosclerosis causes hardening and thickening of major blood vessels. ☐ _____

Subject Matter   **2**   Another good title for this passage would be
- ☐ a. Overweight with High Blood Pressure.
- ☐ b. Kinds of Cardiovascular Diseases.
- ☐ c. Fats and Carbohydrates.
- ☐ d. Avoiding Cardiovascular Diseases.   _____

Supporting Details   **3**   A person will gain from aerobic exercise if he or she
- ☐ a. raises and maintains the heart and breathing rates on a regular basis.
- ☐ b. monitors the heart rate while exercising.
- ☐ c. eats fats and carbohydrates for energy.
- ☐ d. takes a break after every 10 minutes of vigorous exercise.   _____

Conclusion   **4**   We can conclude that the more risk factors a person has for cardiovascular disease, the
- ☐ a. fewer the chances of getting the disease.
- ☐ b. greater the chances of getting the disease.
- ☐ c. more likely it is that the person smokes.
- ☐ d. less likely it is that the person is overweight.   _____

Clarifying Devices   **5**   The sentence "If oxygen-rich blood doesn't reach the brain, a stroke results" is an example of
- ☐ a. persuasion.
- ☐ b. narration.
- ☐ c. definition.
- ☐ d. cause and effect.   _____

Vocabulary in Context   **6**   In this passage <u>contract</u> means
- ☐ a. an agreement between two people.
- ☐ b. to form words like "don't" and "can't."
- ☐ c. to tighten or make shorter.
- ☐ d. to get or bring on oneself.   _____

Add your scores for questions 1–6. Enter the total here and on the graph on page 215.   **Total Score**   _____

39 Bigger and Bigger

Throughout the 20th century, Japanese towns and cities grew rapidly, until today about 80 percent of the Japanese people live in urban areas. The growth of towns and cities, called *urbanization,* happens in two ways. One way is by natural population increase, when more people are born than die. The second way is by rural-urban migration, when people move to the cities from the country. As cities prosper and grow, industries and services that involve many people both as workers and consumers grow to meet the needs of the increasing population. New industries and services <u>emerge</u> to support the growing businesses, and the region experiences an upward spiral of growth.

The urban areas on the Japanese island of Honshu continue to grow as they attract more people, industry, and business. These urban areas contain nearly two-thirds of Japan's population and manufacturing. City suburbs are filling in the rural spaces between the towns and cities, and Japan's efficient and fast transportation system links them all.

Four major cities on Honshu—Tokyo, Kawasaki, Chiba, and Yokohama—have grown together into one of Japan's largest urban areas. Two other large urban areas have developed on Honshu. The area around the city of Nagoya forms one, and the cities of Osaka, Kyoto, and Kobe form the other. At the present time these three areas are growing toward one another to form one long, enormous urban area. A single urban system this large is called a megalopolis. This Japanese megalopolis on Honshu, stretching from Tokyo in the east all the way to Kobe in the west, is called the Tokaido megalopolis.

Main Idea 1

	Answer	Score
Mark the *main idea*	M	15
Mark the statement that is *too broad*	B	5
Mark the statement that is *too narrow*	N	5

a. Japanese urbanization is leading to a megalopolis. ☐ _____

b. Japan has experienced rural-urban migration. ☐ _____

c. Japan has large urban areas. ☐ _____

Subject Matter   **2**   This passage is mostly about
☐ a. what a megalopolis is.
☐ b. a system of rural-urban migration.
☐ c. how a megalopolis is forming in Japan.
☐ d. a fast transportation system in Japan.   _____

Supporting   **3**   The urban areas of Honshu
Details   ☐ a. are shrinking.
☐ b. contain two-thirds of Japan's population.
☐ c. are not part of Japan.
☐ d. are far from the megalopolis.   _____

Conclusion   **4**   A megalopolis is the result of
☐ a. natural growth.
☐ b. deliberate planning.
☐ c. fast commuter trains.
☐ d. poverty.   _____

Clarifying   **5**   The phrase *an upward spiral* in the last sentence of
Devices   the first paragraph is a metaphor for
☐ a. decreasing population and industry.
☐ b. circular population.
☐ c. repetitious numbers of workers and consumers.
☐ d. ever-increasing population and industry.   _____

Vocabulary   **6**   In this passage <u>emerge</u> means to
in Context   ☐ a. become connected.
☐ b. come into being.
☐ c. become well known.
☐ d. meet the needs of people.   _____

Add your scores for questions 1–6. Enter the total here   Total
and on the graph on page 215.   Score   _____

40 The Romance of Arthur

Most cultures have some sort of hero who represents the best values of what its people believe in. The unusual thing about King Arthur is that legends of his heroism have persisted for several centuries and spread far beyond England, the place where they began.

The earliest stories of King Arthur represent him as a warrior who fought and subdued the invading Norsemen in the years around A.D. 700. This much of the Arthurian tale is probably based on fact. Whether called Arthur or not, there is a body of evidence supporting the existence of such a warrior. It is the later embellishments of the tale whose authenticity is questionable. According to these, Arthur was born in a castle in Tintagel, on the stormy western coast of England, and because he was the illegitimate son of King Uther Pendragon, he was spirited away by the magician Merlin and his true identity kept from him. He became king after freeing the sword Excalibur from the stone into which it was thrust. He married the beautiful Guinevere and assembled in his court all the noblest knights of the land, including Lancelot, with whom Guinevere would later be unfaithful to him. He was finally defeated in battle by his illegitimate son Mordred, and his body was spirited away to the isle of Avalon.

This romantic tale greatly appealed to the English and the French in the Middle Ages, when the code of chivalry—ideal qualities of knighthood—constituted an important part of many stories. Tales of the heroism of Galahad, Percival, Gawain, and many other of Arthur's knights were circulated as well.

In England today, there are many sites claiming a piece of the Arthurian legend. There is a ruined castle at Tintagel. Near Glastonbury are the remains of an ancient abbey where Arthur's and Guinevere's bodies were supposedly <u>exhumed</u> in the 12th century. Neither of these proves that the legend is true, but they do keep its mystique alive.

Main Idea	1		
		Answer	**Score**
Mark the *main idea*		M	15
Mark the statement that is *too broad*		B	5
Mark the statement that is *too narrow*		N	5

a. There are many tales of King Arthur. ☐ _____

b. The story of King Arthur became more detailed over the centuries. ☐ _____

c. Arthur was betrayed by Lancelot and Guinevere. ☐ _____

Subject Matter   **2**   Another good title for this passage would be
☐ a. Kings in the Seventh Century.
☐ b. The Knights of the Round Table.
☐ c. Real or Legend?
☐ d. Arthur's Marriage to Guinevere.   _____

Supporting Details   **3**   King Arthur's father was
☐ a. Lancelot.
☐ b. Avalon.
☐ c. Mordred.
☐ d. Uther Pendragon.   _____

Conclusion   **4**   The writer seems to feel that the truth about Arthur is that he
☐ a. existed.
☐ b. was married to Guinevere.
☐ c. had many knights.
☐ d. was born at Tintagel.   _____

Clarifying Devices   **5**   The information in the second paragraph is mostly presented in
☐ a. spatial order.
☐ b. order from latest to earliest.
☐ c. order from earliest to latest.
☐ d. order from least persuasive to most persuasive.   _____

Vocabulary in Context   **6**   Exhumed means
☐ a. dug up from the grave.
☐ b. buried.
☐ c. quarreled over.
☐ d. built a church around.   _____

Add your scores for questions 1–6. Enter the total here and on the graph on page 215.   **Total Score**   _____

41 Just Like Jack and the Beanstalk

Giants figure prominently in children's stories, usually in an extremely negative role. You probably read such tales in your early years and enjoyed rooting for the "little guy" who plots to outwit the evil giant. Are such tremendously enlarged copies of human beings actually possible, or do they only exist in the imagination?

An examination of what happens to surface areas and volumes as you enlarge a three-dimensional geometric figure can help to permanently banish the idea of giants from our everyday world. Begin with a cube with a length, width, and height of 5 feet, and then double those three dimensions—that is, multiply them by 2. The result when you do this is that the surface area increases by the square of 2 (2^2), or becomes four times as large. The volume increases by the cube of 2 (2^3), or becomes eight times as large. (You can prove to yourself that these conclusions are valid by computing the surface areas and volumes of the original cube as well as of the enlarged one. Use the formulas $A = S^2$ and $V = S^3$.)

So how does this information <u>translate</u> to giants? Think for a moment about the human body as it is scaled upward to giant-sized dimensions. The weight, or volume, of the body will increase eightfold, but the *strength* of the body will increase only with the cross-sectional surface area of the bones; that is, it will only increase fourfold. The weight will be so much greater than the strength that a giant couldn't stand or walk, must less threaten a person of standard dimensions.

The fact that giant-sized villains appear to be structurally impossible without some newly engineered increase in bone strength may occur to you the next time you hear a tale with a giant villain, but this scientific knowledge probably will not prevent you from enjoying the story anyway.

Main Idea	1			
			Answer	Score
	Mark the *main idea*		M	15
	Mark the statement that is *too broad*		B	5
	Mark the statement that is *too narrow*		N	5

a. As the dimensions of a cube are doubled, volume increases eightfold. ☐ _____

b. Solid objects have length, surface area, and volume. ☐ _____

c. A simple enlarging experiment can explain why giants are not possible. ☐ _____

Subject Matter   **2**   Another good title for this passage would be
- ☐ a. Why Giants Are Always Evil.
- ☐ b. Finding the Volume of a Giant.
- ☐ c. Are Giants Possible?
- ☐ d. Famous Giants in Folktales.   _____

Supporting Details   **3**   If the dimensions of a cube were doubled, its surface area would become
- ☐ a. twice as large.
- ☐ b. four times as large.
- ☐ c. eight times as large.
- ☐ d. twelve times as large.   _____

Conclusion   **4**   A giant would not be strong enough to stand because
- ☐ a. its legs would be short.
- ☐ b. its bones could not support its weight.
- ☐ c. it would be too tall.
- ☐ d. its bones would be too thick.   _____

Clarifying Devices   **5**   The example used to make the point about giants is
- ☐ a. a square 2 feet on each side.
- ☐ b. a square 5 feet on each side.
- ☐ c. a cube 2 feet on each edge.
- ☐ d. a cube 5 feet on each edge.   _____

Vocabulary in Context   **6**   In this passage <u>translate</u> means
- ☐ a. change from one language into another.
- ☐ b. carry from one place to another.
- ☐ c. relate to or correspond to.
- ☐ d. change from numbers into words.   _____

Add your scores for questions 1–6. Enter the total here and on the graph on page 215.   **Total Score**   _____

42 The Earth Moved

Earthquakes can happen anywhere on Earth, but these natural geological events are more common in some areas than in others. The lithosphere—a 60-mile thickness of the earth's crust and the uppermost layer of its mantle—is separated into huge slabs called tectonic plates. These plates are constantly colliding, and the rock within them accumulates great stresses after many years of continuous grinding. Eventually the stresses exceed the strength of the rock, causing it to suddenly shift position and explosively discharge seismic waves of energy.

The seismic waves travel outward from the focus, or point of origin inside the lithosphere, and <u>span</u> the earth at speeds of about 15,000 miles per hour. However, only waves in the vicinity of the earthquake's epicenter, the point on the earth's surface directly above the focus, will be strong enough to cause damage. The fastest waves to arrive at the epicenter are primary, or P, waves that push and pull as they travel. P waves are not very big and often can be heard but not felt. The secondary, or S, waves are the next to arrive. S waves produce a side-to-side shaking as they travel, thus causing people and things near the epicenter to shake from side to side. The slowest waves, surface waves, produce a rolling movement. Surface waves may be violent enough to reduce entire cities to rubble, to kill or injure thousands of people, and to create faults, or cracks, deep in the rock of the earth's surface.

Scientists often know where an earthquake will occur, but they cannot accurately predict its timing. Earthquake preparation—that is, the education of people so they know what to do during an earthquake and the construction of earthquake-resistant buildings, bridges, and roads—may minimize an earthquake's aftereffects.

Main Idea	1		
		Answer	**Score**
	Mark the *main idea*	M	15
	Mark the statement that is *too broad*	B	5
	Mark the statement that is *too narrow*	N	5

a. Only waves near an earthquake's epicenter are likely to cause damage. ☐ ____

b. Earthquakes are natural events that originate from deep within the earth. ☐ ____

c. Earthquakes occur in many places on the earth. ☐ ____

Subject Matter   **2**   The main purpose of this passage is to
- ☐ a. define epicenters.
- ☐ b. explain the formation of faults.
- ☐ c. describe types of seismic waves.
- ☐ d. tell what happens in an earthquake.   _____

Supporting Details   **3**   An epicenter is
- ☐ a. the point on the earth's surface just above an earthquake's point of origin.
- ☐ b. a large slab of the earth's crust.
- ☐ c. the exact point where an earthquake begins.
- ☐ d. a huge, rolling wave of energy.   _____

Conclusion   **4**   The most destructive waves produced by a quake are
- ☐ a. seismic waves.
- ☐ b. surface waves.
- ☐ c. S waves.
- ☐ d. P waves.   _____

Clarifying Devices   **5**   Which of these terms does the writer _not_ define?
- ☐ a. mantle
- ☐ b. lithosphere
- ☐ c. focus
- ☐ d. earthquake preparation   _____

Vocabulary in Context   **6**   In this passage <u>span</u> means
- ☐ a. the length of a bridge.
- ☐ b. to extend across.
- ☐ c. an individual's lifetime.
- ☐ d. to build a support over.   _____

Add your scores for questions 1–6. Enter the total here and on the graph on page 215.   **Total Score**   _____

43 Very Separate, Very Unequal

Apartheid was the South African policy of racial segregation that benefited the white minority and discriminated against the black majority. From 1948 to 1994, apartheid helped the white minority in South Africa keep political power.

What were some of the effects of apartheid? Apartheid forcibly removed millions of black people into predominately black homelands and townships that were far from the nearest town or city. Schools, health care, water, sanitation, and transportation in these areas were <u>rudimentary</u> at best. Most of the people in the settlements were impoverished and had little opportunity for employment. Young men migrated to the white areas to work in the mines and factories, while the elderly, children, women, and disabled people remained in the homelands.

How did the apartheid system begin to crumble? A number of foreign governments and human rights organizations demanded an end to the system. Trade sanctions and divestment (the withdrawal of investment by foreign companies) pressured the government to change its policies. However, the biggest challenge came from within South Africa. The African National Congress, the KwaZulu-dominated Inkatha group, the churches of South Africa, and the trade union movements all spoke out for a democratic future.

When did apartheid finally come to an end? The politics of apartheid ended in 1994 when South Africa held its first democratic election. All South Africans were able to vote for the first time. The result was the election of the African National Congress candidate, Nelson Mandela, as South Africa's first black president.

Main Idea	1		
		Answer	**Score**
Mark the *main idea*		M	15
Mark the statement that is *too broad*		B	5
Mark the statement that is *too narrow*		N	5

a. Under apartheid, black people were moved to townships. ☐ _____

b. South Africa has a troubled history. ☐ _____

c. South Africa had a policy of apartheid but was forced to dismantle it. ☐ _____

Score 15 points for each correct answer.

Subject Matter 2 This passage is mostly about how apartheid
- ☐ a. promised a democratic future.
- ☐ b. discriminated against black people.
- ☐ c. created jobs in mines and factories.
- ☐ d. pressured governments into trade agreements.

_____

Supporting Details 3 People living in the settlements
- ☐ a. worked in mines and factories.
- ☐ b. were poor and had little work.
- ☐ c. were only women.
- ☐ d. were members of the African National Congress.

_____

Conclusion 4 Apartheid ended because of
- ☐ a. the white minority's desire for a black president.
- ☐ b. full employment opportunities for blacks.
- ☐ c. the growing prosperity within South Africa.
- ☐ d. economic and political pressures.

_____

Clarifying Devices 5 The questions at the beginnings of paragraphs
- ☐ a. are not intended to be answered.
- ☐ b. introduce the topics of the paragraphs.
- ☐ c. come from South African newspapers.
- ☐ d. are not related to what follows them.

_____

Vocabulary in Context 6 In this passage rudimentary means
- ☐ a. undeveloped.
- ☐ b. discourteous.
- ☐ c. completely adequate.
- ☐ d. to be learned or studied. first.

_____

Add your scores for questions 1–6. Enter the total here and on the graph on page 215.

Total Score

_____

44 Theater from the Heart

A common piece of advice offered to writers is "Write what you know about." Playwright Luis Valdez followed this advice to create important dramas about the Mexican-American community that he grew up in.

Valdez, the son of migrant workers, began writing plays in college. Soon after graduating in 1964 he founded a group called El Teatro Campesino, of which he became resident playwright, and originally wrote and helped the group produce brief, one-act plays about the need for a farm workers' union. These short plays, known as *actos,* employed comedy and farce to drive home political points.

Soon, however, El Teatro Campesino broadened its literary and political <u>base</u>. Valdez wanted to dramatize the entire Mexican American experience, and he wanted to approach it from many perspectives. The first play he authored that reflected this new mindset was *Dark Root of a Scream.* Its setting is a wake for a Chicano who had fought unwillingly in the Vietnam War. *Bernabé,* another play from this period, portrays the earth symbolically as a woman who supported the troops during the Mexican Revolution. Valdez labeled both of these plays *mitos,* or myths; their general purpose was to stand back and take a long view of Chicano viewpoints in areas like art, religion, and science. Valdez also began developing dramas he called *corridos,* in which traditional Mexican ballads were sung on stage while actors acted out their meaning.

Valdez continues to write and to find new ways to present Chicano life on the stage. In two well-known works—*The Tent of the Underdogs,* about the struggles of a Mexican immigrant, and *Zoot Suit,* based on the true story of a 1942 murder trial in Los Angeles—he combined elements of *actos, mitos,* and *corridos* to create dramas of both artistic strength and strong political message.

Main Idea 1

	Answer	Score
Mark the *main idea*	M	15
Mark the statement that is *too broad*	B	5
Mark the statement that is *too narrow*	N	5

a. Luis Valdez's plays present various aspects of Chicano life. ☐ ____

b. Luis Valdez has written many plays over the years. ☐ ____

c. An *acto* is a short, farcical play. ☐ ____

88

Score 15 points for each correct answer.   **Score**

Subject Matter **2** This passage is mostly about
- ☐ a. Luis Valdez's life.
- ☐ b. features of Luis Valdez's plays.
- ☐ c. El Teatro Campesino.
- ☐ d. the Mexican-American experience.   _____

Supporting Details **3** In this passage a *mito* is a
- ☐ a. foolish character in a play.
- ☐ b. type of play.
- ☐ c. young, inexperienced playwright.
- ☐ d. farm worker.   _____

Conclusion **4** Valdez was interested in
- ☐ a. getting justice for wrongs done to him.
- ☐ b. returning to work in the fields.
- ☐ c. producing plays by various Chicano writers.
- ☐ d. creating dramas with new and unique elements.   _____

Clarifying Devices **5** The expression *drive home* in the second paragraph is used to mean
- ☐ a. get in a car and travel.
- ☐ b. return to Mexico.
- ☐ c. strongly emphasize.
- ☐ d. hit with a hammer.   _____

Vocabulary in Context **6** In this passage base means
- ☐ a. having little value.
- ☐ b. a low singing voice.
- ☐ c. quarreled over.
- ☐ d. supporting part or foundation.   _____

Add your scores for questions 1–6. Enter the total here and on the graph on page 215.

Total Score   _____

45 An Intense Beam of Light

Our society uses lasers in many areas of science, medicine, communications, industry, and the military. We also utilize lasers in such commonplace devices as bar code scanners, radar speed-detectors, CD and videodisk players, and laser pointers. Laser technology is relatively new, but a <u>theoretical</u> laser was proposed by Albert Einstein in 1917. It wasn't until 1960, however, that technology allowed for construction of the first laser. That laser was made of a solid ruby medium (a substance that transmits energy) that produced an intense beam of pure red light. Lasers today are made of a variety of materials, each of which emits an intense beam of light having one pure color.

The word *laser*—an acronym for **l**ight **a**mplification by **s**timulated **e**mission of **r**adiation—describes how the device works. A laser has three main parts: an energy source, such as intense ordinary light; a medium of ions, molecules, or atoms; and a mirror at either end of the medium—one mirror to reflect the light that strikes it and one to output part of the light. The atoms of the medium exist at low- and high-energy levels. When the energy source activates, the low-energy atoms absorb the energy and become excited to a higher level. Some of the excited atoms spontaneously radiate light waves in random directions and then return to their low-energy level. Many of the light waves become trapped between the mirrors, staying within the medium and striking high-energy atoms. The high-energy atoms become stimulated and emit light of the same wavelength as the light wave that stimulated them. The emitted light amplifies the passing light wave. By repeatedly activating the energy source, the cycle continues, making the light wave bigger and stronger. Eventually some of the wave bursts through the output mirror as a laser beam—a tremendously powerful radiating light wave.

Main Idea	1		
		Answer	**Score**
	Mark the *main idea*	M	15
	Mark the statement that is *too broad*	B	5
	Mark the statement that is *too narrow*	N	5

a.	Our society uses lasers in many different areas.	☐
b.	The first laser produced an intense beam of pure red light.	☐
c.	*Laser* is an acronym for the words that describe how a laser works.	☐

Score 15 points for each correct answer.   **Score**

Subject Matter   2   The purpose of this passage is to
- ☐ a. identify the uses of lasers in our society.
- ☐ b. describe the history of lasers.
- ☐ c. explain how lasers work.
- ☐ d. compare low-energy atoms with high-energy atoms.

_____

Supporting Details   3   The following is not part of today's lasers:
- ☐ a. an energy source.
- ☐ b. a ruby.
- ☐ c. a medium of ions or molecules.
- ☐ d. a pair of mirrors.

_____

Conclusion   4   We can conclude that the light wave reflects back and forth within the laser until
- ☐ a. the low-energy atoms become excited.
- ☐ b. spontaneous light radiation occurs.
- ☐ c. the medium becomes weak.
- ☐ d. the wave has enough energy to escape.

_____

Clarifying Devices   5   To demonstrate what an acronym is, the writer
- ☐ a. uses italicized type for the first letters of words.
- ☐ b. underlines the word.
- ☐ c. compares it to an abbreviation.
- ☐ d. tells how many parts there are.

_____

Vocabulary in Context   6   <u>Theoretical</u> means
- ☐ a. very small.
- ☐ b. based on theory, not fact.
- ☐ c. very large.
- ☐ d. capable of causing accidents.

_____

Add your scores for questions 1–6. Enter the total here and on the graph on page 215.   **Total Score**   _____

46 The Toss of a Coin

In a coin-tossing experiment involving one coin, the probability of the coin landing heads up is expressed by the fraction $\frac{1}{2}$. If there is more than one coin involved, is the probability of getting all heads still represented by this same fraction? To determine probability in more complex situations, it is necessary first to <u>ascetain</u> the possible ways in which the experimental coins can land. For an experiment consisting of two coins, there are just four distinguishable ways that the coins can land—HH, HT, TH, and TT. This information can be represented by the sequence 1, 2, 1 because there is 1 way of getting two heads-up coins (HH), 2 ways of getting one heads-up coin (HT or TH), and 1 way of getting zero heads-up coins (TT). This number sequence 1, 2, 1 can be used to determine the numerators in the four probability fractions, with the denominator of each fraction being the sum of the three numbers—1 + 2 + 1, or 4. The probability of getting two heads-up coins is therefore the fractional number $\frac{1}{4}$; of getting one heads-up coin, $\frac{2}{4}$ or $\frac{1}{2}$; and of getting none, $\frac{1}{4}$.

As the number of coins in the experiment increases, the probability fractions can be found by using a device called Pascal's Triangle, an arrangement of numbers in which each number is the sum of the two numbers directly above it. The fourth row of Pascal's Triangle is used for a three-coin tossing experiment by first adding the row numbers to get the denominator 8 and then using the four different row numbers as the numerators in the fractions. Following this procedure, you would discover that when tossing three coins, the probability of getting three heads is $\frac{1}{8}$; of getting two heads is $\frac{3}{8}$; of getting heads once is $\frac{3}{8}$; and of getting no heads is $\frac{1}{8}$. The greater the number of coins, the lower the probability of getting all heads, as extending Pascal's Triangle for yourself would prove.

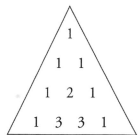

Main Idea	1		
		Answer	**Score**
	Mark the *main idea*	M	15
	Mark the statement that is *too broad*	B	5
	Mark the statement that is *too narrow*	N	5

a. Pascal's Triangle can be used to write probabilities in coin-toss experiments. ☐ _____

b. Probability shows up in coin tossing. ☐ _____

c. Two coins can fall HH, HT, TH, or TT. ☐ _____

Score 15 points for each correct answer.   **Score**

Subject Matter   **2**   This passage is mostly concerned with
- ☐ a. definitions of terms used in probability.
- ☐ b. understanding numerators and denominators.
- ☐ c. finding probabilities in coin-tossing experiments.
- ☐ d. methods for constructing Pascal's Triangle.   _____

Supporting Details   **3**   You toss two coins. The probability that only one of the coins lands heads up is
- ☐ a. $\frac{1}{8}$.
- ☐ b. $\frac{1}{4}$.
- ☐ c. $\frac{1}{2}$.
- ☐ d. $\frac{3}{8}$.   _____

Conclusion   **4**   The next row of Pascal's Triangle will contain
- ☐ a. 5 numbers.
- ☐ b. 6 numbers.
- ☐ c. 2 numbers.
- ☐ d. 1 number.   _____

Clarifying Devices   **5**   The information in this passage is arranged from
- ☐ a. simplest to most difficult.
- ☐ b. most difficult to easiest.
- ☐ c. earliest to latest.
- ☐ d. latest to earliest.   _____

Vocabulary in Context   **6**   In this passage the word <u>ascertain</u> means to
- ☐ a. deny.
- ☐ b. compute.
- ☐ c. find out.
- ☐ d. divide.   _____

Add your scores for questions 1–6. Enter the total here and on the graph on page 215.   **Total Score**   _____

47 You Have the Right to Remain Silent

Ernesto Miranda, sent to jail for the kidnapping and assualt of a Phoenix, Arizona, woman, appealed his case to a higher court on the grounds that he had been forced to incriminate himself. The facts before the United States Supreme Court were that Miranda was <u>interrogated</u> at length following his arrest and that he signed a confession that was used to convict him. Miranda's lawyer argued that the confession had been forced and that the police had not warned Miranda that he did not have to answer. Miranda was also not told that anything he said voluntarily could be used against him in court. This, Miranda's lawyer insisted, was unconstitutional.

On June 16, 1966, the Supreme Court agreed, ordered a retrial for Miranda, and issued the following majority opinion.

> Prior to any questioning, the person must be warned that he has the right to remain silent, that any statement he does make may be used as evidence against him, and that he has a right to the presence of an attorney, either retained or appointed. The defendant may waive effectuation of these rights, provided the waiver is made voluntarily, knowingly, and intelligently. If however, he indicates in any manner and at any stage of the process that he wishes to consult with an attorney before speaking, there can be no questioning.

This decision led to the Miranda Rule. Police must inform a suspect of his or her rights, which are the right to remain silent and the right to have an attorney present.

Ernesto Miranda was retried, convicted again, and served prison time until he was paroled in 1972. In 1976 Miranda, who was 34 years old, was stabbed to death during a fight in a bar.

Main Idea   1 ───────────────────────────────

	Answer	Score
Mark the *main idea*	M	15
Mark the statement that is *too broad*	B	5
Mark the statement that is *too narrow*	N	5

a. The United States Supreme Court heard Ernesto Miranda's appeal. ☐ _____

b. Ernesto Miranda was sent to jail for kidnapping and assault. ☐ _____

c. The Supreme Court's Miranda decision clarified the rights of a crime suspect. ☐ _____

Score 15 points for each correct answer.   **Score**

Subject Matter   **2**   The Miranda case had mostly to do with the
    ☐ a. rights of police officers.
    ☐ b. rights of an accused attorney.
    ☐ c. rights of an arrested individual.
    ☐ d. guilt or innocence of Ernesto Miranda.   _____

Supporting   **3**   Ernesto Miranda appealed his case on the grounds
Details   that
    ☐ a. he was not guilty.
    ☐ b. he had been forced to incriminate himself.
    ☐ c. police had not informed him that he was
        under arrest.
    ☐ d. he had not signed a confession.   _____

Conclusion   **4**   The U.S. Supreme Court agreed that Miranda's
rights had been violated and that this was
    ☐ a. questionable.
    ☐ b. interrogation procedure.
    ☐ c. unconstitutional.
    ☐ d. newsworthy.   _____

Clarifying   **5**   The indenting of the third paragraph on both
Devices   right and left margins tells the reader that this is
    ☐ a. quoted material.
    ☐ b. legal jargon.
    ☐ c. paraphrased material.
    ☐ d. a list.   _____

Vocabulary   **6**   The word <u>interrogated</u> means
in Context   ☐ a. warned.
    ☐ b. interrupted.
    ☐ c. opposed.
    ☐ d. questioned.   _____

Add your scores for questions 1–6. Enter the total here   **Total**
and on the graph on page 215.   **Score**   _____

48 Stepping Lively

In the early years of the 20th century a new sense of freedom and daring began to pervade popular American culture. When ragtime music, with its <u>jerky</u>, uneven rhythms, crossed over from black performance halls into mainstream society, the result was a whole series of new, unusual, and often downright silly dances through which young people of the era flaunted their independence from the past.

Some have claimed that the so-called animal dances were *the* ragtime dances, and in fact they were the rage among both black and white young people in the years around World War I. In dances with names such as the kangaroo dip, the bunny hug, and the eagle rock, partners performed steps that attempted to imitate the gait and mannerisms of various animals. Because some of these dances, like the grizzly bear, involved tight embraces as well as silly movements, they were roundly denounced by the older generation. Yet these were not improvised dances: they had to be done right, and dance schools sprang up all over the country to show people how.

The fox trot was another development of this era, but despite its name, it was not truly an animal dance. Its originator, a music hall performer named Henry Fox, developed a trotting sort of step that was to be performed to ragtime. It was a jerky, uneven dance of four slow steps back, followed by seven or eight quick ones forward. This step, in a much smoother form, persists today, but a lot of the fun has been stripped from it.

Of all the dances associated with this era, undoubtedly the best known is the Charleston, named after the South Carolina city where black dockworkers were first found doing it. The frenzied kicks and arm movements of the Charleston as it evolved were easy enough for almost anyone to do and quickly made it a national favorite.

Main Idea	1		
		Answer	**Score**
Mark the *main idea*		M	15
Mark the statement that is *too broad*		B	5
Mark the statement that is *too narrow*		N	5

a.	The 1900s brought many new dances.	☐	____
b.	Silly, ragtime-based steps introduced a new era of dances in the early 1900s.	☐	____
c.	Dances associated with animals became all the rage.	☐	____

Score 15 points for each correct answer.　　　　**Score**

Subject Matter　**2**　This passage deals with the early 1900s and
　　　　☐ a. what life was like then.
　　　　☐ b. popular dance steps of the era.
　　　　☐ c. why the young rebelled against the old.
　　　　☐ d. the characteristics of ragtime music.　　　____

Supporting　**3**　The fox trot was
Details　　　☐ a. an animal dance.
　　　　☐ b. originated by Henry Fox.
　　　　☐ c. a smooth, slow dance.
　　　　☐ d. a dance specifically designed for younger
　　　　　　 people.　　　____

Conclusion　**4**　It is fair to say that during the era discussed in
　　　　the passage,
　　　　☐ a. people were nostalgic for the past.
　　　　☐ b. modern ideas and attitudes began to form.
　　　　☐ c. many laws were broken.
　　　　☐ d. strict separation of the races was an
　　　　　　 important idea among the young.　　　____

Clarifying　**5**　The writer of this passage uses details to present
Devices　　　the dances as
　　　　☐ a. immoral.
　　　　☐ b. boring.
　　　　☐ c. short-lived.
　　　　☐ d. fun.　　　____

Vocabulary　**6**　In this passage <u>jerky</u> means
in Context　　☐ a. a kind of dried meat.
　　　　☐ b. stupid.
　　　　☐ c. with sudden starts and stops.
　　　　☐ d. very loud.　　　____

Add your scores for questions 1–6. Enter the total here　**Total**
and on the graph on page 215.　**Score**　____

49 Is It Real, or Is It . . . ?

You pause in your descent from the mountaintop and walk out onto a rocky overhang. With one more step, you're standing at the edge. You cautiously look down, careful not to lose your balance. You're taken aback by the startling landscape. Nowhere else in the solar system have you seen such a spectacular view—a mix of cliffs and plateaus painted in vivid hues of yellow-browns and dark reddish-purples. You're still in awe as you turn away, eager to explore Mars's Mariner Valley below.

Although the passage above reads like science fiction, it describes what you could experience if you were to visit a virtual-reality lab. Virtual reality engages the user in a computer-generated environment that simulates, or imitates, reality. The user wears special equipment, often in the form of a head-mounted-display (HMD) such as goggles or a headset. Inside the HMD are two tiny video screens, one in front of each eye. The computer sends a slightly different image onto each screen, thus creating an illusion of depth. This false <u>perception</u> gives the user the feeling of being in the midst of a three-dimensional world. Sensors in the HMD track the user's head movements and inform the computer to update the scene on the video screens in "real time" with each movement. Some virtual reality systems may also include sensors in gloves or bodysuits that let the user interact more fully with the virtual environment.

You may be familiar with virtual reality from the "realistic" video games that totally immerse players in a three-dimensional, interactive world. Scientists, however, continue to explore virtual reality as a learning tool. Applications of this science include such areas as space exploration, medicine, pilot training, architecture, chemistry, biotechnology, engineering—and even driver's education.

Main Idea   1

	Answer	Score
Mark the *main idea*	M	15
Mark the statement that is *too broad*	B	5
Mark the statement that is *too narrow*	N	5

a. Virtual reality is a computer-generated environment that simulates reality. ☐ _____

b. The mind can be tricked through various computer devices. ☐ _____

c. Some video games use virtual reality. ☐ _____

Score 15 points for each correct answer. **Score**

Subject Matter **2** This passage is concerned with
- ☐ a. why people like science fiction.
- ☐ b. the Mariner Valley of Mars.
- ☐ c. how virtual reality works.
- ☐ d. applications of science technology. _____

Supporting
Details **3** The HMD contains two video screens to
- ☐ a. track the user's movements.
- ☐ b. simulate a game.
- ☐ c. fill the space in front of the eyes.
- ☐ d. create an illusion of depth. _____

Conclusion **4** The HMD, data gloves, and bodysuit create
the illusion that the user is
- ☐ a. an active member of a real environment.
- ☐ b. playing a computer game.
- ☐ c. watching a film.
- ☐ d. a bit confused by the world. _____

Clarifying
Devices **5** The author italicized the first paragraph to
- ☐ a. give readers something different to look at.
- ☐ b. present details about virtual reality.
- ☐ c. discuss HMD tracking systems.
- ☐ d. signal a different type of writing. _____

Vocabulary
in Context **6** In this passage <u>perception</u> means
- ☐ a. heat or electricity.
- ☐ b. observation or understanding.
- ☐ c. the act of clarifying something.
- ☐ d. the ability to make a sound conclusion. _____

Add your scores for questions 1–6. Enter the total here **Total**
and on the graph on page 215. **Score** _____

50 Drawing on the Definition

If you are ever uncertain about how to draw a particular geometric shape, you can rely on the fact that definitions of geometric figures usually indicate how to draw or construct them. Familiar examples include the square ("four right angles and four equal sides"), the rectangle ("four right angles and opposite sides parallel"), and the right triangle ("one right angle and three sides of any length"). Curved figures can be more difficult to draw than ones with straight sides, so it can be helpful to review the definitions of these figures when you have a need to create them. For a circle, any point on its curve is equidistant from the center, and this distance from the center, called the *radius*, would be the length of a string used to make the circle. Thus when you are making a circle, fasten one end of the string to the center point, tie the other end of the string to a pencil, and <u>sweep</u> completely around to draw the shape.

Another familiar curved figure is the ellipse. This egg-shaped figure appears very difficult to draw, but a review of the underlying definition provides the appropriate clue. An ellipse, like a circle, has a center point, but it also has two focus points (A and B). The definition says that the sum of lines such as AC and BC, which connect the focus points to the curve of the ellipse, must be constant, no matter where the lines connect to the curve. In the diagram, the string is fastened to points A and B. To draw the ellipse, stretch the string with a pencil to point C and sweep completely around, keeping the string tight as you proceed. You'll end up with an ellipse.

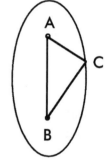

Main Idea	1		Answer	Score
	Mark the *main idea*		M	15
	Mark the statement that is *too broad*		B	5
	Mark the statement that is *too narrow*		N	5

a. An ellipse has two focus points. ☐ _____

b. Geometric shapes can all be drawn. ☐ _____

c. Understanding a definition can help you find a way to draw a geometric figure. ☐ _____

Score 15 points for each correct answer.

Subject Matter 2   Another good title for this passage would be
- [ ] a. Drawing Geometric Shapes.
- [ ] b. Writing Definitions for Geometric Shapes.
- [ ] c. Using Focus Points.
- [ ] d. Equations for Shapes in Geometry. _____

Supporting Details 3   The distance from the center to a point on a circle is called the
- [ ] a. diameter.
- [ ] b. curve.
- [ ] c. focus point.
- [ ] d. radius. _____

Conclusion 4   Based on the descriptions in this passage,
- [ ] a. it is easier to draw a circle than an ellipse.
- [ ] b. it is easier to draw an ellipse than a circle.
- [ ] c. an ellipse can be either circular or oval.
- [ ] d. a piece of string should be used in drawing a rectangle. _____

Clarifying Devices 5   The quoted material in the first paragraph is
- [ ] a. statements made by mathematicians.
- [ ] b. instructions for drawing right angles
- [ ] c. definitions.
- [ ] d. instructions for drawing circles. _____

Vocabulary in Context 6   In this passage the word <u>sweep</u> means
- [ ] a. move completely around.
- [ ] b. search thoroughly.
- [ ] c. clean or clear away.
- [ ] d. remove or erase. _____

Add your scores for questions 1–6. Enter the total here and on the graph on page 215.

Total Score _____

51 1968: A Watershed Year

Some historians mark 1968 as a watershed year in the United States civil rights movement. They see it as a turning point in the flow of events and a changing point in the way people thought about their country's problems. One changing point of view was that civil rights demonstrations had gotten out of hand. Many Americans called for law and order, but violence seemed to be escalating. Malcolm X, a leader of the Nation of Islam, who proclaimed that blacks needed to be strong, independent, and achieve equality and justice by any means necessary, had been assassinated in 1965. And in 1968 the Rev. Martin Luther King, Jr., a founder of the Southern Christian Leadership Conference and people's last best hope for change through nonviolent means, was also shot down.

Americans had become accustomed to nonviolent protesters. Now they were confronted by more militant activists such as Stokely Carmichael and by the Black Power movement. And the clear and single-purpose fight against segregation waned as more complicated issues of poverty and discrimination came to the forefront. In 1966 and 1967 poverty, rage, and hopelessness prompted riots in more than 100 U.S. cities, destroying the very neighborhoods that civil rights activists were trying to improve. The King assassination brought even more rage and rioting across the country.

The United States was also sending troops to Vietnam during this period, and military personnel were dying. The Tet offensive in January 1968 sparked the growing antiwar effort against U.S. military involvement in Vietnam. This new cause siphoned increasing attention, energy, and resources away from the civil rights movement.

From 1968 on, civil rights concerns about equality would broaden to include basic human rights as well, such as decent homes, health care, jobs, and education.

Main Idea 1

	Answer	Score
Mark the *main idea*	M	15
Mark the statement that is *too broad*	B	5
Mark the statement that is *too narrow*	N	5

a. People's views of the civil rights movement changed around 1968. ☐ _____

b. The civil rights movement went through some changes. ☐ _____

c. In 1968 many Americans were dying in Vietnam. ☐ _____

Subject Matter   2   This passage is mostly about
- ☐ a. Malcolm X and Martin Luther King, Jr.
- ☐ b. causes of change in the civil rights movement.
- ☐ c. protests against the Vietnam War.
- ☐ d. violent protests and counterprotests.   _____

Supporting Details   3   The Vietnam War affected the civil rights movement by
- ☐ a. destroying black neighborhoods.
- ☐ b. taking attention away from it.
- ☐ c. resolving many civil rights issues.
- ☐ d. requiring that civil rights leaders be drafted.   _____

Conclusion   4   The last paragraph suggests that
- ☐ a. civil rights no longer concerns Americans.
- ☐ b. the scope of the civil rights movement changed.
- ☐ c. the civil rights movement is over.
- ☐ d. the civil rights movement in the United States was ineffective.   _____

Clarifying Devices   5   Stokely Carmichael is given as an example of
- ☐ a. a militant activist.
- ☐ b. a nonviolent protester.
- ☐ c. an assassinated civil rights leader.
- ☐ d. an antiwar protester.   _____

Vocabulary in Context   6   Waned means
- ☐ a. became ill.
- ☐ b. increased the cost of.
- ☐ c. lost importance.
- ☐ d. disagreed.   _____

Add your scores for questions 1–6. Enter the total here and on the graph on page 216.   **Total Score**   _____

52 Squiggles and Colors on Canvas

Abstract expressionism, the first truly American artistic movement of the 20th century, came to prominence in the years just after World War II. Not really part of a movement in the sense that their work had uniform stylistic traits, these painters, all living around New York City, were nonetheless united in their recognition that the world could now be ended with the touch of a button. In the face of the terror of the hydrogen bomb, painters had to approach art from a new perspective.

The main belief of the abstract expressionists was that the painter's canvas was a surface on which to act rather than to reproduce a specific image—in other words, the method of painting, not what resulted from it, was the primary consideration.

One of the best known abstract expressionists was Jackson Pollock. Detractors claim that his giant canvases look like nothing more than paint thrown at a surface; and indeed, this is one of the methods Pollock employed. Laying an unstretched canvas on the ground, Pollock would walk around or on it, flinging and dribbling paint as his arm flew in a controlled arch. His work, along with that of Willem de Kooning, who also produced largely abstract canvases to which paint was obsessively applied, belongs to the *action school* of abstract expressionism.

The other wing of the movement might be called the *color-field school,* artists who experimented with large flat planes of either thick or thinly washed color. Perhaps the best-known of these painters is Mark Rothko, who created canvases filled with soft-edged rectangles. Rothko did not <u>slather</u> the canvas with paint; instead his rectangles often overlapped each other with thinly applied colors, the background of the canvas always remaining recognizable. As with other abstract expressionists, he was seeking effect rather than image, but felt that his paintings nonetheless conveyed basic human emotions.

Main Idea   1 ———————————————————————————

	Answer	Score
Mark the *main idea*	M	15
Mark the statement that is *too broad*	B	5
Mark the statement that is *too narrow*	N	5

a. World War II initiated new art styles.	☐	____
b. Pollock dribbled paint on canvases.	☐	____
c. Abstract expressionists were unified by a concern with the method of painting.	☐	____

Score 15 points for each correct answer.   **Score**

Subject Matter 2 Another good title for this passage is
- [ ] a. Pollock and de Kooning.
- [ ] b. It's the Effect, Not the Image.
- [ ] c. Why Is Form More Important than Color?
- [ ] d. Getting Artistic Training in New York.   _____

Supporting Details 3 Abstract expressionism came to prominence
- [ ] a. after World War I.
- [ ] b. during World War II.
- [ ] c. after World War II.
- [ ] d. during the Vietnam War.   _____

Conclusion 4 In an abstract expressionist painting you might expect to see
- [ ] a. an unusual application of paint.
- [ ] b. a picture of a sunset.
- [ ] c. a canvas with no paint on it.
- [ ] d. a family portrait.   _____

Clarifying Devices 5 The purpose of the last two paragraphs is to
- [ ] a. show why many people dislike abstract expressionism.
- [ ] b. explain the two schools of abstract expressionism.
- [ ] c. praise abstract expressionism.
- [ ] d. show why art movements don't last long.   _____

Vocabulary in Context 6 <u>Slather</u> means to
- [ ] a. paint with a tiny brush.
- [ ] b. destroy.
- [ ] c. stretch.
- [ ] d. spread in large amounts.   _____

Add your scores for questions 1–6. Enter the total here and on the graph on page 216.   **Total Score**   _____

53 Weathering

Mountains, plains, and coastlines seem solid and immovable beneath our feet, but in reality the earth around us is in a state of constant change. It's changing along shores as powerful waves pound into the rock of a cliff. It's changing on windy days as airborne particles gouge into the surface of anything in their path. It's changing both on sweltering, sunny days and on frigid, snowy days. The <u>disintegration</u> of rock that takes place at or near the surface of the earth is called weathering.

Physical weathering occurs when a force is applied to rock, causing it to disintegrate into its basic components. The principal sources of physical weathering are temperature change, which expands and contracts rock particles and thus breaks rock apart; frost action, which condenses water vapor in cooling air to form water that seeps into cracks in rock; and organic activity, which occurs when plants and other organisms grow and burrow into cracks in rock, causing the rock to crumble over time.

Chemical weathering occurs when substances such as water, sulfuric acid, and plant acids cause changes in the mineral composition or chemical makeup of rock. Many minerals in rocks react chemically with substances in the damp atmosphere. Limestone, for example, is weathered by the carbon dioxide in rainwater, which slowly eats away the rock.

While weathering breaks down rocks to form loose material or rock minerals, erosion removes the material and rock minerals from their original location and transports them to other locations. These combined forces of weathering and erosion have been shaping the familiar landscapes of the earth for millions of years.

Main Idea	1		
		Answer	**Score**
	Mark the *main idea*	**M**	15
	Mark the statement that is *too broad*	**B**	5
	Mark the statement that is *too narrow*	**N**	5

a. The earth around us is in a state of constant change. ☐ _____

b. Chemical weathering results from changes in the chemical makeup of rock. ☐ _____

c. Weathering is an ongoing process caused by physical and chemical processes. ☐ _____

Subject Matter **2** Another good title for this passage would be
- [ ] a. Weather Patterns and Climate.
- [ ] b. The Changing Face of the Earth.
- [ ] c. Our Eroding Mountains.
- [ ] d. Rocks, Minerals, and Fragments. _____

Supporting Details **3** Physical weathering may be caused by all of the following *except*
- [ ] a. frost action.
- [ ] b. plant acids.
- [ ] c. temperature change.
- [ ] d. organic activity. _____

Conclusion **4** A good example of weathering is
- [ ] a. heavy ice breaking chunks off a rockface.
- [ ] b. water removing sand from a beach and putting it elsewhere.
- [ ] c. wind breaking the windows in a building.
- [ ] d. heavy rain causing rivers to flood. _____

Clarifying Devices **5** The writer introduces the concept of weathering by
- [ ] a. presenting examples that we might be familiar with.
- [ ] b. describing mountains, plains, and coasts.
- [ ] c. explaining how wind speeds constantly change.
- [ ] d. defining physical and chemical processes. _____

Vocabulary in Context **6** In this passage <u>disintegration</u> means
- [ ] a. breaking into parts.
- [ ] b. uniting into a whole.
- [ ] c. creation of newer, larger substances.
- [ ] d. restoration to a previous condition. _____

Add your scores for questions 1–6. Enter the total here and on the graph on page 216. **Total Score** _____

54 Zeno's Paradoxes

Paradoxes are statements that may be true but seem to say opposite things. Some people find paradoxes enjoyable and thought-provoking while others find them frustrating, but most mathematicians would agree that these puzzling situations have played an important role in the history of philosophical thought.

Zeno of Elea (495–435 B.C.) was a Greek philosopher now best known for inventing several paradoxes that caused mathematicians to question the very nature of time and space. In one of Zeno's paradoxes, the fast-running Achilles and a tortoise run a race, but the tortoise is allowed a head start because he is so much slower than Achilles. Zeno contends that Achilles can't win the race because he must first reach the place from which the tortoise started, but when Achilles reaches that location the tortoise has departed and therefore is ahead. The argument is repeated over and over, thereby proving that the more slowly moving tortoise is always ahead of Achilles.

In another paradox, Zeno demonstrates that any motion at all is actually impossible! To proceed from point A to point B, an object must first reach the middle of the distance; but before it reaches the middle, it must first reach the quarter mark; and so on. The object can never get from point A to point B; in fact, the motion can never even begin.

These types of paradoxes are usually explained by <u>positing</u> that both space and time are infinitely divisible; that is, the number of points on a line segment—or the number of instants in a time interval—has nothing to do with its length. However, since most of us are as perplexed by these infinite categories as by the original paradoxes themselves, Zeno's conundrums remain as intriguingly annoying as they have been for more than 2,000 years.

Main Idea	1	Answer	Score
	Mark the *main idea*	M	15
	Mark the statement that is *too broad*	B	5
	Mark the statement that is *too narrow*	N	5

a. Zeno's paradoxes challenged assumptions about space and time.	☐	_____
b. Paradoxes are statements that may be true but seem to say opposite things.	☐	_____
c. In one of Zeno's paradoxes, Achilles never passes the tortoise.	☐	_____

Score 15 points for each correct answer.   Score

Subject Matter   **2** This passage is mainly about
☐ a. various kinds of infinite categories.
☐ b. the history of Greek philosophy.
☐ c. the meaning of paradox.
☐ d. two paradoxes involved with motion.   _____

Supporting Details   **3** In the paradox about Achilles and the tortoise,
☐ a. the tortoise always wins.
☐ b. Achilles always wins.
☐ c. sometimes Achilles wins, and sometimes the tortoise does.
☐ d. neither one wins.   _____

Conclusion   **4** It is probably the case that Elea is or was a
☐ a. family of Greek philosophers.
☐ b. place in Greece.
☐ c. famous school of philosophers.
☐ d. Greek church or temple.   _____

Clarifying Devices   **5** The writer of the passage describes two of Zeno's paradoxes
☐ a. and then refers to several others.
☐ b. and then proves they are false.
☐ c. but does not fully explain how they work.
☐ d. but then points out that they are no longer important.   _____

Vocabulary in Context   **6** In this passage the word <u>positing</u> means
☐ a. setting in a fixed position.
☐ b. proposing.
☐ c. denying.
☐ d. drawing a diagram of.   _____

Add your scores for questions 1–6. Enter the total here and on the graph on page 216.   Total Score   _____

109

55 Good, Bad, or in Between

Sigmund Freud's work as a psychological theorist generated many terms and concepts. Among the most essential terms are those describing what he conceived to be the three major components of personality: the id, the ego, and the superego. For Freud, the human mind functioned as a battleground. It was the scene of a never-ending struggle among the three opposing forces of id, ego, and superego, as they struggled for supremacy of the human personality.

The id is what Freud called in his earlier writing "the unconscious." It represents blind impulse and energy and it operates according to the pleasure principle. The id demands immediate satisfaction regardless of circumstances and possible undesirable effects.

The ego represents reason and common sense. The ego understands that immediate gratification is usually impossible and often unwise. It operates according to the reality principle. With the formation of the ego, the individual becomes a self, instead of merely an animal that is driven only by urges and needs. The ego may temporarily repress the urges of the id with the fear of external punishment. Eventually, however, a person internalizes the punishment—it becomes part of him or her.

The superego is this internalization of punishment. The superego uses guilt and self-reproach to enforce rules and produce good behavior. When a person does something acceptable to the superego, the person experiences pride and self-satisfaction. The superego represents the rules and standards of adult society. It is often described as the conscience, but it is much more <u>punitive</u>, unforgiving, and irrational than a conscience.

Main Idea 1		Answer	Score
Mark the *main idea*		M	15
Mark the statement that is *too broad*		B	5
Mark the statement that is *too narrow*		N	5

a. Sigmund Freud was a psychological theorist.	☐	____
b. Individuals are driven in part by urges and needs.	☐	____
c. Freud's theory of personality has three major components.	☐	____

Score 15 points for each correct answer. Score

Subject Matter 2 This passage focuses on
☐ a. the only theory of human personality.
☐ b. Freud's theory of human personality.
☐ c. the ego and the superego.
☐ d. the history of human personality study. _____

Supporting Details 3 The ego operates according to
☐ a. the reality principle.
☐ b. the pleasure principle.
☐ c. an economic principle.
☐ d. a self-satisfaction principle. _____

Conclusion 4 According to Freud's theories, which part of the personality would most likely be responsible for developing the rules and regulations for a school?
☐ a. id
☐ b. ego
☐ c. superego
☐ d. unconscious _____

Clarifying Devices 5 Which of the following is a simile for Freud's view of the human mind?
☐ a. It is like a battleground.
☐ b. It is like an animal.
☐ c. It is like a blind impulse.
☐ d. It is like a person experiencing self-satisfaction. _____

Vocabulary in Context 6 The word <u>punitive</u> means
☐ a. forgetful.
☐ b. sensitive.
☐ c. thoughtful.
☐ d. seeking to punish. _____

Add your scores for questions 1–6. Enter the total here and on the graph on page 216. Total
Score _____

56 Tales of the Terrible Past

It is not the job of fiction writers to analyze and interpret history. Yet by writing about the past in a vivid and compelling manner, storytellers can bring earlier eras to life and force readers to consider them seriously. Among those taking on the task of recounting history are some black writers who attempt to examine slavery from different points of view.

Nobel Prize-winning author Toni Morrison deals specifically with the legacy of slavery in her book *Beloved*. The main character in this novel, a former slave called Sethe, lives in Ohio in the years following the Civil War, but she cannot free herself from her horrific memories. Through a series of flashbacks and bitter reminiscences, the reader learns how and why Sethe escaped from the plantation she had lived on; the fate of her husband, who also tried to escape; and finally, what happened to the child called Beloved. Morrison's scenes of torture and murder are vivid and strongly convey the desperation of the slaves and the cruelty of their owners.

Charles Johnson's *Middle Passage* approaches slavery from a different, yet no less violent, vantage point. His main character, Rutherford Calhoun, is a ne'er-do-well free black American who stows away on a slave ship bound for Africa to collect its "cargo." Put to work after he is discovered, Calhoun witnesses firsthand the <u>appalling</u> conditions in which the captured Africans are transported. When they finally rebel and take over the ship, he finds himself in the middle—and is forced to come to terms with who he is and what his values are.

Neither *Beloved* nor *Middle Passage* is an easy read, but both exemplify African American writers' attempts to bring significant historical situations alive for a modern audience.

Main Idea	1	Answer	Score
	Mark the *main idea*	**M**	15
	Mark the statement that is *too broad*	**B**	5
	Mark the statement that is *too narrow*	**N**	5

a.	Many novelists have written books about the past.	☐	____
b.	Conditions on slave ships were awful.	☐	____
c.	Toni Morrison and Charles Johnson wrote novels dealing with different aspects of slavery.	☐	____

Score 15 points for each correct answer.   **Score**

Subject Matter   **2** This passage is mostly about
- [ ] a. the causes of slavery in America.
- [ ] b. black writers in the late 20th century.
- [ ] c. why Morrison and Johnson wrote the books they did.
- [ ] d. two novels that deal with slavery.

_____

Supporting Details   **3** *Beloved* is set
- [ ] a. on a slave ship.
- [ ] b. on a plantation before the Civil War.
- [ ] c. in Ohio after the Civil War.
- [ ] d. in an African town.

_____

Conclusion   **4** The writer seems to feel that
- [ ] a. everyone should read Morrison's and Johnson's novels.
- [ ] b. the books are worthwhile but challenging.
- [ ] c. black writers should ignore racial issues.
- [ ] d. we will repeat the past if we don't learn about it.

_____

Clarifying Devices   **5** The writer emphasizes that the two books are similar in their
- [ ] a. use of flashbacks.
- [ ] b. treatment of women.
- [ ] c. criticism of whites.
- [ ] d. portrayal of violence.

_____

Vocabulary in Context   **6** The word <u>appalling</u> means
- [ ] a. terrible.
- [ ] b. surprising.
- [ ] c. guilty.
- [ ] d. unrealistic.

_____

Add your scores for questions 1–6. Enter the total here and on the graph on page 216.   **Total Score**   _____

57 Bacteria Killers

In 1928 Scottish scientist Alexander Fleming was searching for methods of treating infections. He found that a mold of the genus *Penicillium* had accidentally contaminated a culture of bacteria and stopped its growth. Fleming named the mold's antibacterial substance penicillin. He recognized the therapeutic potential of his discovery, but it produced inconsistent results as a treatment against infections. Fleming's penicillin proved to be impure and weak. It was not until 1941 that two scientists, Howard Florey and Ernst Chain, came up with a purer, more stable penicillin. During World War II, methods were developed to mass produce the drug so that it could fight infections in injured Allied troops. By the end of the war, penicillin was made available to the general public. Penicillin soon became the miracle drug of the 20th century.

Penicillin is an antibiotic, or a chemical produced by living organisms—usually bacteria or molds—that retard or stop the growth of bacteria. Antibiotics weaken the cell walls of reproducing bacteria, causing the new cells to grow abnormally. After several days of treatment with antibiotics, few bacterial cells survive. Along with penicillin, other widely used antibiotics are ampicillin and streptomycin. These antibiotics are used to fight infectious diseases, such as meningitis, pneumonia, strep throat, and staph infections.

In recent years, antibiotics have become less effective. One reason may be that they have been used too frequently. Scientists have discovered that bacteria can develop a <u>resistance</u> to antibiotics by forming genetic mutations. These genetic changes let the mutants survive and reproduce. While scientists continue to search for new sources of antibiotics, they caution doctors not to overprescribe these drugs.

Main Idea   1 —————————————————————

	Answer	Score
Mark the *main idea*	M	15
Mark the statement that is *too broad*	B	5
Mark the statement that is *too narrow*	N	5

a. Antibiotics work by killing harmful bacteria that cause infectious diseases. ☐ ____

b. Penicillin affects reproducing bacteria. ☐ ____

c. Antibiotics include penicillin, ampicillin, and streptomycin. ☐ ____

Score 15 points for each correct answer.   **Score**

Subject Matter   **2**   The purpose of this passage is to
     ☐ a. introduce Alexander Fleming.
     ☐ b. explain the use of antibiotics in World War II.
     ☐ c. discuss antibiotics and how they work.
     ☐ d. describe ampicillin and streptomycin.   _____

Supporting   **3**   Penicillin acts on bacteria by weakening
Details
     ☐ a. cell reproduction.
     ☐ b. the cell walls.
     ☐ c. their immune systems.
     ☐ d. protein development.   _____

Conclusion   **4**   From the last paragraph, we can conclude that
overprescription of antibiotics makes
     ☐ a. harmful bacteria resistant to the drugs.
     ☐ b. the drugs more effective.
     ☐ c. mutant bacteria weaker.
     ☐ d. new sources of antibiotics.   _____

Clarifying   **5**   The author begins this passage by
Devices
     ☐ a. defining penicillin.
     ☐ b. explaining cell division.
     ☐ c. contrasting the uses of antibiotics.
     ☐ d. describing the development of penicillin.   _____

Vocabulary   **6**   In this passage <u>resistance</u> means
in Context
     ☐ a. the opposing troops during World War II.
     ☐ b. weakness.
     ☐ c. the ability not to be affected by.
     ☐ d. assist.   _____

Add your scores for questions 1–6. Enter the total here   **Total**
and on the graph on page 216.   **Score**   _____

58 A Creative Leap

Your own memories of algebra classes may contradict the notion of creativity. Perhaps you were unfortunate enough to be exposed only to lesson after lesson of mind-numbing drill. To gain an appreciation for the creative side of algebra, consider for a moment the supremely creative notion embedded in the familiar algebraic phrase, *Let* x *equal.*

To refresh your memory of how this phrase appears, consider a problem in which you are to find two consecutive integers, or whole numbers, with a sum of 35. The usual solution strategy is to begin by saying, "Let x equal the first integer and then $x + 1$ equals the second integer." The solution proceeds with the equation $x + (x + 1) = 35$. The solution, or x, is the smaller of the two integers, 17. That is, 17 plus 18 equals 35. The problem has been solved by letting x stand for the smaller unknown number.

This type of algebraic problem-solving is usually taught in such a humdrum manner that the surprising and creative part of the process is lost. The magic of the approach is that, faced with a problem about consecutive integers which may sound completely incomprehensible, a student is directed to take the optimistic leap that a solution has already been found! The idea of letting x equal the solution assumes two things. First, there exists a solution. And, second, the student can <u>forge</u> ahead, following the specified steps, and eventually reach the happy event of finding that solution. The creative part of algebra is not in the cleverness of the problem-solving strategies but rather in the wonderful and comforting notion that a solution always exists and that, somehow, you will be able to find it.

Main Idea	1		
		Answer	**Score**
	Mark the *main idea*	M	15
	Mark the statement that is *too broad*	B	5
	Mark the statement that is *too narrow*	N	5

a. Using the unknown x in algebra is an act of creativity. ☐ ____

b. Many algebraic solutions are extremely creative. ☐ ____

c. Problems about consecutive integers can be solved with algebraic equations. ☐ ____

Score 15 points for each correct answer.   **Score**

Subject Matter **2** This passage is mainly about
  ☐ a. problems about consecutive integers.
  ☐ b. increasing a person's creativity.
  ☐ c. the importance of drill problems in algebra.
  ☐ d. using the variable x to write equations.   _____

Supporting Details **3** The two consecutive integers that have a sum of 35 are
  ☐ a. 16 and 17.
  ☐ b. 17 and 17.
  ☐ c. 17 and 18.
  ☐ d. impossible to figure out without algebra.   _____

Conclusion **4** If a math problem asks you to find the time it takes to drive a distance, you could start by writing Let x equal
  ☐ a. the distance in miles.
  ☐ b. the speed in miles per hour.
  ☐ c. the time in hours.
  ☐ d. two consecutive integers.   _____

Clarifying Devices **5** The writer of the passage conveys a fondness for algebra by
  ☐ a. showing you a way to solve a problem.
  ☐ b. emphasizing how creative it is.
  ☐ c. downplaying the importance of drill.
  ☐ d. describing practical uses for it.   _____

Vocabulary in Context **6** In this passage the word <u>forge</u> means
  ☐ a. advance gradually but steadily.
  ☐ b. harden over a fire.
  ☐ c. form or create.
  ☐ d. fake a solution.   _____

Add your scores for questions 1–6. Enter the total here and on the graph on page 216.   **Total Score**   _____

59 Looking for Mr. Spenser

Kilcolman Castle, on Kilcolman Hill in County Cork, Ireland, is one of hundreds of small castles found throughout the Irish countryside. But Kilcolman Castle had a famous resident in the late 1500s. He was the English poet Edmund Spenser. Kilcolman Castle is where Spenser wrote *The Faerie Queene,* considered to be the greatest epic poem of the Elizabethan Age. Four hundred years later, in the late 1990s, Irish graduate students, volunteers, architects, archaeologists, and historians searched for clues of Spenser's presence in the now-ruined castle.

The first task was to look at the surviving masonry and the surrounding terrain. Shrubbery and ivy were cleared away, cattle manure was removed from the cellar, and the land was surveyed. Over the next three years a geophysical survey was undertaken to locate buried archaeological features. A geophysical survey is done by measuring variations in the soil's resistance to electricity every three feet. The purpose is to locate buried walls and pits. A laptop computer helps the archaeologist map the finds right in the field.

Although the site proved to be rich in <u>domestic</u> artifacts, such as fragments of pottery from storage and serving vessels and a pewter spoon handle and dish fragment, few artifacts could be associated with Spenser. Among personal items found that may have belonged to the poet were pins, a spur, the bronze tip of a dagger scabbard, and metal fittings for furniture or trunks. The four seasons of field work did, however, produce a plan of the castle enclosure, reveal the different construction phases of the tower-house, locate and identify other structures, and keep alive the possibility of learning still more about life in the Elizabethan age.

Main Idea	1		Answer	Score
	Mark the *main idea*		M	15
	Mark the statement that is *too broad*		B	5
	Mark the statement that is *too narrow*		N	5

a. Archaeologists are aided in their work by computers. ☐ _____

b. Archaeologists have studied castles in Ireland ☐ _____

c. A ruined castle in Ireland helped to reveal Elizabethan life. ☐ _____

Score 15 points for each correct answer.   **Score**

Subject Matter   **2**   This passage is mainly about
- ☐ a. Spenser and his poetry.
- ☐ b. castle construction.
- ☐ c. the Elizabethan age.
- ☐ d. an archaeological project.   _____

Supporting
Details   **3**   One of the uncovered artifacts that may have belonged to Edmund Spenser was
- ☐ a. a map.
- ☐ b. a pewter spoon handle.
- ☐ c. the bronze tip of a dagger scabbard.
- ☐ d. a laptop computer.   _____

Conclusion   **4**   The excavation at Kilcolman Castle
- ☐ a. uncovered no valuable information.
- ☐ b. uncovered information, but not what the archaeologists were looking for.
- ☐ c. completely changed people's views about life in Ireland.
- ☐ d. was a waste of time and resources.   _____

Clarifying
Devices   **5**   The word _Although_ at the beginning of the third paragraph signals
- ☐ a. an example.
- ☐ b. a contrast.
- ☐ c. an argument.
- ☐ d. a reason.   _____

Vocabulary
in Context   **6**   In this passage <u>domestic</u> means
- ☐ a. related to the home.
- ☐ b. a household servant.
- ☐ c. tame.
- ☐ d. not of a foreign country.   _____

**Add your scores for questions 1–6. Enter the total here
and on the graph on page 216.**

Total
Score   _____

60 Making Drama from History

Sometimes when students first discover that Shakespeare has written history plays, they are skeptical about whether compelling dramas can be created from long-ago events. Because the playwright is Shakespeare, the answer is an <u>unequivocal</u> yes.

Though Shakespeare wrote plays, such as *Julius Caesar,* that focused on historical figures from ancient Rome, the works generally categorized as history plays are 10 dramas dealing with English rulers, all but two set in the 15th century. In these plays Shakespeare considers royal issues important to people of the era, such as who had the right to the throne at various times and what qualities a good ruler should have.

Shakespeare got much of the basic information for his plays from historical reference books such as Holinshed's *Chronicles.* But Shakespeare used his own devices to bring individuals to life. For example, it a was common belief at the time that Richard III, king from 1483 to 1485, was evil for seizing power after his brother's death. But Shakespeare goes much further: he creates in Richard a total villain who fascinates with his cleverness even as he horrifies with his wickedness.

In the tetralogy, or group of four plays, dealing with kings Henry IV and Henry V, Shakespeare closely examines the attributes of a good ruler. His portrayal of the young Henry V, known as Prince Hal, is particularly well developed. Hal is initially characterized, in *Henry IV, Part I,* as a foolish, frivolous fellow who wastes his time with the roguish Falstaff—incidentally, one of Shakespeare's most inspired comical figures. His father the king despairs that Hal will ever develop the qualities of a competent ruler. Yet by the end of *Henry IV, Part II,* when the old king is dying, Hal has rejected Falstaff and stepped forward to assume his regal role. In *Henry V* he will reveal himself as an ideal ruler of the period, who invades and conquers France.

Main Idea   1 ——————————————————————————

	Answer	Score
Mark the *main idea*	M	15
Mark the statement that is *too broad*	B	5
Mark the statement that is *too narrow*	N	5

a. Shakespeare wrote 10 history plays.	☐	____
b. Shakespeare's history plays portray various conflicts of English kings.	☐	____
c. Shakespeare used historical references as sources of information.	☐	____

Score 15 points for each correct answer.   **Score**

Subject Matter   **2**   Another good title for this passage would be
                    ☐ a. Dramatizing the Lives of Kings.
                    ☐ b. All About Prince Hal and His Father.
                    ☐ c. Richard III, a Villain.
                    ☐ d. How Shakespeare Used His Sources.   _____

Supporting   **3**   Prince Hal became
Details   ☐ a. King Henry IV.
                    ☐ b. King Henry V.
                    ☐ c. King Henry VI.
                    ☐ d. Falstaff's jailer.   _____

Conclusion   **4**   It is probably true that Shakespeare's audiences
saw the history plays as
                    ☐ a. boring.
                    ☐ b. untrue.
                    ☐ c. dealing with much familiar material.
                    ☐ d. dealing with much unfamiliar material.   _____

Clarifying   **5**   The writer explains the term *tetralogy* through
Devices   ☐ a. comparison and contrast.
                    ☐ b. description.
                    ☐ c. definition.
                    ☐ d. a list of four titles.   _____

Vocabulary   **6**   Unequivocal means
in Context   ☐ a. unlikely.
                    ☐ b. medieval.
                    ☐ c. untruthful.
                    ☐ d. without doubt.   _____

Add your scores for questions 1–6. Enter the total here   Total
and on the graph on page 216.   Score   _____

61 A Multiuse Substance

Think of all the things around you that are made of glass; windows, containers, cookware, lightbulbs, eyeglasses, and decorative pieces are just a few possibilities. Glass is a hard, transparent material with a lustrous appearance and great durability. Such physical properties make glass very popular, but the chemical properties of glass are what allow us to fashion the various sizes, shapes, thicknesses, and colors needed to produce such a wide range of commonplace glass commodities.

Glass is made by heating a mixture of solid materials, such as sodium carbonate, limestone, and sand (silicon dioxide) until the atoms of the raw materials react. Some of the sand reacts with the limestone to form calcium silicate and carbon dioxide; the rest of the sand reacts with the sodium carbonate. The result is a three-dimensional network of silicon-oxygen bonds that in the short range of a few atomic distances are arranged regularly but in the long range have no regular pattern. This atomic structure makes the substance soft and <u>pliable</u> as it gradually passes into the liquid state, at which point it can be blown, rolled, or pressed into just about any shape. As the liquid cools, it thickens until it forms a shiny, hard, and very brittle solid.

Commercial glasses are usually silicates of sodium and calcium, but other elements and compounds may be substituted to produce different kinds of glass. Optical glass and cut-glass tableware, for example, are composed of sand, potassium carbonate, and lead oxide. Colored glasses are produced with the addition of various metals: manganese for purple, chromium for green, cobalt and copper for blue, silver for yellow, selenium for red, and calcium fluoride for white. The pale-green color common to glass bottles comes from iron compounds in the sand.

Main Idea	1		
		Answer	**Score**
	Mark the *main idea*	M	15
	Mark the statement that is *too broad*	B	5
	Mark the statement that is *too narrow*	N	5

a. Many items in our everyday world are made of glass. ☐ _____

b. The atomic structure of glass makes it soft and pliable. ☐ _____

c. Glass is a shiny, hard material that can be molded into various sizes and shapes. ☐ _____

Score 15 points for each correct answer.   **Score**

Subject Matter   **2**   This passage is mostly concerned with the
- ☐ a. commodities around us.
- ☐ b. chemical properties of glass.
- ☐ c. physical appearance of glass.
- ☐ d. chemical name for sand.   _____

Supporting Details   **3**   Glass is soft and pliable as a liquid but hard and brittle as a solid because
- ☐ a. glass is heated until it becomes a liquid.
- ☐ b. it breaks easily when dropped.
- ☐ c. its atoms do not have a regular pattern.
- ☐ d. glass can be molded into just about any shape.   _____

Conclusion   **4**   A piece of green cut glass probably would *not* contain
- ☐ a. calcium.
- ☐ b. chromium.
- ☐ c. potassium carbonate.
- ☐ d. lead oxide.   _____

Clarifying Devices   **5**   The progression in this passage is
- ☐ a. in chronological order.
- ☐ b. in spatial order.
- ☐ c. from the less familiar to the more familiar.
- ☐ d. from the more familiar to the less familiar.   _____

Vocabulary in Context   **6**   The word <u>pliable</u> means
- ☐ a. rigid.
- ☐ b. fixed.
- ☐ c. flexible.
- ☐ d. immovable.   _____

Add your scores for questions 1–6. Enter the total here and on the graph on page 212.   **Total Score**   _____

62 What's Rational About That?

Glance through the table of contents of a grammar school or high school mathematics textbook and you are likely to encounter the term *rational number*. While you are familiar with whole numbers, fractions, decimals, and percents, you may well wonder what a rational number is and how you passed through your school mathematics classes without encountering one.

In fact, you did learn definitions, computation, and applications for rational numbers, although they may not have been identified as such in your classes. A rational number is any number that can be expressed as a ratio of two whole numbers, and so $\frac{4}{5}$ (the ratio of 4 to 5), $\frac{2}{3}$ (ratio of 2 to 3), and in fact all fractions are members of the set of rational numbers. Also included are all terminating decimals such as 0.25 (equal to $\frac{1}{4}$ or 1 to 4) and repeating decimals like 0.333 . . . (equal to $\frac{1}{3}$ or 1 to 3). Percents are rational numbers, too, as any percent has an <u>implied</u> denominator of 100; for example, 35 percent equals the ratio 35 to 100, or 35 out of 100 parts. Even ordinary, everyday whole numbers are members of the set of rational numbers, since a whole number such as 4 can be written as $\frac{4}{1}$ or the ratio 4 to 1. So your math classes have involved work with all these types of rational numbers as you learned to compute, estimate, and solve problems with them.

This brief description of the major subsets of the rational numbers may give you the impression that *all* numbers are rational, but that is not the case. For example, the square root of the number 9 is 3, a rational number. But the square roots of numbers such as 5 and 10 do not equal whole numbers and cannot be expressed as ratios. So the square roots of numbers that are not exactly divisible are not rational numbers.

Main Idea   1

	Answer	Score
Mark the *main idea*	M	15
Mark the statement that is *too broad*	B	5
Mark the statement that is *too narrow*	N	5

a. Not all square roots are rational numbers. ☐ _____

b. Many different types of numbers are studied in school math classes. ☐ _____

c. Rational numbers include all types of numbers that can be written as ratios. ☐ _____

Score 15 points for each correct answer.   Score

Subject Matter   **2**   This passage is mostly concerned with
- [ ] a. persuading you to like math.
- [ ] b. explaining problems that use ratios.
- [ ] c. the definition of the term *rational number.*
- [ ] d. describing how to find square roots.   _____

Supporting   **3**   The number .25 is an example of
Details
- [ ] a. a square root.
- [ ] b. an irrational number.
- [ ] c. a terminating decimal.
- [ ] d. a repeating decimal.   _____

Conclusion   **4**   When whole numbers are written as ratios, the
second number in the ratio must always be
- [ ] a. 1.
- [ ] b. 0.
- [ ] c. larger than 1.
- [ ] d. a decimal.   _____

Clarifying   **5**   The passage explains what rational numbers are by
Devices
- [ ] a. defining categories of numbers.
- [ ] b. giving examples.
- [ ] c. proving theorems.
- [ ] d. showing examples that use computation.   _____

Vocabulary   **6**   In this passage <u>implied</u> means
in Context
- [ ] a. not necessary.
- [ ] b. proven.
- [ ] c. made up of fractions.
- [ ] d. not stated directly.   _____

Add your scores for questions 1–6. Enter the total here   Total
and on the graph on page 216.   Score   _____

63 Suu Kyi's Struggle

The prestigious 1991 Nobel Peace Prize went to Daw Aung San Suu Kyi (dah ông san sōo chē). The Nobel Committee chose to honor her for her "nonviolent struggle for democracy and human rights." Suu Kyi could not be present in Oslo, Norway, on December 10, 1991, to accept her award because she was under house arrest in the capital city of Yangon, Myanmar (the former Rangoon, Burma), in Southeast Asia.

Suu Kyi's political activities as leader of the National League of Democracy (NLD) began in 1988 when, at the age of 46, she returned to Burma to assist her ill mother. Her father, U Aung San, had fought for the <u>liberation</u> of Burma, first from the British and then from the Japanese in World War II. He was assassinated in 1947, when Suu Kyi was two years old.

When Suu Kyi returned to Burma, she was propelled into politics by the violent protests in that country. The protests forced the resignation of U Ne Win, the country's longtime military strongman. Suu Kyi's political involvement resulted in her being placed under house arrest in 1989 and kept isolated for six years. The governing military council held parliamentary elections in May 1990, and in spite of Suu Kyi's isolation, her party, the NLD, won 392 of the 485 contested seats. The military council ignored the results.

In announcing her selection for the Nobel Peace Prize, the committee said, "Suu Kyi's struggle is one of the most extraordinary examples of civil courage in Asia in recent decades." Although no longer under house arrest, her activities are still closely monitored and her closest supporters are in jail, but Daw Aung San Suu Kyi remains committed to the struggle for a free and democratic Burma.

Main Idea   1

	Answer	Score
Mark the *main idea*	M	15
Mark the statement that is *too broad*	B	5
Mark the statement that is *too narrow*	N	5

a. The Nobel Peace Prize was awarded to Suu Kyi for her efforts to bring democracy to Burma. ☐ _____

b. Many have struggled for freedom in Burma. ☐ _____

c. Suu Kyi is the leader of the NLD. ☐

Score 15 points for each correct answer.   **Score**

Subject Matter   **2**   This passage is mostly about
☐ a. how Suu Kyi caused political upheaval.
☐ b. Suu Kyi's family.
☐ c. why Suu Kyi won the Nobel Prize.
☐ d. the meaning of human rights.   _____

Supporting   **3**   Suu Kyi is the daughter of
Details   ☐ a. U Ne Win, Burmese military strongman.
☐ b. Yangon Myanmar, the former Rangoon.
☐ c. U Aung San, who was active in the liberation
of Burma.
☐ d. a Nobel Peace Prize winner.   _____

Conclusion   **4**   The writer of this passage considers Suu Kyi to be a
☐ a. violent protester.
☐ b. strong, committed leader.
☐ c. political troublemaker.
☐ d. person with limited influence.   _____

Clarifying   **5**   The first and final paragraphs of this passage are
Devices   organizationally related because they both
☐ a. tell of Suu Kyi's family.
☐ b. describe Suu Kyi's house arrest.
☐ c. use Suu Kyi's full name.
☐ d. explain what the Nobel Prize was awarded for.   _____

Vocabulary   **6**   The word <u>liberation</u> means
in Context   ☐ a. freedom.
☐ b. honor.
☐ c. recognition.
☐ d. reorganization.   _____

Add your scores for questions 1–6. Enter the total here   Total
and on the graph on page 216.   Score   _____

64 **Getting Inside Characters' Heads**

Though nearly all novelists report what at least some of the characters in their works are thinking about, few writers attempt to recreate all of the thoughts and half thoughts that race constantly through any individual's mind. Those writers who do, rely on a technique called stream of consciousness.

Consider for a moment what goes on in your own mind at any given moment. You may be consciously thinking, for example, of what you are reading on this page. Below this conscious level, however, hundreds of other impressions might be floating about—a concert you attended last night, a sudden noise outside, a sight in the room as you glance up that makes you think of something related. Most of these images or ideas are half-formed and fleeting, and usually you are barely aware of them. Yet a writer using stream of consciousness attempts to put this jumble of concepts onto the printed page.

Many novels include short snatches of stream of consciousness, usually characterized by long or half-formed sentences and free association from one idea to the next. Few writers attempt to sustain the technique for long stretches, though there are some notable exceptions. James Joyce uses the technique extensively throughout his novel *Ulysses,* the story of one character's experiences—and reflections—as he wanders through Dublin on a single day. William Faulkner uses it in *The Sound and the Fury* to probe the thoughts of three characters, including one of limited mental ability. Virginia Woolf uses it in *The Waves,* as she allows the reader to inhabit the minds of six friends as they pass through the stages of their lives. These works are some of the most challenging yet critically <u>acclaimed</u> novels of the 20th century.

Main Idea	1	Answer	Score
	Mark the *main idea*	M	15
	Mark the statement that is *too broad*	B	5
	Mark the statement that is *too narrow*	N	5

a.	Stream of consciousness is a technique that some writers use.	☐ ____
b.	In stream of consciousness writers attempt to show the thoughts passing through characters' minds.	☐ ____
c.	Much thinking involves association, or one thought suggesting another.	☐ ____

Subject Matter   **2**   Another good title for this passage would be
☐ a. The Genius of Joyce and Faulkner.
☐ b. A History of Stream of Consciousness.
☐ c. Stream of Consciousness Novels.
☐ d. Great Novelists of the 20th Century.   _____

Supporting   **3**   *Ulysses* is a novel that
Details
☐ a. traces the stages of its characters' lives.
☐ b. presents three individuals from the same
family.
☐ c. is set in England.
☐ d. takes place in a single day.   _____

Conclusion   **4**   Stream of consciousness is a
☐ a. technique that most readers enjoy.
☐ b. difficult technique to pull off successfully.
☐ c. technique used by most writers today.
☐ d. way of analyzing historical events.   _____

Clarifying   **5**   The writer explains "stream of consciousness" by
Devices
☐ a. asking the reader to consider his or her own
thought processes.
☐ b. giving examples from novels.
☐ c. explaining who originated the term.
☐ d. giving a dictionary definition.   _____

Vocabulary   **6**   <u>Acclaimed</u> means
in Context
☐ a. criticized.
☐ b. praised.
☐ c. ridiculed.
☐ d. copied.   _____

Add your scores for questions 1–6. Enter the total here   **Total**
and on the graph on page 216.   **Score**   _____

65 Infection Makers

Contraction of a viral disease such as a common cold, the flu, chicken pox, mumps, measles, mononucleosis, polio, or hepatitis is an inescapable part of life. In fact, every living thing—whether it's a plant, fungi, algae, protozoa, animal, or bacteria—can be infected by a type of virus specific to that organism. A virus is an infectious noncellular structure of genetic material, either DNA (deoxyribonucleic acid) or RNA (ribonucleic acid), that is usually surrounded by a protein coat. The sole purpose of a virus is to produce more viruses. A virus cannot, however, <u>multiply</u> or grow independently because a virus is not a cell. Instead a virus must infect, or enter, a living cell, called a host, and use the host's cell structures to reproduce more viruses. Eventually the infected host cell releases the new viruses, and then the host cell usually dies. The released viruses go on to infect other cells.

When a virus infects one or more cells of a body tissue, the infection causes the synthesis and secretion of proteins called interferons. These proteins strengthen the cell membrane of adjacent healthy cells so the virus cannot penetrate those cells. Sometimes, however, the virus succeeds in spreading to "other" cells. Then the human immune system activates and starts killing the viruses outside the cells as well as any infected cells themselves. Eventually the virus is eliminated and the organism returns to good health.

Vaccination is often the best protection against viral disease. A vaccine contains weakened or dead viruses that no longer cause the disease. Upon entering the body, a vaccine triggers the immune system to produce antibodies that kill the weakened viruses. Vaccination often results in a lifelong immunity against further infection.

Main Idea	1		
		Answer	**Score**
	Mark the *main idea*	M	15
	Mark the statement that is *too broad*	B	5
	Mark the statement that is *too narrow*	N	5

a. A viral infection causes the secretion of proteins called interferons. ☐ _____

b. Viruses infect people by invading a host cell and reproducing, but then the body's immune system fights back ☐ _____

c. Viruses are structures that attack cells. ☐ _____

Score 15 points for each correct answer.   **Score**

Subject Matter   **2**   The purpose of this passage is to
- [ ] a. define the role of interferons.
- [ ] b. explain the penetration of a host cell.
- [ ] c. describe the impact of a virus on a healthy organism.
- [ ] d. identify types of viral disease.   _____

Supporting Details   **3**   A virus cannot function independently because it
- [ ] a. has too much genetic material.
- [ ] b. is too small.
- [ ] c. usually kills the host cell.
- [ ] d. is not a cell with the structures necessary for growth and reproduction.   _____

Conclusion   **4**   We can conclude from the second paragraph that the "other" cells infected by the virus were
- [ ] a. not adjacent to the infected tissue.
- [ ] b. surrounded by a protein coat.
- [ ] c. synthesized and secreted proteins.
- [ ] d. killing the viruses outside the cells.   _____

Clarifying Devices   **5**   A device the author uses to help the reader understand the type of genetic material in a virus is
- [ ] a. quotation marks.
- [ ] b. parenthetical notes.
- [ ] c. a definition.
- [ ] d. an example.   _____

Vocabulary in Context   **6**   In this passage, the word <u>multiply</u> means
- [ ] a. live.
- [ ] b. reproduce.
- [ ] c. calculate.
- [ ] d. magnify.   _____

Add your scores for questions 1–6. Enter the total here and on the graph on page 216.   **Total Score**   _____

66 Precision and Common Sense

Consider the following anecdote and look for the mathematical misconception that underlies its humor. A small child was looking at fossils in a museum and asked a guard how old the fossils were. When the guard responded that they were 30 million and 8 years old, the child's skeptical parent asked where the age estimate came from. The guard answered that he had been working at the museum for eight years and had been told the fossils were 30 million years old when he started work.

The mathematical error embodied in the anecdote is that of misinterpreting the precision of the number 30 million. In the story 30 million years was never intended as a precise time period, but rather should have been <u>construed</u> to mean "about 30 million years" or even "between 25 and 35 million years." The degree of imprecision is unknown from just the information given in the anecdote and could only be determined from locating the scientist who made the estimate.

If a number is the sum or product of other numbers, the precision of that number is much affected by the precision of its component parts. Let's say two people are measuring the length and width of a room to determine its area. If one person estimates the width visually as about 10 feet while the other person carefully measures to the nearest inch, an area computed in square inches would have a meaningless precision.

Thus, common sense should be used generously when interpreting numbers used as measurements or counts. Before accepting any number literally, pause and think about the accuracy with which the original measurement or estimation was worked out.

Main Idea 1 ——————————————————

	Answer	Score
Mark the *main idea*	M	15
Mark the statement that is *too broad*	B	5
Mark the statement that is *too narrow*	N	5

a. Some numbers are more specific than others. ☐ ____

b. The age of any fossil is just an estimate. ☐ ____

c. It is important to describe or specify the precision of numbers used in scientific work. ☐ ____

Subject Matter   **2**   Another good title for this passage would be
- ☐ a. 30,000,008 Years Old?
- ☐ b. Imprecise Numbers in Archaeology.
- ☐ c. Measuring the Ages of Fossils.
- ☐ d. Finding Areas by Measuring Lengths.   _____

Supporting Details   **3**   Using the number 30 million to describe the age of dinosaurs is very
- ☐ a. precise.
- ☐ b. imprecise.
- ☐ c. inaccurate.
- ☐ d. confusing.   _____

Conclusion   **4**   If you subtract a very imprecise number from one that is extremely precise, the answer will be
- ☐ a. a sum.
- ☐ b. given in square feet.
- ☐ c. very precise.
- ☐ d. very imprecise.   _____

Clarifying Devices   **5**   The purpose of the introductory paragraph is to
- ☐ a. show how uninformed museum workers can be.
- ☐ b. provide an example using simple arithmetic.
- ☐ c. introduce a concept by telling a story.
- ☐ d. give a clear definition of a million.   _____

Vocabulary in Context   **6**   In this passage <u>construed</u> means
- ☐ a. recorded.
- ☐ b. understood.
- ☐ c. computed.
- ☐ d. measured.   _____

Add your scores for questions 1–6. Enter the total here and on the graph on page 216.   Total Score   _____

67 Domestic Violence

The National Coalition Against Domestic Violence defines domestic violence as "a pattern of behavior with the effect of establishing power and control over another person through fear and <u>intimidation</u>." Domestic violence is viewed as any violent or threatening behavior between family members. This includes abuse between former husbands and wives and between unmarried partners who live together. It is the leading cause of injury to women in the United States, with more than an estimated 2 million women being severely beaten in their homes each year. According to the U.S. Attorney General's office, 94 percent of violence between partners involves a man beating a woman.

Violence in the home was not publicly addressed until the 1970s, when women began to demand their rights. Women working together established local shelters and domestic abuse hotlines. They pressured states to enact and enforce domestic abuse prevention laws. Groups of battered women filed class-action suits against police departments and court officers who failed to arrest and prosecute abusers. Domestic violence began to be viewed as a crime, and cases were moved from the civil to the criminal courts.

Long overdue education and training programs about the nature and effects of domestic abuse became available for police officers, prosecutors, and judges. Programs were also aimed at the abusive men to help them understand and stop being abusers. And domestic violence awareness programs were started in schools. With domestic violence out in the open, there is increased awareness, better prevention, and more help for those who are abused.

Main Idea	1	Answer	Score
	Mark the *main idea*	M	15
	Mark the statement that is *too broad*	B	5
	Mark the statement that is *too narrow*	N	5

a. Violence and threatening behavior are never appropriate. ☐ ____

b. Domestic violence has been recognized as a crime and steps have been taken to deal with it. ☐ ____

c. Programs for abusive men are aimed at helping them change their behavior. ☐ ____

Subject Matter   **2**   This passage is mostly about
☐ a. shelters for battered women.
☐ b. programs for abusive men.
☐ c. court cases about domestic violence.
☐ d. domestic violence and what is being done
about it.   _____

Supporting   **3**   According to this passage, domestic violence
Details
☐ a. is the result of alcoholism.
☐ b. affects about 20 million U.S. women.
☐ c. started in the 1970s.
☐ d. is the leading cause of injury to women.   _____

Conclusion   **4**   The last sentence of this passage suggests that
the problem
☐ a. may be able to be solved.
☐ b. is too difficult to solve.
☐ c. no longer exists.
☐ d. is not big enough to worry about.   _____

Clarifying   **5**   The information in this passage is organized
Devices   through
☐ a. personal narrative.
☐ b. problem and solution.
☐ c. fact and opinion.
☐ d. case study.   _____

Vocabulary   **6**   In this passage <u>intimidation</u> means
in Context
☐ a. closeness.
☐ b. threats of violence.
☐ c. lack of tolerance.
☐ d. disagreement.   _____

Add your scores for questions 1–6. Enter the total here   Total
and on the graph on page 216.   Score   _____

68 Building the Wright Way

When the history of 20th-century architecture is written, the name of Frank Lloyd Wright will be prominent in the story. Though he built many larger buildings, Wright is known as much for the way he revolutionized home design.

Wright was born in Richland Center, Wisconsin, in the 1860s and moved to Chicago as a young man to work with renowned architect Louis Sullivan, who assigned Wright to supervise his firm's residential designs. Several of Wright's early houses were two-story, turreted structures that from the exterior were not too dissimilar to many of the Victorian houses currently in vogue. But then a radical change began to appear in his style, and he started to build houses that he felt harmonized with the great open spaces of Illinois. These houses, in the so-called "prairie style," were generally low, wide structures with overhanging roofs meant to provide shade from the summer heat. Windows were generally tall and narrow, often of decorated glass, and were a prominent feature in many houses. Interiors typically featured large open living spaces and, because Wright felt people didn't spend much time in those rooms, small bedrooms and kitchens. Though he built many houses in this style in Oak Park and other Chicago suburbs, probably the most famous is the Robie House on Chicago's South Side, completed in 1906.

In 1935 Wright designed and constructed Fallingwater, sometimes called the most famous nonroyal residence in the world. This house was commissioned by Edgar J. Kaufmann, who asked Wright to take the waterfall on his rural Pennsylvania property into consideration in the home design. Wright responded to this request by building the house *over* the waterfall, using reinforced concrete slabs to make the house seem to be floating in air. The unique design of this residence, so perfectly harmonized with its surroundings, could almost by itself immortalize Wright.

Main Idea	1	Answer	Score
	Mark the *main idea*	**M**	15
	Mark the statement that is *too broad*	**B**	5
	Mark the statement that is *too narrow*	**N**	5

a.	Frank Lloyd Wright built homes of new and unusual designs.	☐ ____
b.	Frank Lloyd Wright was a world-famous architect.	☐ ____
c.	Wright built many houses in Illinois.	☐ ____

Score 15 points for each correct answer.   **Score**

Subject Matter   **2**   This passage is mostly about
- ☐ a. the large buildings that Wright built.
- ☐ b. the houses that Wright built.
- ☐ c. Wright's early life in Wisconsin.
- ☐ d. Wright's relationship with Louis Sullivan.   _____

Supporting Details   **3**   Fallingwater is a house
- ☐ a. in the prairie style.
- ☐ b. with turrets.
- ☐ c. that Wright built for his family.
- ☐ d. built over a waterfall.   _____

Conclusion   **4**   When he designed and built houses, Wright
- ☐ a. tried to make them as costly as possible.
- ☐ b. tried to make them as inexpensive as possible.
- ☐ c. tried to make them appropriate to their environment.
- ☐ d. never consulted with his clients in advance.   _____

Clarifying Devices   **5**   Which phrase best describes the significance of Fallingwater?
- ☐ a. most famous nonroyal residence in the world
- ☐ b. commissioned by Edgar J. Kaufmann
- ☐ c. reinforced concrete slabs
- ☐ d. a house in rural Pennsylvania   _____

Vocabulary in Context   **6**   Renowned means
- ☐ a. misunderstood.
- ☐ b. restored.
- ☐ c. difficult.
- ☐ d. famous.   _____

Add your scores for questions 1–6. Enter the total here and on the graph on page 216.   **Total Score**   _____

69 Seeing Double

Twinning, the process that leads to a multiple birth, takes place in the early stages of the reproductive process. The egg cell from the female and the sperm cell from the male are specialized cells called gametes, each of which contains one half of the genetic information needed to form a complete fetus. During fertilization, the female gamete and the male gamete unite to form a zygote, or a fertilized egg, that contains the combined genetic information from both parent cells.

When a zygote undergoes mitosis, or cell division, it splits into two (or more) parts that contain the exact genetic information. Each part develops into an embryo that is genetically identical to the other and is of the same sex. Since the separate embryos are formed from a single zygote, the identical twins are called monozygotic (MZ) twins. Usually MZ twins share a common placenta and amniotic sac.

When two separate zygotes are present to form two unique embryos, dizygotic (DZ) twins, or fraternal twins, form. The presence of two zygotes is a result of multiple ovulations within a single menstrual cycle, and as part of the continued birth process a placenta is formed for each zygote. Since DZ twins come from two separate zygotes, they are no more genetically similar than are other <u>siblings</u> and thus may be of either sex.

Multiple births have increased since fertility drugs were introduced in the 1960s to help couples who have difficulty conceiving. Fertility drugs often cause the release of more than one egg from the ovary, thus increasing the chance of multiple births of DZ twins.

Main Idea   1

	Answer	Score
Mark the *main idea*	M	15
Mark the statement that is *too broad*	B	5
Mark the statement that is *too narrow*	N	5

a. Whether twins are identical or fraternal depends on how many zygotes are present. ☐ _____

b. Monozygotic twins are genetically identical and are of the same sex. ☐ _____

c. Twin births are fairly common occurrences. ☐ _____

Score 15 points for each correct answer.   **Score**

Subject Matter   **2** The purpose of this passage is to
- [ ] a. define *monozygotic* and *dizygotic*.
- [ ] b. explain the process of twinning.
- [ ] c. describe fertilization.
- [ ] d. discuss mitosis.   _____

Supporting Details   **3** During twinning, the specific process that results in the formation of monozygotic twins is
- [ ] a. ovulation.
- [ ] b. mitosis.
- [ ] c. reproduction.
- [ ] d. fertilization.   _____

Conclusion   **4** If the prefix *mono* in *monozygotic* means "one," then the prefix *di* in *dizygotic* must mean
- [ ] a. multiple.
- [ ] b. two.
- [ ] c. split in half.
- [ ] d. a choice.   _____

Clarifying Devices   **5** To help the reader understand why identical and fraternal twins are different, the writer
- [ ] a. describes the union of the two gametes.
- [ ] b. explains monozygotic twinning and then dizygotic twinning.
- [ ] c. contrasts fertilization and mitosis.
- [ ] d. discusses the effects of fertility drugs.   _____

Vocabulary in Context   **6** The word <u>siblings</u> means
- [ ] a. split personalities.
- [ ] b. female and male gametes.
- [ ] c. the genetic relationship between twins.
- [ ] d. brothers and sisters.   _____

Add your scores for questions 1–6. Enter the total here and on the graph on page 216.   **Total Score**   _____

70 What's It Worth to You?

Perhaps you have made a major purchase recently, one for which a sales clerk asked if you wanted to purchase replacement insurance. This type of insurance is offered for appliances and electronics and usually involves your receiving a replacement item if your new purchase breaks during some specified time period, such as the first year.

Is there some kind of mathematical principle you can use to decide whether you should buy this type of insurance, or must you simply guess whether or not your new purchase will break in the specified time period? As in many everyday problem-solving situations, mathematics can provide you with some assistance in your decision making. To determine whether you should purchase the replacement insurance, it will be necessary to compute what statisticians call the expected cost. An example will serve to <u>illuminate</u> both the mathematical principle and the computations involved.

If the purchased item costs $60 and the insurance is $20, you need one more number to find the expected cost—the probability of the item breaking or failing in the specific time period. Let's say that probability is 25%; that is, 25% or one fourth of the items are returned for replacement in the time period. If insurance is not purchased, the expected cost will be the sum of two quantities, one representing the situation in which the item breaks down and one for the situation in which it does not. If the item fails, the expected cost is 25% of the sum of $60 plus $60 (that second $60 is because you have to purchase the item a second time), or $30. If the item does not fail, the expected cost is 75% of $60. Adding these two amounts, $30 plus $45, results in $75, and since this is less than the total for purchasing insurance ($60 plus $20 is $80), the replacement insurance is not a wise choice in this situation.

Main Idea 1 ─────────────────────────────

	Answer	Score
Mark the *main idea*	**M**	15
Mark the statement that is *too broad*	**B**	5
Mark the statement that is *too narrow*	**N**	5

a. Understanding insurance involves many mathematical applications. ☐ ____

b. Figuring expected cost helps in deciding if you need replacement insurance. ☐ ____

c. Expected cost is the sum of two quantities. ☐ ____

Score 15 points for each correct answer.   **Score**

Subject Matter   **2**   This passage is mostly concerned with figuring out
☐ a. the rising cost of insurance.
☐ b. how to get refunds for defective products.
☐ c. when you need replacement insurance.
☐ d. how to know whether a product will fail.   _____

Supporting   **3**   If a product has a failure rate of 25%, then about
Details   what fraction of the items will fail or break in the
given time period?
☐ a. one fourth
☐ b. one third
☐ c. one half
☐ d. three fourths   _____

Conclusion   **4**   If you buy replacement insurance and your new
purchase breaks down, you
☐ a. get your money back.
☐ b. get a new product exactly the same as the
one that broke.
☐ c. can pick a new product of equal value.
☐ d. must purchase the insurance a second time.   _____

Clarifying   **5**   The passage explains expected cost by
Devices   ☐ a. defining replacement insurance.
☐ b. explaining insurance probabilities.
☐ c. giving failure rates for various products.
☐ d. giving an example of how it works.   _____

Vocabulary   **6**   In this passage the word <u>illuminate</u> means to
in Context   ☐ a. decorate with candles.
☐ b. brighten with lights.
☐ c. make understandable.
☐ d. prove.   _____

Add your scores for questions 1–6. Enter the total here   **Total**
and on the graph on page 216.   **Score**   _____

71 Unwritten History

The integration of history and archaeology has led to the study of people who have often been denied a voice in traditional history because of race, class, or gender. The historical archaeologist challenges traditional <u>interpretations</u> of the past and questions written sources of history. The historical archaeologist goes directly to the people for evidence of the people's history. The following two examples show historical archaeology at work.

While digging a site for an office tower in lower Manhattan, New York City, workers unearthed the bones of some 400 bodies buried in an 18th-century ceme-tery for African slaves. The information held in this cemetery provided data about the health of enslaved Africans prior to the American Revolution. Half of the 400 skeletons belonged to children under the age of 12. Nearly half of those were infants. Of the children who survived infancy, half showed signs of illness and malnutrition. Evidence of cultural continuity from Africa to the New World was found in a heart-shaped design of tacks hammered into one coffin lid. The design is thought to be a ritual symbol of the Akan people of Africa's Ghana and Ivory Coast.

The second example is found in the excavations at Southern plantations by Charles H. Fairbanks in the 1960s. Fairbanks's research pieced together information from the enslaved people. By excavating slave cabins, he found that Africans ate a variety of wild local plants, hunted game with guns, trapped and ate raccoons and opossums, caught mullet and catfish in tidal streams, and cooked in their homes. And like the evidence of the New York coffin design, Fairbanks's evidence also showed that African culture and identity—expressed in the people's pottery, food, and architecture—had been preserved in the New World.

Main Idea	1		
		Answer	**Score**
	Mark the *main idea*	M	15
	Mark the statement that is *too broad*	B	5
	Mark the statement that is *too narrow*	N	5

a. Historical archaeologists study cemeteries and plantations. ☐ _____

b. Historical archaeologists study the nonwritten evidence of people lives. ☐ _____

c. Historical archaeology is a field of study. ☐ _____

Score 15 points for each correct answer.   **Score**

Subject Matter   **2**   This passage mostly focuses on
- [ ] a. why historical archaeology is important.
- [ ] b. what historical archaeology can show about poor or enslaved people.
- [ ] c. how historical archaeology is changing today.
- [ ] d. comparing classical archaeology and historical archaeology.   _____

Supporting Details   **3**   The Manhattan cemetery yielded information about the
- [ ] a. health of African slaves.
- [ ] b. diet of African slaves.
- [ ] c. clothing of African slaves.
- [ ] d. literacy rate of African slaves.   _____

Conclusion   **4**   Fairbanks's excavations show that slaves on Southern plantations
- [ ] a. often went hungry.
- [ ] b. were excellent cooks.
- [ ] c. had a fair amount of leisure time.
- [ ] d. had a varied diet.   _____

Clarifying Devices   **5**   The term *historical archaeology* is explained through
- [ ] a. a dictionary definition.
- [ ] b. a question-and-answer format.
- [ ] c. definition and examples.
- [ ] d. comparison and contrast.   _____

Vocabulary in Context   **6**   In this passage <u>interpretations</u> means
- [ ] a. questions.
- [ ] b. evaluations.
- [ ] c. translations.
- [ ] d. summaries.   _____

Add your scores for questions 1–6. Enter the total here and on the graph on page 216.   **Total Score**   _____

72 Not What You Say, but How You Say It

To create memorable lines of poetry or fiction, a writer may rely on a number of techniques. Similes and metaphors, which compare unlike items either directly or indirectly, are commonly used devices, as is—at least in poetry—the making of non-living objects to come alive through personification. Many writers pride themselves on creating vivid imagery— word pictures that appeal to the senses. You have probably been familiar with these techniques since you were in elementary school.

Here are a few literary devices that you may not know. Symbolism gives a concrete object, such as a forest, a deeper, more abstract meaning: perhaps in a story it represents a place of freedom for the characters. When every element in a story, or the whole story, has a deeper meaning, then the symbolism becomes *allegory*. A modern-day example of allegory is the novel *Animal Farm,* which is not only a story about animals but a commentary on the oppressiveness of the Russian Revolution.

Three wording techniques that can help writers express themselves in a creative manner are *oxymoron, synecdoche,* and *metonymy.* An oxymoron is a pairing of words that puts together two contradictory concepts, such as *wise fool* or *deafening silence.* By juxtaposing opposites in this manner, the writer suggests a new meaning beyond that of the original words. Synecdoche and metonymy are both shorthand ways of expressing concepts, though they are formed in rather opposite ways. In synecdoche the writer uses a part of something to stand for the whole (*all hands on deck* means "all workers on deck"); in metonymy one word or phrase is substituted for another with which it is associated (*the Colonies* for "the 13 original colonies.")

Main Idea	1	Answer	Score
	Mark the *main idea*	M	15
	Mark the statement that is *too broad*	B	5
	Mark the statement that is *too narrow*	N	5
	a. Writers use many literary devices.	☐	____
	b. Certain literary devices are not that familiar to readers.	☐	____
	c. Metonymy and synecdoche are formed in rather opposite ways.	☐	____

144

Score 15 points for each correct answer. **Score**

Subject Matter **2** This passage mostly focuses on
- [ ] a. well-written poems and short stories.
- [ ] b. less familiar literary devices.
- [ ] c. the novel *Animal Farm*.
- [ ] d. why creative writers must be imaginative. _____

Supporting Details **3** In an oxymoron,
- [ ] a. a part stands for the whole.
- [ ] b. a broad term stands for a narrower one.
- [ ] c. two contradictory terms are put together.
- [ ] d. two unlike items are compared. _____

Conclusion **4** Allegories are usually written to
- [ ] a. amuse the reader.
- [ ] b. make a point or teach a lesson.
- [ ] c. show off the writer's use of language.
- [ ] d. explain the steps in a difficult process. _____

Clarifying Devices **5** Italic type is used in this passage
- [ ] a. for unfamiliar terms only.
- [ ] b. for unfamiliar terms and for examples.
- [ ] c. to highlight foreign words.
- [ ] d. for titles of poems. _____

Vocabulary in Context **6** Juxtaposing means
- [ ] a. measuring.
- [ ] b. lying about.
- [ ] c. making the imaginary seem real.
- [ ] d. placing side by side. _____

Add your scores for questions 1–6. Enter the total here **Total**
and on the graph on page 216. **Score** _____

73 A Chain of Life

The organisms in a community have a common link in that each organism is food for the next. A food chain shows the transfer of energy from one organism to another in a community. The chain begins with producers that make their own food. Green plants, for example, are producers that obtain chemical energy through photosynthesis. During photosynthesis green plants transform the sun's radiant energy into the chemical energy that plants use for life. The energy in the green plants is transferred to other organisms in the community when consumers, or organisms that cannot produce their own food, feed on the plants and obtain the energy and nutrients stored in them. All animals are consumers because they must eat green plants or other animals to obtain energy. When a producer or a consumer dies, its body <u>decomposes</u> into minerals and gases that are then used by plants when they convert the sun's radiant energy into chemical energy. Thus another food chain begins in the community.

Scientists, after closely examining food chains, have found that toxic chemicals, such as some pesticides and herbicides that are sprayed in an environment, can be passed through a food chain. The toxins build up in a consumer's body as it eats more contaminated food, which may be producers, consumers, or both, in the environment. Eventually in a process called biological magnification, high concentrations of poison accumulate in the bodies of consumers and kill them. Since humans have a very long life span of eating plants and animals from food chains, there is serious concern that we are likely to experience biological magnification. Some doctors, who have seen an increase in the types and numbers of cancers striking children and young adults, believe that humans already are being affected by toxic chemicals in food chains.

Main Idea	1		
		Answer	**Score**
	Mark the _main idea_	M	15
	Mark the statement that is _too broad_	B	5
	Mark the statement that is _too narrow_	N	5

a. Organisms in a community transfer energy by feeding off one another, but they may also pass contaminants. ☐ _____

b. Consumers eat producers or other consumers. ☐ _____

c. Food chains are of interest to scientists. ☐ _____

Score 15 points for each correct answer.   **Score**

Subject Matter   **2**   The primary purpose of this passage is to
- ☐ a. define photosynthesis.
- ☐ b. explain biological magnification.
- ☐ c. describe the workings of a food chain.
- ☐ d. tell about man-made influences that can be transferred through a food chain.

_____

Supporting Details   **3**   Consumers in a food chain
- ☐ a. cannot produce their own food.
- ☐ b. obtain chemical energy through photosynthesis.
- ☐ c. do not experience biological magnification.
- ☐ d. are mostly pesticides.

_____

Conclusion   **4**   The author's tone at the end of this article shows
- ☐ a. no feelings.
- ☐ b. amusement.
- ☐ c. anger.
- ☐ d. concern.

_____

Clarifying Devices   **5**   The first paragraph of this selection
- ☐ a. compares and contrasts.
- ☐ b. explains a process.
- ☐ c. narrates an episode.
- ☐ d. persuades through facts and details.

_____

Vocabulary in Context   **6**   Another word for <u>decomposes</u> is
- ☐ a. decays.
- ☐ b. reproduces.
- ☐ c. doubles.
- ☐ d. generates.

_____

Add your scores for questions 1–6. Enter the total here and on the graph on page 216.   **Total Score** _____

74 A Visual Illusion

You probably imagine that you can visually distinguish straight lines and edges from those that are curved, judging from your experiences or instincts whether a line <u>veers</u> away from a perfect horizontal or vertical. Most people do possess a good sense of whether something is straight or curved, owing perhaps to a perceptive ability that we are all born with. But the distinction between straight and curved is not always as clearcut as it might seem. Your eyes and mind can be fooled into thinking that a curved line exists where in actuality there is only a set of straight lines.

The figure that accompanies this passage demonstrates one way to blur the distinction between what is straight and what is curved. The example construction is based on connecting numbered pairs of points in a specified manner—in this case, 12 straight lines are drawn, with the result that a curve approximating that of a quarter circle emerges. The 24 connected points are positioned at equal distances along the two sides of a right, or 90 degree, angle. By varying the size of the angle as well as the number and positioning of the points, a wide variety of interesting and attractive "curved" figures can be created from straight line segments.

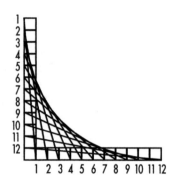

Main Idea 1

	Answer	Score
Mark the *main idea*	M	15
Mark the statement that is *too broad*	B	5
Mark the statement that is *too narrow*	N	5

a. Straight lines can be positioned to create the illusion of a curve. ☐ ____

b. Many people are tricked by visual illusions. ☐ ____

c,. A right angle is used in creating one illusion of a curve. ☐ ____

Subject Matter   **2**   This passage is mainly about
- ☐ a. drawing lines within right angles.
- ☐ b. characteristics of curved lines.
- ☐ c. characteristics of straight lines.
- ☐ d. creating a specific type of visual illusion.   _____

Supporting Details   **3**   The curve in the diagram
- ☐ a. is actually made from 12 straight lines.
- ☐ b. can only be seen from a certain angle.
- ☐ c. contains 24 small line segments.
- ☐ d. creates a 90 degree angle.   _____

Conclusion   **4**   The final sentence of this passage suggests that by varying the size of the angle, you might be able to draw
- ☐ a. larger circles.
- ☐ b. part of an oval.
- ☐ c. various sizes of rectangles.
- ☐ d. longer straight lines.   _____

Clarifying Devices   **5**   The points along the sides of the angle are numbered to
- ☐ a. prove there are more than 10 points on each side of the angle.
- ☐ b. show that the angle has 90 degrees.
- ☐ c. demonstrate how to connect them.
- ☐ d. make the figure look like a graph.   _____

Vocabulary in Context   **6**   In this passage <u>veers</u> means
- ☐ a. moves away from.
- ☐ b. becomes parallel with.
- ☐ c. zig zags.
- ☐ d. continues without ending.   _____

Add your scores for questions 1–6. Enter the total here and on the graph on page 216.   **Total Score**   _____

75 **Growing Your Brain**

Jean Piaget (1896–1980), an influential experimenter and theorist in developmental psychology, identified changes in the way children think at different stages in their development. Piaget stated that there are four distinctly different periods of mental development and that each involves increasingly more complex thought processes.

The first stage is *sensorimotor,* lasting from birth to the beginning of language, or about the first year and half of life. In this period of development, children function at a practical, nonsymbolic level.

The second stage is *preoperational,* which includes the early childhood years up to the age of six or seven. This is a stage of egocentrism in which children are incapable of taking into account the point of view of others. They learn to use language, symbols, and mental imagery. Putting objects in sequence, from first to last or smallest to largest, is difficult, as is understanding past, present, and future.

The *concrete operational* stage consists of the elementary school years until the age of 11. Children in this stage normally acquire the ability to organize and relate experiences into an ordered pattern. They begin to understand reversibility—that altering an object or event's properties— such as its shape, form, size, or color— does not change its basic properties. They also understand multiple classification and are capable of classifying items according to more than one <u>attribute</u>.

The *formal operational* stage consists of the years of middle school, beginning around the age of 11. A new form of thinking emerges as children begin to manipulate symbols and ideas and to think abstractly. They can develop and test hypotheses, make inferences, draw conclusions, and engage in problem solving.

Main Idea	1		
		Answer	**Score**
Mark the *main idea*		**M**	15
Mark the statement that is *too broad*		**B**	5
Mark the statement that is *too narrow*		**N**	5

a. New thinking emerges for children in the middle school years. ☐ _____

b. Theories about mental processes are part of the study of psychology. ☐ _____

c. Piaget's theory identified four stages of intellectual development. ☐ _____

Score 15 points for each correct answer.   **Score**

Subject Matter   **2**   The information in this passage has mostly to
                             do with the field of
                             ☐ a. philosophy.
                             ☐ b. interpersonal relations.
                             ☐ c. sociology.
                             ☐ d. child psychology.   _____

Supporting   **3**   Between the ages of 7 and 11 most children are
Details   likely to be in the
                             ☐ a. sensorimotor stage.
                             ☐ b. preoperational stage.
                             ☐ c. concrete operational stage.
                             ☐ d. formal operational stage.   _____

Conclusion   **4**   Children in the preoperational stage would be
                             most likely to
                             ☐ a. refuse to share toys with others.
                             ☐ b. enjoy a game that required helping a partner.
                             ☐ c. group their toys into the categories of
                                    vehicles, dolls, and games.
                             ☐ d. make an inference from a story they hear.   _____

Clarifying   **5**   Words like *sensorimotor* and *formal operational* are
Devices   italicized in this passage because they
                             ☐ a. are words Piaget made up.
                             ☐ b. are key words.
                             ☐ c. represent the exact words of a speaker.
                             ☐ d. are part of a list.   _____

Vocabulary   **6**   In this passage <u>attribute</u> means
in Context   ☐ a. give credit to.
                             ☐ b. share with a group.
                             ☐ c. quality.
                             ☐ d. belief.   _____

Add your scores for questions 1–6. Enter the total here   **Total**
and on the graph on page 216.   **Score**   _____

76 Equilateral and Equiangular

From the standpoint of aesthetic appeal, no class of geometric figures can compare with the regular polygons. These rotationally symmetric shapes have such a satisfying completeness that they have found extensive applications in all the visual arts.

The first, or simplest, of the regular polygons is that with the least number of sides, the equilateral triangle. You have observed this shape in yield signs from the window of a moving car, as well as in other types of informational or cautionary signs. This three-sided exemplar of the class of regular polygons <u>evidences</u> the distinctive characteristics of the group—to be designated "regular," a polygon must possess sides and angles of equal dimension. It is not sufficient to have just all equal sides or all equal angles, as shown by the four-sided rhombus, a polygon with four equal sides but lacking the necessary four equal angles (two sides are diagonal). Thus a rhombus is not regular, and the four-sided polygon that does have this distinction is the familiar square.

Perhaps the most convenient method of constructing regular polygons involves using the central angles of a circle. To illustrate the procedure to be followed, consider the regular pentagon, the equilateral and equiangular polygon with five sides. Draw any circle, mark the center point, and divide the total central angle measure of 360 degrees by 5 to get 72. Using a protractor, divide the circle into five equal sectors, each with a central angle of 72 degrees. Connect the points on the rim of the circle and you will have—subject to the accuracy of your construction techniques—a perfect regular pentagon. Using this construction approach, you may enjoy creating for yourself regular polygons with six sides (hexagons), seven sides (heptagons), eight sides (octagons), and so forth. One caution: if your intent is to create a regular figure with a large number of sides, be sure to begin your drawing activity with a very large circle!

Main Idea   1 ─────────────────────────────

	Answer	Score
Mark the *main idea*	M	15
Mark the statement that is *too broad*	B	5
Mark the statement that is *too narrow*	N	5

a. To construct a regular polygon with 5 sides, first divide 360 degrees by 5. ☐ _____

b. A few geometric figures are regular polygons. ☐ _____

c. Regular polygons are visually pleasing and easy to construct with central angles. ☐ _____

Subject Matter   **2**   This passage is mainly about
- ☐ a. measuring angles.
- ☐ b. flat shapes with all equal sides and angles.
- ☐ c. triangles with three equal sides.
- ☐ d. names for different kinds of polygons.   _____

Supporting   **3**   The angles of a rhombus are
Details
- ☐ a. less than 90 degrees.
- ☐ b. more than 90 degrees.
- ☐ c. all the same size.
- ☐ d. not all the same size.   _____

Conclusion   **4**   A protractor is a tool used to
- ☐ a. measure and draw angles.
- ☐ b. measure circles.
- ☐ c. draw straight line segments.
- ☐ d. draw equilateral triangles.   _____

Clarifying   **5**   The material in parentheses in this passage is used for
Devices
- ☐ a. definitions.
- ☐ b. information unrelated to the topic.
- ☐ c. explanatory notes.
- ☐ d. side comments by the writer.   _____

Vocabulary   **6**   In this passage the word <u>evidences</u> means
in Context
- ☐ a. surprises.
- ☐ b. denies.
- ☐ c. shows clearly.
- ☐ d. contradicts.   _____

Add your scores for questions 1–6. Enter the total here   **Total**
and on the graph on page 217.   **Score**   _____

77 Time Passes, Seasons Change

Living in an age of renowned religious painters, Pieter Bruegel the Elder was perhaps the most important essentially <u>secular</u> artist of the 16th century. Bruegel did his share of religious works as well, but he is far better known for paintings that give a glimpse of the life of the common people, the peasants, in his native Flanders.

Toward the end of his life Bruegel did a series of paintings commonly referred to as "The Months" that in many ways may be called the high point of his work. The five remaining paintings from the series portray a mountainous landscape and peasants performing typical activities in it in all seasons except spring.

The general view of all five paintings is very similar, for each looks down from a high point onto a wide and winding river that seems to lead out to a sea. The atmosphere of one of the paintings, *Hunters in the Snow,* portrays the dull, leaden skies and snow-covered environment of midwinter as well as the harshness of life, for the hunters are returning almost empty-handed. By contrast the late summer painting, *The Harvest,* depicts rich, golden fields of grain and a group of peasants pausing in their work for a pleasant midday meal. The other three paintings in the series—*The Gloomy Day, Haymaking,* and *The Return of the Herd*—represent typical scenes from late winter, midsummer, and autumn.

Since so few details of Bruegel's life are known to us, this series of paintings has raised many questions. For a long time, for example, debate raged among art critics as to whether the full series consisted of six or twelve paintings, though the consensus has finally settled on the former figure. Which work is to be considered first in the series is another mystery, as is, of course, the fate of the missing painting.

Main Idea	1		
		Answer	**Score**
	Mark the *main idea*	**M**	15
	Mark the statement that is *too broad*	**B**	5
	Mark the statement that is *too narrow*	**N**	5

a. Bruegel was a famous 16th-century painter. ☐ _____

b. Bruegel's paintings of "The Months" show typical scenes of peasant life throughout the year. ☐ _____

c. No painting in the series shows spring. ☐ _____

Score 15 points for each correct answer. **Score**

Subject Matter **2** This passage focuses primarily on
- [ ] a. painters of the 16th century.
- [ ] b. an overview of Bruegel's work.
- [ ] c. Bruegel's paintings of "The Months."
- [ ] d. a painting called *Hunters in the Snow.*

_____

Supporting Details **3** All five remaining paintings in the series "The Months"
- [ ] a. can be found in museums.
- [ ] b. are situated in the fields around a castle.
- [ ] c. have a winding river running through them.
- [ ] d. are painted in bright colors.

_____

Conclusion **4** Each painting in the series probably represents
- [ ] a. one month.
- [ ] b. two months.
- [ ] c. three months.
- [ ] d. a particular festival of the year.

_____

Clarifying Devices **5** The author conveys a sense of the paintings by
- [ ] a. telling about Bruegel's brush strokes and other techniques.
- [ ] b. describing their content.
- [ ] c. presenting them in chronological order.
- [ ] d. explaining why Bruegel painted them.

_____

Vocabulary in Context **6** Secular means
- [ ] a. religious.
- [ ] b. of the nonreligious world.
- [ ] c. talented.
- [ ] d. having to do with peasants.

_____

Add your scores for questions 1–6. Enter the total here and on the graph on page 217. Total Score

_____

78 Real-World Robots

When you think of a robot, do you envision a shiny, metallic device having the same general shape as a human being, performing humanlike functions, and responding to your questions in a monotone voice accentuated by high-pitched tones and beeps? This is the way many of us imagine a robot, but in the real world a robot is not <u>humanoid</u> at all. Instead a robot often is a voiceless, box-shaped machine that efficiently carries out repetitive or dangerous functions usually performed by humans. Today's robot is more than an automatic machine that performs one task again and again. A modern robot is programmed with varying degrees of artificial intelligence—that is, a robot contains a computer program that tells it how to perform tasks associated with human intelligence, such as reasoning, drawing conclusions, and learning from past experience.

A robot does not possess a human shape for the simple reason that a two-legged robot has great difficulty remaining balanced. A robot does, however, move from place to place on wheels and axles that roll and rotate. A robot even has limbs that swivel and move in combination with joints and motors. To find its way in its surroundings, a robot utilizes various built-in sensors. Antennae attached to the robot's base detect anything they bump into. If the robot starts to teeter as it moves on an incline, a gyroscope or a pendulum inside it senses the vertical differential. To determine its distance from an object and how quickly it will reach the object, the robot bounces beams of laser light and ultrasonic sound waves off obstructions in its path. These and other sensors constantly feed information to the computer, which then analyzes the information and corrects or adjusts the robot's actions. As science and technology advance, the robot too will progress in its functions and use of artificial-intelligence programs.

Main Idea	1	Answer	Score
	Mark the *main idea*	M	15
	Mark the statement that is *too broad*	B	5
	Mark the statement that is *too narrow*	N	5

a. A robot, aided by artificial intelligence, can perform certain human functions. ☐ ____

b. Today's robots move on wheels and axles. ☐ ____

c. Robots can be useful to people. ☐ ____

Score 15 points for each correct answer.   **Score**

Subject Matter   **2**   Another good title for this passage would be
  ☐ a. Robots: Taking the Place of Humans.
  ☐ b. Artificial Intelligence Programs.
  ☐ c. Today's Robots and How They Function.
  ☐ d. Modern-Day Sensors.   _____

Supporting   **3**   Artificial intelligence is
Details
  ☐ a. the unnatural way in which robots move.
  ☐ b. a voiceless, box-shaped machine that
    performs repetitive tasks.
  ☐ c. sensors such as antennae and a gyroscope.
  ☐ d. a computer program that imitates human
    intellectual processes.   _____

Conclusion   **4**   The last paragraph suggests that future robots will be
  ☐ a. more humanlike in behavior and actions.
  ☐ b. more like automatic machines.
  ☐ c. better able to move on inclines.
  ☐ d. better equipped with laser light sensors. _____

Clarifying   **5**   The writer begins the passage by comparing
Devices
  ☐ a. the shape of a human being with a box.
  ☐ b. a modern robot with a fictional robot.
  ☐ c. an imaginary machine with a human.
  ☐ d. a computer program with artificial
    intelligence.   _____

Vocabulary   **6**   The word <u>humanoid</u> means
in Context
  ☐ a. lacking human characteristics.
  ☐ b. anything having the appearance of a
    humanoid.
  ☐ c. being void or vacant.
  ☐ d. having a human form or characteristics. _____

Add your scores for questions 1–6. Enter the total here **Total**
and on the graph on page 217.   **Score** _____

79 Psychological Research

Psychologists use a research approach just as other scientists do. They develop hypotheses, which are possible explanations for what they have observed, and scientific methods to test the hypotheses. There are three main techniques used in psychological research.

Naturalistic observation, the first technique, involves watching the behavior of human beings and animals in their natural environment. The researcher looks for broad patterns of behavior. Psychologists conducting such studies try to observe a <u>representative</u> sample. This sample should be a large, typical group that reflects the total population. Naturalistic observation is usually used to gain insights and ideas for later testing.

Systematic assessment, the second technique, includes case histories, surveys or public opinion polls, and standardized tests. These are used to examine people's thoughts, feelings, and personality traits. Systematic assessments enable psychologists to gather information that they could not get by naturalistic observation. The accuracy of this information depends on well-designed studies and truthful, complete responses from participating individuals.

The third technique, experimentation, allows scientists to test a theory under controlled conditions as they attempt to discover or confirm cause-and-effect relationships. The researcher randomly divides subjects into two groups. One group is the experimental group and the other is the control group. The condition to be tested is changed only for the experimental group. If the experimental group behaves differently from the control group, then the tested condition probably caused the difference.

Main Idea 1		Answer	Score
Mark the *main idea*		M	15
Mark the statement that is *too broad*		B	5
Mark the statement that is *too narrow*		N	5
a. Psychologists research individual behavior.	☐		____
b. Psychologists develop and test hypotheses.	☐		____
c. Psychologists use three techniques in their scientific research.	☐		____

Score 15 points for each correct answer.　　　　　　Score

Subject Matter　　**2**　This passage is primarily focused on
　　　　　　　　　☐ a. hypotheses, explanation, and observation.
　　　　　　　　　☐ b. naturalistic observation, systematic
　　　　　　　　　　　assessment, and experimentation.
　　　　　　　　　☐ c. people's thoughts, feelings, personalities.
　　　　　　　　　☐ d. individual behavior and scientific manner.　　_____

Supporting　　**3**　Case histories, surveys, and standardized
Details　　　　　assessment are part of
　　　　　　　　　☐ a. experimentation.
　　　　　　　　　☐ b. naturalistic observation.
　　　　　　　　　☐ c. systematic assessment.
　　　　　　　　　☐ d. people's personality traits.　　_____

Conclusion　　**4**　A psychologist watching children at play on a
　　　　　　　　school playground would most likely be using
　　　　　　　　　☐ a. standardized testing.
　　　　　　　　　☐ b. analysis of cause-effect relationships.
　　　　　　　　　☐ c. experimentation.
　　　　　　　　　☐ d. naturalistic observation.　　_____

Clarifying　　**5**　The words *first, second,* and *third* in this passage
Devices　　　　alert the reader that
　　　　　　　　　☐ a. this is the order of steps in a research study.
　　　　　　　　　☐ b. this is the order of importance.
　　　　　　　　　☐ c. these are items in a list of research techniques.
　　　　　　　　　☐ d. these are the numbers of the paragraphs.　　_____

Vocabulary　　**6**　The word <u>representative</u> in this passage means
in Context　　　☐ a. large.
　　　　　　　　　☐ b. serve as an example of something.
　　　　　　　　　☐ c. natural.
　　　　　　　　　☐ d. a person appointed to speak for others.　　_____

Add your scores for questions 1–6. Enter the total here　　Total
and on the graph on page 217.　　　　　　　　　　Score　　_____

80 Looking Across for Answers

Imagine you are unfortunate enough to be caught in a traffic <u>snarl</u> with the effect that you and your vehicle progress only 45 miles in two entire hours! At this average rate of speed, it will take a total of four hours to cover 90 miles; that is, 45 miles in 2 hours is the same rate as 90 miles in 4 hours.

The equivalency of these two rates is illustrated with the mathematical expression displayed in the box, and is one practical application of using two equal rates to form a proportion. An attribute or property of all proportions that is immensely useful is that the two cross products are of necessity equal. In this example, the two cross products are 45 times 4 and 2 times 90, each pair of factors being diagonally opposite or across from each other.

$$\frac{45 \text{ miles}}{2 \text{ hours}} = \frac{90 \text{ miles}}{4 \text{ hours}}$$

The equivalency of cross products is so useful because it allows you to solve for a missing term in a proportional expression. Continuing with our traffic snarl example, suppose you wish to know how far you may expect to travel in $3\frac{1}{2}$ hours. Set up your proportion using the fractions $\frac{45}{2}$ and $\frac{N}{3.5}$, multiply to find the cross-products, and then solve the resulting simple equation for N. In a like manner, the time required to travel any given distance at this very slow rate of speed can be determined.

This useful cross-product strategy can be applied in the solution of a wide variety of practical applications—almost any situation, in fact, that involves rates, ratios, speeds, and measurement conversions.

Main Idea   1

	Answer	Score
Mark the *main idea*	M	15
Mark the statement that is *too broad*	B	5
Mark the statement that is *too narrow*	N	5

a. Forty-five miles in two hours is equivalent to 90 in four hours. ☐ ____

b. Solving mathematical problems involves an understanding of basic properties. ☐ ____

c. A key property of proportions is that the cross products are equal. ☐ ____

Subject Matter   **2**   This passage is primarily concerned with
- ☐ a. finding average speeds.
- ☐ b. mathematical qualities of speed.
- ☐ c. understanding fractions.
- ☐ d. proportions and how to solve them. _____

Supporting
Details   **3**   The example in the box uses two equal rates to show
- ☐ a. a ratio.
- ☐ b. an average distance.
- ☐ c. an attribute.
- ☐ d. a proportion. _____

Conclusion   **4**   The cross products for the proportion
$\frac{45}{2} = \frac{N}{3.5}$ are
- ☐ a. 45 times 3.5; 2 times N.
- ☐ b. 45 times 2; N times 3.5.
- ☐ c. 45 times N; 2 times 3.5.
- ☐ d. not equal. _____

Clarifying
Devices   **5**   The real-world example of proportion used
in the passage involves figuring out
- ☐ a. distance.
- ☐ b. time.
- ☐ c. speed.
- ☐ d. acceleration. _____

Vocabulary
in Context   **6**   In this passage the word <u>snarl</u> means a
- ☐ a. vicious growl.
- ☐ b. tangled mass.
- ☐ c. dangerous situation.
- ☐ d. confusing situation. _____

Add your scores for questions 1–6. Enter the total here   **Total**
and on the graph on page 217.   **Score** _____

81 Water to Drink

We need water for drinking, bathing, cleaning, and numerous other purposes, but how can we be certain that the water we drink and use is safe? Communities operate water-treatment plants to remove contaminants, harmful microorganisms, and chemicals and to render the water crystal clear, with almost no color, odor, or taste.

Any number of physical and chemical processes can be used to treat water for domestic use. Water entering a water-treatment plant passes through *screening* to remove fish, dead leaves, and other large objects. Then the water undergoes various processes to eliminate impurities that are suspended, or mixed but not dissolved, in the water and to improve its clarity. During *coagulation* and *flocculation,* a chemical coagulant such as aluminum sulfate, ferric sulfate, or sodium aluminate is added to the water to bring small suspended particles together into larger, heavier masses called floc. Next, the water goes through the processes of *clarification* and *sedimentation.* The water, filled with floc and other particles, flows into sedimentation tanks and as the water stands immobile in the tank, the floc and other dense particles settle to the bottom. The clarified water at the top is then skimmed off, but this water still contains impurities. These are removed through *filtration.* In this step, water trickles downward through layers of a filter. Anthracite coal, sand, and gravel make up the layers, which trap most of the remaining suspended particles. A final process involves *disinfection,* which destroys any disease-carrying microbes in the water. This step is accomplished either by applying chlorine or ozone to the water or by exposing the water to ultraviolet radiation. At this point, other processes such as softening, aeration, and fluoridation may be performed to meet a community's drinking water standards.

Main Idea	1		
		Answer	**Score**
	Mark the *main idea*	M	15
	Mark the statement that is *too broad*	B	5
	Mark the statement that is *too narrow*	N	5

a. Water treatment involves processes that make water suitable for drinking. □ ____

b. During filtration, water trickles downward through layers of a filter. □ ____

c. We need water for many purposes in our lives. □ ____

Score 15 points for each correct answer.   **Score**

Subject Matter   **2**   Another good title for this passage would be
    ☐ a. Harmful Microorganisms in Our Water.
    ☐ b. Getting the Lumps Out of Water.
    ☐ c. What Happens at Water Treatment Plants.
    ☐ d. Microbes Are Trickling from Your Faucet.   _____

Supporting   **3**   A chemical coagulant causes
Details
    ☐ a. large objects to become trapped.
    ☐ b. sediment to stand still in the tank.
    ☐ c. disease-carrying microbes to be destroyed.
    ☐ d. particles in the water to clump together.   _____

Conclusion   **4**   We can conclude that we should not
    ☐ a. drink tap water unless it has been processed
        at a water treatment plant.
    ☐ b. care whether water has been processed at a
        water treatment plant.
    ☐ c. apply ozone to our drinking water.
    ☐ d. use physical and chemical processes to treat
        our drinking water.   _____

Clarifying   **5**   To help the reader identify the processes that
Devices   purify our drinking water, the author
    ☐ a. defines each process.
    ☐ b. explains flocculation.
    ☐ c. italicizes the terms.
    ☐ d. describes filtration.   _____

Vocabulary   **6**   The word <u>clarity</u> means
in Context
    ☐ a. smell.
    ☐ b. clearness.
    ☐ c. taste.
    ☐ d. color.   _____

Add your scores for questions 1–6. Enter the total here   **Total**
and on the graph on page 217.   **Score**   _____

82 Flying People and Never-Ending Storms

Beginning in the 1940s and reaching its height in the 1960s, a Latin American literary movement took the publishing world by storm. Writers such as José Donoso in Chile, Jorge Luis Borges and Julio Cortázar in Argentina, Jorge Amado in Brazil, and Gabriel García Márquez in Colombia began writing stories and novels that were often a blend of reality and fantasy, while at the same time frequently commenting on political situations in their respective countries. Out of this rich literary environment came the technique known as *magic realism.*

Magic realism is a style of writing in which fantastic events, such as a character rising from the ground like a bird, are presented as ordinary occurrences in otherwise realistic fiction. These elements, which may also involve dreams and superstitions proving to be true, add a rich and sometimes humorous flavor to fiction without <u>detracting</u> from the overall development of plot.

Specific examples will clarify some of the scope of magic realism. In the short stories of Borges, a complex dream world exists. Sometimes, as in "A Circular Ruin," the suggestion is made that a character who thinks he is dreaming is really only a player in another person's dream. Often, as in "The Garden of Forking Paths," the fantastic or magical elements are interwoven into detective stories or tales of international intrigue.

The novels and stories of García Márquez have more straightforward plots, and the magic realism elements are easier to distinguish. For example, in his master work *One Hundred Years of Solitude,* one of the main characters is well over 100 years old. A tropical storm persists for almost five years without cease. Yet these magic elements merely enrich an already complex tale of five generations of a Colombian family.

Main Idea	1		Answer	Score
		Mark the *main idea*	M	15
		Mark the statement that is *too broad*	B	5
		Mark the statement that is *too narrow*	N	5

a. Magic realism is a style that developed in Latin America. ☐ _____

b. Magic realism puts supernatural and other strange events into ordinary fiction. ☐ _____

c. In magic realism people might fly. ☐ _____

Score 15 points for each correct answer. Score

Subject Matter   **2**   This passage deals most closely with
- [ ] a. the work of Jorge Luis Borges.
- [ ] b. magic realism and how writers use it.
- [ ] c. the Latin American literary renaissance.
- [ ] d. writers from Argentina and Chile.   _____

Supporting   **3**   *One Hundred Years of Solitude* is
Details
- [ ] a. a story about characters in a dream.
- [ ] b. the master work of José Donoso.
- [ ] c. a novel about a family in Colombia.
- [ ] d. a nonfictional account of Argentine politics.   _____

Conclusion   **4**   A good way to read stories with magic realism is to
- [ ] a. try to figure out what the magic realism symbolizes.
- [ ] b. enjoy it but not let it distract you too much.
- [ ] c. realize that the writer is making fun of the reader.
- [ ] d. assume that only Latin Americans can understand it.   _____

Clarifying   **5**   The second paragraph is mainly developed through
Devices
- [ ] a. comparison and contrast.
- [ ] b. narration.
- [ ] c. persuasion.
- [ ] d. definition.   _____

Vocabulary   **6**   Detracting means
in Context
- [ ] a. making a list of.
- [ ] b. adding to.
- [ ] c. taking away from.
- [ ] d. summarizing.   _____

**Add your scores for questions 1–6. Enter the total here
and on the graph on page 217.**   Total
Score   _____

83 The End of a Friendship

Psychoanalytic theories are concerned with the dynamics of behavior. Each theory offers an explanation as to why people feel, think, and act as they do. Sigmund Freud (1856–1939) developed the method of therapy called psychoanalysis, and his theory influenced the work of other major personality theorists who participated or were trained at the Vienna Psychoanalytic Society. One of these theorists was Carl Gustav Jung (1875–1961), who had met Freud in 1907. Early in his career, Jung used Freud's psychoanalytical theories and participated in the psychoanalytic movement. Jung, like Freud, stressed the effects of unconscious ideas on human behavior. However, a series of disagreements led Jung to break with Freud, and their friendship ended in 1913.

Among the disagreements was that Jung believed Freud placed too much importance on sexual instincts. He could not agree with Freud that human energy is essentially sexual in nature, preferring to believe that sexuality is only one example of human psychic energy. Another disagreement Jung had with Freud was that Jung's analytic psychology was more spiritual and mystical than Freud's. Jung believed that personal growth occurred through spiritual rediscovery and renewal. In yet another area of disagreement Jung, unlike Freud, did not believe that personality was fixed by the end of childhood. For Jung, the process of developing a unique self that fulfills one's <u>potential</u> continues throughout life, and the most important structure is the self, which represents a harmony or balance between opposing parts of the personality. The self, Jung believed, could only emerge after the inner conflicts were resolved. The result of these disagreements was Jung's development of an analytic theory that addressed not only mental illness but also spirituality, goals, and growth in adulthood.

Main Idea	1		
		Answer	**Score**
	Mark the _main idea_	**M**	15
	Mark the statement that is _too broad_	**B**	5
	Mark the statement that is _too narrow_	**N**	5
	a. Personality theorists Freud and Jung did not always agree.	☐	_____
	b. Jung's theory of psychology was more spiritual than Freud's.	☐	_____
	c. Freud and Jung developed personality theories.	☐	_____

Subject Matter   **2**   Another good title for this passage is
   ☐ a. How Psychoanalysis Began.
   ☐ b. Freud and Jung: A Lifelong Partnership.
   ☐ c. Freud and Jung: A Difference in Approach.
   ☐ d. What Is a Personality?   _____

Supporting
Details   **3**   Jung was
   ☐ a. trained in Freud's theories.
   ☐ b. one of Freud's teachers.
   ☐ c. a dissenter who did not believe in
       psychology.
   ☐ d. convinced that personality was fixed by the
       end of childhood.   _____

Conclusion   **4**   Jung's theories
   ☐ a. were the same as Freud's.
   ☐ b. had no points of agreement with Freud's.
   ☐ c. kept Freud's theories and expanded on them.
   ☐ d. differed in fundamental ways from Freud's.   _____

Clarifying
Devices   **5**   The basic pattern used to develop this passage is
   ☐ a. a personal narrative.
   ☐ b. chronological order.
   ☐ c. comparison and contrast.
   ☐ d. question and answer.   _____

Vocabulary
in Context   **6**   In this passage <u>potential</u> means
   ☐ a. strength.
   ☐ b. capabilities.
   ☐ c. electric force.
   ☐ d. a drink used as a medicine.   _____

Add your scores for questions 1–6. Enter the total here   **Total**
and on the graph on page 217.   **Score**   _____

84 Only Length Times Width?

Once they have finished their last math course, most people think of the concept of "area" only in the context of rectangular regions. They may compare sizes of houses in square feet or check the coverage abilities of paint in square yards. Since the majority of area applications seem to involve rectangles, it is not surprising that many people think of area as being only the result of multiplying the length of a figure times its width.

Thinking of area only in terms of this formula is quite limiting, however, as the majority of shapes are more complicated than rectangles. In fact, area is a much broader concept than a simple formula. It embodies the notion of a surface covering. In the same way that a length is quantified by relating it to standard linear units such as inches, area is measured in standard square units. The most <u>tangible</u> way of demonstrating area is to use a set of one-inch tiles and have the learner cover, or approximately cover, a flat object such as a drawing of a lamp with the tiles. This exercise emphasizes the fact that almost all areas are approximations and that "multiply the length times the width" applies only to determining areas of rectangles and squares.

Of course many geometric figures *do* have area formulas and these are quite useful in situations where triangles, trapezoids, parallelograms, and their like are involved in problem-solving exercises. But remembering the underlying concept that an area is a covering of standard square units allows you to find the area of *any* shape, no matter how irregular. You can place a transparent square grid over the shape and then count or estimate the number of square units that cover the interior.

Main Idea	1		Answer	Score
	Mark the *main idea*		M	15
	Mark the statement that is *too broad*		B	5
	Mark the statement that is *too narrow*		N	5

a. The important idea about area is that it is a region covered by square units. ☐ _____

b. Figures like triangles and trapezoids use various area formulas. ☐ _____

c. Mathematics involves concepts as well as formulas. ☐ _____

Score 15 points for each correct answer. **Score**

Subject Matter   **2**   This passage primarily helps the reader to
- ☐ a. learn to differentiate area from perimeter.
- ☐ b. think of area as a covering rather than the answer to a formula.
- ☐ c. stop using area formulas.
- ☐ d. see that area is an important math topic.   _____

Supporting   **3**   Multiplying length times width gives the area of
Details
- ☐ a. a trapezoid.
- ☐ b. a parallelogram.
- ☐ c. a rectangle.
- ☐ d. any geometric figure.   _____

Conclusion   **4**   A transparent square grid would be a particularly useful tool to find the area of
- ☐ a. a very large shape.
- ☐ b. a very small shape.
- ☐ c. any shape with four sides.
- ☐ d. an irregular shape.   _____

Clarifying   **5**   The use of one-inch square tiles is described as
Devices   helpful for
- ☐ a. helping learners understand the basic concept of area.
- ☐ b. finding areas of shapes like triangles.
- ☐ c. teaching learners how to draw a grid.
- ☐ d. connecting area and linear measurements.   _____

Vocabulary   **6**   In this passage the word <u>tangible</u> means
in Context
- ☐ a. made out of a touchable substance.
- ☐ b. valuable.
- ☐ c. clear and obvious.
- ☐ d. practical.   _____

Add your scores for questions 1–6. Enter the total here   **Total**
and on the graph on page 217.   **Score**   _____

85 Polymers

We use polymers to make such goods as telephones, television screens, computers, fabrics, combs, baby bottles, carpets, CDs, automobile bumpers, asphalt roads, dishes, artificial body parts, insulation, and pesticides. Each of these products contains synthetic polymers; that is, each is made partly or entirely of substances such as plastic, nylon, acrylic, or silicone. Though some polymers—starch, cotton, rubber, leather, and DNA, for instance—exist naturally, a great many others are synthetic.

In scientific terms, polymers are large molecules made of smaller molecules <u>bonded</u> together. Polymers exist because of a remarkable element—carbon. Atoms of carbon form very strong three-dimensional bonds with other carbon atoms as well as with atoms of hydrogen, oxygen, nitrogen, sulfur, phosphorus, and many other elements. Carbon's unique bonding enables the atoms to combine in varied ways, literally forming millions of different carbon compounds. A polymer results when some of these smaller carbon compounds bond together in long chains, sometimes forming a polymer molecule of hundreds of atoms.

A polymer chemist is a scientist who studies carbon compounds and their properties. The chemist identifies the number and types of atoms in a compound and the pattern in which the atoms bond. Then he or she conducts experiments to observe the compound's reaction to heat and other substances. Through such studies, the chemist discovers how to synthesize molecules with specific desired properties. Chemists have used such procedures to synthesize polymers that vary in hardness, flexibility, softening temperature, and biodegradability. Due to the work of polymer chemists, we are able to use polymers to create numerous indispensable products.

Main Idea	1		
		Answer	**Score**
	Mark the *main idea*	M	15
	Mark the statement that is *too broad*	B	5
	Mark the statement that is *too narrow*	N	5

a.	Carbon's bonding enables atoms to form millions of carbon compounds.	☐	_____
b.	Polymers are used in many products.	☐	_____
c.	Synthetic polymers can be created to fulfill specific needs.	☐	_____

Subject Matter   **2**   Another good title for this passage would be
- [ ] a. The Properties of Plastics.
- [ ] b. The Many Uses of Nylon.
- [ ] c. What Is Silicone?
- [ ] d. Creating Polymers.

_____

Supporting
Details   **3**   A polymer molecule contains
- [ ] a. carbon compounds.
- [ ] b. never more than a few atoms.
- [ ] c. asphalt.
- [ ] d. a combination of natural and synthetic
fibers.

_____

Conclusion   **4**   When polymer chemists first began their studies,
they most likely experimented with
- [ ] a. nylon materials.
- [ ] b. pesticides.
- [ ] c. natural polymers.
- [ ] d. synthetic polymers.

_____

Clarifying
Devices   **5**   The author introduces the topic by presenting
- [ ] a. detailed word pictures.
- [ ] b. scientific studies.
- [ ] c. several different facts.
- [ ] d. specific examples.

_____

Vocabulary
in Context   **6**   In this passage, the word <u>bonded</u> means
- [ ] a. obligated.
- [ ] b. paroled.
- [ ] c. released.
- [ ] d. joined.

_____

Add your scores for questions 1–6. Enter the total here   **Total**
and on the graph on page 217.   **Score**

_____

86 All That Jazz

Of all the musical types that came into flower in America in the 20th century, one with a particularly great influence was jazz. This music, which like so many other forms probably had its origins on slave plantations, developed into a complex, sophisticated genre of remarkable <u>diversity</u> and worldwide appeal.

Most agree that the direct precursor of jazz was ragtime, which was developed by pianist Scott Joplin and others in the 1890s. Ragtime popularized the use of syncopation, a technique whereby a musical line begins with an unaccented beat and moves to an accented one, thus leading the way to the uneven sounds and melodies that are characteristic of jazz. But whereas a ragtime pianist played with a beat that was always consistent, a jazz pianist plays differently with the right and left hands, setting the melody of one against the rhythm of the other.

An important early jazz innovator was Jelly Roll Morton, who claimed to have invented jazz in 1902. Though many dispute his claim, one of his contributions was scoring music that allowed for improvisation, a technique that became a hallmark of jazz. Jelly Roll Morton's band played in New Orleans, where other jazz greats like Louis Armstrong got their start.

Band leader Duke Ellington can be credited with shaping the development of jazz through his own original compositions. In hundreds of carefully composed pieces from the 1920s on, he wrote to the strengths of his individual orchestra members, working their improvisational styles into distinctive, balanced works.

It is hardly an exaggeration to say that there are as many jazz styles as there are jazz performers. Though players may favor one type over another, the strength of jazz is that there are no real boundaries that keep them from free musical expression.

Main Idea	1	Answer	Score
	Mark the *main idea*	M	15
	Mark the statement that is *too broad*	B	5
	Mark the statement that is *too narrow*	N	5

a. Improvisation is an important jazz technique. ☐ _____

b. Jazz is a type of American music. ☐ _____

c. Many players contributed to the development of the musical form jazz. ☐ _____

Subject Matter   **2**   This passage is mostly a
- [ ] a. comparison of jazz and ragtime.
- [ ] b. short history of jazz.
- [ ] c. discussion of Duke Ellington's contributions to jazz.
- [ ] d. discussion of the future of jazz.   _____

Supporting Details   **3**   Jelly Roll Morton claimed to be
- [ ] a. the inventor of jazz.
- [ ] b. the main influence on Louis Armstrong.
- [ ] c. more important than Scott Joplin.
- [ ] d. a band leader who allowed no improvisation.   _____

Conclusion   **4**   In the modern world jazz
- [ ] a. does not change from player to player.
- [ ] b. is no longer popular except among old people.
- [ ] c. has been replaced by soul.
- [ ] d. continues to grow and develop.   _____

Clarifying Devices   **5**   The information in this passage is presented
- [ ] a. in chronological order.
- [ ] b. through spatial description.
- [ ] c. through comparison and contrast.
- [ ] d. through persuasive techniques.   _____

Vocabulary in Context   **6**   In this passage <u>diversity</u> means
- [ ] a. composed of different ethnic groups.
- [ ] b. variety.
- [ ] c. beauty.
- [ ] d. sophistication.   _____

Add your scores for questions 1–6. Enter the total here and on the graph on page 212.   **Total Score** _____

87 A Constant Battle

What is terrorism? Consideration of just a few statistics begins to provide an answer.

- October 1983—U.S. Marine barracks bombed in Beirut: 241 deaths.
- December 1988—Pan Am Flight 103 blown up over Scotland: 270 killed.
- February 1993—New York City's World Trade Center bombed: 6 dead, more than 1,000 injured.
- April 1995—Oklahoma City Federal Building bombed: 169 killed, hundreds injured.

These four acts of terrorism directed against the U. S. Government or its citizens were systematic, <u>premeditated</u>, and calculated; furthermore, they were fueled by extreme hatred. The resulting death, injury, and destruction are merely part of the shock and fear that terrorists want to create, as they also call attention to their causes. The unfortunate commonality in terrorist crimes is that innocent people suffer.

Is there a clear profile of who the terrorist is? Terrorists are people who believe that their cause and their rights are being threatened, and that the violence they create is justified and desirable. However, not all terrorists can be categorized as part of an organized, radical, or extremist group, for some are individuals acting alone in order to assert more direct control over their immediate environment.

What steps can be taken to mitigate the terrorist's threat? Defensive tactics, according to terrorism experts, include tighter building security, more stringent immigration policies to prevent foreign terrorists from entering the United States, and better intelligence information to circumvent terrorist crimes before they occur. However, in a free society, it becomes difficult to simultaneously protect citizens from terrorism and to protect the civil liberties they enjoy.

Main Idea	1	Answer	Score
	Mark the *main idea*	M	15
	Mark the statement that is *too broad*	B	5
	Mark the statement that is *too narrow*	N	5

		Answer	Score
a.	Terrorism, motivated by hatred or belief in a cause, is hard to control.	☐	____
b.	Terrorism is a serious crime.	☐	____
c.	Terrorists may act alone or in groups.	☐	____

Score 15 points for each correct answer.   **Score**

Subject Matter   **2**   This passage presents

☐ a. an explanation of terrorism.

☐ b. details of a terrorist act.

☐ c. the arguments for and against terrorism.

☐ d. an eyewitness account of terrorism.   _____

Supporting Details   **3**   A proposed defensive tactic against terrorism is to have

☐ a. more laws against it.

☐ b. fewer extremist groups.

☐ c. tighter immigration policies.

☐ d. fewer incoming flights from foreign countries.   _____

Conclusion   **4**   The concluding sentence in this passage suggests that

☐ a. terrorism cannot be stopped.

☐ b. the solution to terrorism is not an easy one.

☐ c. civil liberties take precedence over protection from terrorism.

☐ d. citizens will give up their civil liberties in exchange for protection from terrorists.   _____

Clarifying Devices   **5**   The basic pattern used to develop this passage is

☐ a. personal narrative.

☐ b. question-and-answer.

☐ c. chronological order.

☐ d. statement and disagreement.   _____

Vocabulary in Context   **6**   The word <u>premeditated</u> means

☐ a. given great importance.

☐ b. under the influence of prescription drugs.

☐ c. planned beforehand.

☐ d. performed publicly.   _____

Add your scores for questions 1–6. Enter the total here and on the graph on page 217.   **Total Score**   _____

88 Helpful or Harmful?

Radiation in one form or another is part of our everyday lives. Cosmic rays from outer space, radiation from the sun, radioactive elements in the earth's crust, and electro-magnetic radiation from radio waves, television sets, and electricity are sources of "background radiation." The long-term effects of radiation exposure are not fully known. But a branch of science called radiation biology is focused on finding out.

Radiation biologists study the effects of radiation on living tissue. The need for such studies became clear after atomic bombs were dropped on Japan during World War II. The biological effects of exposure to such large amounts of radiation were <u>devastating</u> to thousands of war survivors. High doses of radiation disrupt the mole-cular structure of a body's tissues. These molecular changes trigger a chain of events that can produce gene damage and cell mutations. The results include birth defects, tumors, eye cataracts, brain convulsions, nausea, and other injuries.

Radiation biologists believe, however, that small amounts of radiation exposure are of greater benefit than harm. Medical science, for example, commonly uses small amounts of radiation to diagnose and treat disease. Radioactive iodine helps doctors to diagnose thyroid problems. Radioactive isotopes let doctors trace the path of food molecules through the digestive system. Radiology procedures assist doctors in detecting tumors, brain activity, weakened heart muscle, and other conditions. Such procedures include the use of x-rays, PET (positron emission tomography) scans, CAT (computerized axial tomography) scans, and MRI (magnetic resonance imaging). As long as exposure to radiation is carefully controlled, people's life can be prolonged rather than destroyed.

Main Idea	1		
		Answer	**Score**
	Mark the *main idea*	M	15
	Mark the statement that is *too broad*	B	5
	Mark the statement that is *too narrow*	N	5
	a. Radiation is all around us.	☐	_____
	b. Radiation biologists have learned that radiation can be helpful as well as harmful.	☐	_____
	c. High doses of radiation disrupt the molecular structure of a body's tissues.	☐	_____

Subject Matter   **2**   Another good title for this passage would be
☐ a. Radioactive Elements on Earth.
☐ b. Radiation Exposure During World War II.
☐ c. Types of Radiation.
☐ d. The Pros and Cons of Radiation.   _____

Supporting   **3**   Birth defects, tumors, eye cataracts, and other
Details   disorders are the result of
☐ a. exposure to background radiation.
☐ b. changes in the molecular structure of tissue.
☐ c. MRIs.
☐ d. radiology procedures such as x-rays, CAT
scans, PET scans, and MRI.   _____

Conclusion   **4**   This passage suggests that radiation from the
atomic bombs dropped in Japan
☐ a. had very little effect on people.
☐ b. was harmful only.
☐ c. was both helpful and harmful.
☐ d. was helpful only.   _____

Clarifying   **5**   In the first paragraph, the term *background*
Devices   *radiation* means
☐ a. the long-term effects of radiation.
☐ b. the effects of radiation on living tissue.
☐ c. a fairly steady radiation level in the
environment.
☐ d. a molecular change from radiation exposure.   _____

Vocabulary   **6**   Another word for <u>devastating</u> is
in Context   ☐ a. ruinous.
☐ b. restorative.
☐ c. wholesome.
☐ d. beneficial.   _____

Add your scores for questions 1–6. Enter the total here   Total
and on the graph on page 217.   Score   _____

The triangular illustration shown below demonstrates one of the many different links between geometric and arithmetic concepts—the notion of triangular numbers. The particular triangular number shown is 10, the fourth in the series that begins with 1, 3, and 6. A triangular number can be represented by a triangular arrangement of dots such as the one in the drawing and is one example of a class of numbers called figurate or polygonal. The geometric aspect of triangular numbers is obvious; the arithmetic connection is a little less apparent, but begins to emerge if you write each triangular number as the sum of a series of <u>consecutive</u> integers. Following 1, 3, 6, and 10, the next six triangular numbers in the series are 15, 21, 28, 36, 45, 55.

The sums of series of consecutive odd integers form another set of figurate numbers that may be represented by square arrays of dots. The successive sums $1 + 3 = 4$, $1 + 3 + 5 = 9$, $1 + 3 + 5 + 7 = 16$, and so on result in the number sequence 1, 4, 9, 16, 25, etc., the same sequence that is formed when you square each of the integers 1, 2, 3, 4, 5, ... Figurate numbers contain many interesting relationships for the curious and persistent to uncover, and one such is hidden in this brief introduction. Try adding adjacent, or bordering, pairs of triangular numbers and observe the emerging number sequence until a familiar pattern begins to show.

4th

1 ○

2 ○–○

3 ○–○–○

4 ○–○–○–○

$1 + 2 + 3 + 4 = 10$

Main Idea	1	Answer	Score
	Mark the *main idea*	M	15
	Mark the statement that is *too broad*	B	5
	Mark the statement that is *too narrow*	N	5

a. Square and triangular numbers are two kinds of figurate numbers. ☐ _____

b. The fourth triangular number is 10. ☐ _____

c. Number patterns can be interesting and surprising. ☐ _____

Subject Matter   **2**   This passage is mostly concerned with
☐ a. applications of triangles and squares.
☐ b. numbers that can be shown with geometric arrangements of dots.
☐ c. finding squares of numbers.
☐ d. finding sums of number sequences.   _____

Supporting Details   **3**   The third triangular number is
☐ a. 3.
☐ b. 6.
☐ c. 10.
☐ d. 15.   _____

Conclusion   **4**   Adding bordering pairs of triangular numbers creates a sequence of
☐ a. square numbers.
☐ b. odd numbers.
☐ c. even numbers.
☐ d. fractions.   _____

Clarifying Devices   **5**   The illustration shows that the fourth triangular number is the sum of
☐ a. 1 + 3 + 5.
☐ b. 1 + 3 + 5 + 7.
☐ c. 1 + 2 + 3.
☐ d. 1 + 2 + 3 + 4.   _____

Vocabulary in Context   **6**   In this passage the word <u>consecutive</u> means
☐ a. added to other numbers.
☐ b. not equal.
☐ c. following one another in order.
☐ d. complimentary.   _____

Add your scores for questions 1–6. Enter the total here and on the graph on page 217.   **Total Score**   _____

90 Seeing the World Centuries Ago

If you enjoy looking through travel books by such familiar authors as Arthur Frommer or Eugene Fodor, it will not surprise you to learn that travel writing has a long and venerable history. Almost from the earliest annals of recorded time individuals have found ready audiences for their accounts of journeys to strange and exotic locales

One of the earliest travel writers, a Greek geographer and historian named Strabo, lived around the time of Christ. Though Strabo is known to have traveled from east of the Black Sea west to Italy and as far south as Ethiopia, he also used details gleaned from other writers to extend and enliven his accounts. His multivolumed work *Geography* provides the only surviving account of the cities, peoples, customs, and geographical peculiarities of the whole known world of his time.

Two other classic travel writers, the Italian Marco Polo and the Moroccan Ibn Battutah, lived in roughly the same time period. Marco Polo traveled to China with his father and uncle in about A.D.1275 and remained there 16 or 17 years, visiting several other countries during his travels. When Marco returned to Italy he dictated his memoirs, including stories he had heard from others, to a scribe, with the resulting book *Il milione* being an instant success. Though difficult to <u>attest</u> to the accuracy of all he says, Marco's book impelled Europeans to begin their great voyages of exploration.

Ibn Battutah's interest in travel began on his required Muslim journey to Mecca in 1325, and during his lifetime he journeyed through all the countries where Islam held sway. His travel book the *Rihlah* is a personalized account of desert journeys, court intrigues, and even the effect of the Black Death in the various lands he visited. In almost 30 years of traveling it is estimated that Ibn Battutah covered more than 75,000 miles.

Main Idea	1		
		Answer	**Score**
	Mark the *main idea*	M	15
	Mark the statement that is *too broad*	B	5
	Mark the statement that is *too narrow*	N	5

a. Some early travel writing comes from around the time of Christ. ☐ _____

b. Three early travel writers described many new locations to their audiences. ☐ _____

c. Travel writing has always been popular. ☐ _____

Score 15 points for each correct answer.   **Score**

Subject Matter   **2**   This passage is mostly about
- ☐ a. why people find travel writing exciting.
- ☐ b. the literary style of three early travel writers.
- ☐ c. where three early travel writers went and wrote about.
- ☐ d. how to write a travel book.   _____

Supporting
Details   **3**   Ibn Battutah traveled
- ☐ a. to China.
- ☐ b. to Ethiopia.
- ☐ c. throughout the Muslim world.
- ☐ d. for 16 or 17 years.   _____

Conclusion   **4**   The books of the three writers were popular because
- ☐ a. they listed good places to stay.
- ☐ b. they told of strange and exotic locales.
- ☐ c. they explained the best routes to get to places.
- ☐ d. all of their stories were firsthand accounts.   _____

Clarifying
Devices   **5**   The overall organization of this passage is through
- ☐ a. chronological order.
- ☐ b. spatial description.
- ☐ c. travel writers' personal narratives.
- ☐ d. persuasive details.   _____

Vocabulary
in Context   **6**   In this passage <u>attest</u> means to
- ☐ a. give an examination to.
- ☐ b. draw a map of.
- ☐ c. tell lies to.
- ☐ d. give proof of.   _____

Add your scores for questions 1–6. Enter the total here   **Total**
and on the graph on page 217.   **Score**   _____

91 *¡Huelga!*

A cry of "*¡Huelga!*—Strike!" rang out over the vineyards in 1965 as the National Farm Workers Association was finally feeling powerful enough to stop work and demand pay raises from three of the largest California grape growers. Two growers agreed to recognize the farm workers' union and increase the pay, but the nation's largest table grape producer did not agree, and the strike continued. Organizations, individuals, political leaders, and religious leaders lent their support to the union. The National Farm Workers Association organized rallies, marches, hunger strikes, and asked Americans to not buy California grapes unless the grapes had the union label.

The leader of these workers was César Chávez (1927–1993). A teenaged Chávez had left his family's migrant life years ago to take a job pruning vines and picking grapes near Delano, California. During World War II he served in the U.S. Navy, but after the war he began to organize Mexican-American farm workers. His intention was to improve the living and working conditions of the migrant farm workers, who, Chávez believed, would continue to remain powerless unless they had their own union.

In September 1962, he founded the National Farm Workers Association in Fresno, California, and traveled through the California grapefields trying to convince workers of the benefits of union membership. We can help you stand up to your Anglo bosses, Chávez told them, and help you get decent wages and working conditions. The union strike and the nationwide boycott finally, in 1970, convinced the largest vineyards and most other California table grape growers to agree to the union contract, a contract that helped to improve salaries and conditions for union farm workers.

Main Idea	1		
		Answer	**Score**
	Mark the *main idea*	M	15
	Mark the statement that is *too broad*	B	5
	Mark the statement that is *too narrow*	N	5

a. Mexican-American grape pickers struck successfully for better pay and conditions. ☐ _____

b. The National Farm Workers Association is a union. ☐ _____

c. César Chávez had been a picker. ☐ _____

Score 15 points for each correct answer. **Score**

2 This passage is mainly about
    ☐ a. the life of César Chávez.
    ☐ b. the success of the National Farm
         Workers' strike.
    ☐ c. the Mexican-American heritage.
    ☐ d. agricultural developments in the grapefields. _____

Supporting
Details 3 The National Farm Workers called for a boycott of
    ☐ a. wine.
    ☐ b. hiring migrant farm workers.
    ☐ c. nonunion table grapes.
    ☐ d. grape growers. _____

Conclusion 4 The migrant workers' union was effective insofar as
    ☐ a. government laws were passed to improve
         their wages and living conditions.
    ☐ b. the public decided to buy and eat grapes.
    ☐ c. the boycott and strike convinced grape
         growers to honor a contract.
    ☐ d. César Chávez began pruning vines. _____

Clarifying
Devices 5 The purpose of the second paragraph is to
    ☐ a. give background information about the
         union leader.
    ☐ b. explain how the union is organized.
    ☐ c. describe the daily life of a migrant worker.
    ☐ d. list important events in the union's history. _____

Vocabulary
in Context 6 The word <u>strike</u> in this passage means to
    ☐ a. hit.
    ☐ b. set on fire by rubbing.
    ☐ c. cross out.
    ☐ d. stop work. _____

Add your scores for questions 1–6. Enter the total here   **Total**
and on the graph on page 217.   **Score** _____

92 The Impossible Equation

Introductory algebra deals with the solutions of various types of equations, some simple and others quite complex. Each solution of an equation is a number that, when substituted into the equation, results in a true statement. Some equations have more than one solution. For example, $x^2 - 5x + 6 = 0$ is solved by substituting either the number 2 or the number 3 for the letter variable x.

In the history of mathematics, one very simple-appearing equation must have caused tremendous frustration for mathematicians because, on the one hand, it appeared so <u>trivial</u> but, on the other hand, no one could find a whole number or a fractional number for a solution. The annoyingly simple equation is $x^2 + 1 = 0$, and some brief experimentation should convince you that no number of the ordinary sort will make this equation true.

What kind of number, if any, can be thought of as the solution to $x^2 + 1 = 0$? Years ago, some mathematicians preferred to say that equations of this type had no solution, or were "absurd." Solutions of these equations were called meaningless, or impossible, or imaginary. Other mathematicians felt that $x^2 + 1 = 0$ and the related set of equations $x^2 + a = 0$, where a is greater than 0, had to have some kind of solution, so it was proposed to just *define* a solution, and the imaginary number i was eventually accepted to equal the square root of negative 1. Squaring i gives negative 1 and so the solution to $x^2 + 1 = 0$ is the imaginary number i, a member of a larger set called the complex numbers that take the form $a + bi$.

The imaginary and complex numbers should not be thought of as being without reality—they obey the standard laws of arithmetic and are just as real, in their own way, as familiar everyday whole numbers.

Main Idea   1 ————————————————————————————

	Answer	Score
Mark the *main idea*	M	15
Mark the statement that is *too broad*	B	5
Mark the statement that is *too narrow*	N	5

a. Imaginary and complex numbers are advanced mathematical concepts. ☐ ____

b. The equation $x^2 + 1 = 0$ has no immediately obvious solution. ☐ ____

c. Imaginary numbers were invented to solve equations of the form $x^2 + a = 0$. ☐ ____

Subject Matter   **2**   This passage is mainly about
    ☐ a. ways to solve equations.
    ☐ b. the invention of imaginary numbers.
    ☐ c. equations that have no reality.
    ☐ d. the development of difficult equations.   _____

Supporting   **3**   Equations like $x^2 + 1 = 0$ were called "absurd" since
Details   ☐ a. no ordinary sort of number could solve them.
    ☐ b. it was a waste of time to work with them.
    ☐ c. there were thousands of possible solutions.
    ☐ d. there were three or four solutions, but all
       were silly.   _____

Conclusion   **4**   The passage implies that finding solutions to
equations
    ☐ a. is a very important issue for mathematicians.
    ☐ b. is usually difficult or impossible.
    ☐ c. always involves using imaginary and complex
       numbers.
    ☐ d. is too elementary for most mathematicians.   _____

Clarifying   **5**   The equation $x^2 - 5x + 6 = 0$ is given as an
Devices   example of an equation
    ☐ a. that cannot be solved.
    ☐ b. that can be solved.
    ☐ c. with only one possible solution.
    ☐ d. requiring the use of imaginary numbers.   _____

Vocabulary   **6**   In this passage the word <u>trivial</u> means
in Context   ☐ a. always equal to zero.
    ☐ b. the simplest possible example.
    ☐ c. of little significance or value.
    ☐ d. unusual.   _____

Add your scores for questions 1–6. Enter the total here   **Total**
and on the graph on page 217.   **Score**   _____

93 Forever Warm

Environmental scientists continue to issue warnings about global warming, or the possible increase in average global atmospheric temperatures. Is there any legitimate concern about the earth's temperature rising a few degrees? In fact, a surface temperature increase of just a few degrees could lead to a partial melting of the polar icecaps, resulting in a major rise in sea levels. Some scientists predict that by the middle of the 21st century sea levels could rise by three or more feet. If sea levels rise as expected, coastal areas or tidal cities, such as New York and London, as well as of the best low-lying agricultural areas would experience regular flooding. In Bangladesh, where the Ganges River reaches the sea, such flooding could <u>displace</u> 15 million people. Scientists also believe that global warming may cause more frequent extreme weather patterns. Stronger winds, more destructive hurricanes, and particularly devastating droughts would become normal events. The major climatic zones may also shift, thus affecting some of the most fertile and productive agricultural areas on earth.

Global warming is caused when heat radiated by the earth's surface becomes trapped in the lower atmosphere by gases, such as water vapor (H_2O), carbon dioxide (CO_2), and methane (CH_4), and is reradiated back to the earth's surface, thereby warming it. Although some of this "greenhouse effect" occurs naturally in the atmosphere, the effect intensifies as atmospheric greenhouse gases increase. Human actions, such as the burning of fossil fuels and the destruction of tropical rain forests, add to the greenhouse gases, particularly carbon dioxide, in the atmosphere and thus increase the warming of the earth's surface. If global warming occurs as many scientists predict, the repercussions will be severe for ecosystems and human populations on earth.

Main Idea   1 ──────────────────────────────

	Answer	Score
Mark the *main idea*	M	15
Mark the statement that is *too broad*	B	5
Mark the statement that is *too narrow*	N	5

a. Global warming may very well happen. ☐ ____

b. Global warming may have severe repercussions for the entire earth. ☐ ____

c. Sea levels could rise by three or more feet by the middle of the 21st century. ☐ ____

Subject Matter   **2**   This passage is concerned with the

☐ a. scientists who study earth's environment.

☐ b. polar icecaps and why they melt.

☐ c. regular flooding of coastal areas.

☐ d. consequences of the increase in average
atmospheric temperatures around the earth. _____

Supporting
Details   **3**   Some scientists predict that in 50 years,

☐ a. there will be no winter weather on earth.

☐ b. the earth will be uninhabitable.

☐ c. seas could rise three or more feet.

☐ d. New York City and London will disappear. _____

Conclusion   **4**   The effects of global warming as described in
this passage

☐ a. seem likely to happen.

☐ b. are certain to happen.

☐ c. are based on faulty ideas.

☐ d. cannot be prevented at this late date. _____

Clarifying
Devices   **5**   The writer presents "greenhouse effect" by

☐ a. explaining the chemical names of the gases.

☐ b. giving an explanation of the process.

☐ c. listing the results of careful measurements.

☐ d. defining the major climatic zones. _____

Vocabulary
in Context   **6**   In this passage, the word <u>displace</u> means to

☐ a. incur the disapproval of.

☐ b. force to flee from home.

☐ c. put in a particular position.

☐ d. restore to a former position. _____

Add your scores for questions 1–6. Enter the total here   **Total**
and on the graph on page 217.   **Score** _____

187

94 Isn't It Absurd?

There was a time when it was very much in vogue to create dramas in which characters discussed topics like the nothingness of existence and their personal inability to control their fates. Such works were produced by a movement called, appropriately enough, the theater of the absurd, which constituted an important dramatic force among European and American playwrights in the 1950s.

Absurdist playwrights used various vehicles to present their point of view, which in essence was that the meaning of life is uncertain at best. Setting their characters in unlikely or bizarre locations was one technique; another was presenting dialogue which, at least on the surface, seemed devoid of meaning.

One of the best known absurdist writers is Samuel Beckett, whose frequently produced play *Waiting for Godot,* in which characters wait uncertainly for another who may never arrive, has the minimal setting and lack of plot characteristic of absurdism. In another Beckett play, *Happy Days,* one of the two characters is involuntarily buried in sand up to her waist, though she never comments on her situation.

Other well-known absurdist dramatists include the Frenchman Jean Genét, the Romanian Eugène Ionesco, and the British Harold Pinter. Genét wrote plays such as *The Maids,* which explore identity problems through characters that are sometimes doubles of each other. Ionesco is the creator of such works as *Rhinoceros,* a drama in which nearly all the characters are of their own <u>volition</u> transformed into the huge horned animal. In dramas like *The Birthday Party,* Pinter has menacing outsiders break into a situation and terrorize the characters with strange, often absurd questions.

It would be a mistake to think that such dramas lack meaning, since they all through their various devices explore and comment on what it means to be human.

Main Idea	1	Answer	Score
	Mark the *main idea*	M	15
	Mark the statement that is *too broad*	B	5
	Mark the statement that is *too narrow*	N	5

		Answer	Score
a.	Theater of the absurd explored life's meaning—or lack of meaning.	☐	_____
b.	Plays convey many modern ideas.	☐	_____
c.	Theater of the absurd often used strange settings and minimal plots.	☐	_____

Score 15 points for each correct answer.   **Score**

Subject Matter   **2**   Another good title for this passage would be
- [ ] a. Experimental Drama of the 1950s.
- [ ] b. Playwrights Without Ideas.
- [ ] c. Beckett, A Master of the Absurd.
- [ ] d. Rational vs. Irrational Drama.   _____

Supporting Details   **3**   Writers of absurdist dramas came
- [ ] a. only from America.
- [ ] b. only from Europe.
- [ ] c. mostly from countries that were Communist.
- [ ] d. from both Europe and America.   _____

Conclusion   **4**   The phrase "the huge horned animal" refers to
- [ ] a. Ionesco.
- [ ] b. a playwright Ionesco didn't like.
- [ ] c. the main character in a play.
- [ ] d. a rhinoceros.   _____

Clarifying Devices   **5**   The first two paragraphs of this passage are intended to
- [ ] a. surprise the reader.
- [ ] b. give background for the topic.
- [ ] c. describe important plays.
- [ ] d. make a case that this kind of drama is worthwhile.   _____

Vocabulary in Context   **6**   Volition means
- [ ] a. decision or choice.
- [ ] b. anger.
- [ ] c. laziness.
- [ ] d. weakness or exhaustion.   _____

Add your scores for questions 1–6. Enter the total here and on the graph on page 217.   **Total Score**   _____

95 Phobias

Phobias are intense, unrealistic fears that are <u>disproportionate</u> to the danger of an object or situation. People who suffer from phobias avoid the situations or objects that they fear, an avoidance that usually disrupts their daily lives. The National Institute of Mental Health has reported that 5.1 to 12.5 percent of Americans have phobias. Phobias are the most common psychiatric illness among women and the second most common psychiatric illness among men over 25.

Phobias may be divided into three classes:

1. Simple phobias, such as the fear of small animals, harmless snakes, heights, darkness, heights, or closed spaces.
2. Social phobias, such as the fear of speaking in public, eating in public, being out in public, or attending social gatherings.
3. Agoraphobia, the fear of being in situations where escape might be difficult or embarrassing, or in which help might not be available if one has an anxiety attack.

Agoraphobia is the most complex and debilitating of all phobias. People with agoraphobia tend to avoid crowds, movie theaters, tunnels, bridges, and public transportation. The range of avoided situations may be so great that people suffering from agoraphobia find themselves unable to leave their homes.

Phobias are treatable through either behavior therapy or medication. In behavior therapy, a trained therapist helps the patient confront the feared object or situation in a carefully planned, gradual way in order to learn to control the physical reactions of fear. With medication, which is the preferred treatment for social phobia and agoraphobia, both anxiety and panic can be controlled.

Main Idea	1	Answer	Score
	Mark the *main idea*	M	15
	Mark the statement that is *too broad*	B	5
	Mark the statement that is *too narrow*	N	5

a.	Agoraphobia is a severe phobia.	☐ ____
b.	Fears can cause people problems.	☐ ____
c.	Phobias are unrealistic fears that usually respond to treatment and medication.	☐ ____

Subject Matter   2   Another good title for this passage is
☐ a. Agoraphobia: A Fear of Everything.
☐ b. Working with a Therapist.
☐ c. Why People Are Afraid.
☐ d. Recognizing and Overcoming Irrational Fears.   _____

Supporting Details   3   The number of Americans with phobias is
☐ a. more than 15 percent.
☐ b. less than 5 percent.
☐ c. between 5.1 and 12.5 percent.
☐ d. 17.6 percent.   _____

Conclusion   4   Phobias are considered a psychiatric illness because
☐ a. they are complex.
☐ b. they are treatable only at the National Institute of Mental Health.
☐ c. they are an unrealistic overreaction to objects and situations.
☐ d. they are contagious.   _____

Clarifying Devices   5   The list of phobias is presented
☐ a. alphabetically.
☐ b. from least to most severe.
☐ c. from most to least severe.
☐ d. in the order of importance.   _____

Vocabulary in Context   6   Disproportionate means
☐ a. out of proportion.
☐ b. able to be measured.
☐ c. disrespectful.
☐ d. extremely large.   _____

Add your scores for questions 1–6. Enter the total here and on the graph on page 217.   **Total Score**   _____

96 Just Rolling Along

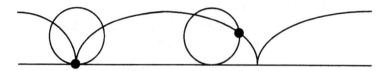

Here is a thought experiment to test your spatial visualization skills. Imagine a rolling bicycle wheel with a painted red spot on its rim, and trace out the path or curve followed by the red spot as the bicycle wheel moves along. This curve, well-known and much studied since the time of Galileo in the 1600s, is called the cycloid, and it has a variety of interesting properties.

If you found the rolling-circle thought experiment too difficult, you can generate a more tangible cycloid by attaching a pen to a bicycle wheel so that the pen is perpendicular to the wheel. Now roll the wheel along next to a piece of paper and the pen will trace out the loops, or arches, of the cycloid for you.

Two diverse properties of this graceful curve include the fact it is the strongest shape for the arch of a bridge, and that an object rolling down the curve will reach the bottom in the same time regardless at which point on the cycloid it begins its journey. A geometrical oddity is that the length of one complete arch equals the perimeter of the square that could be circumscribed around the circle that generated the arch.

Can the cycloid be represented by a mathematical equation in the manner in which lines, circles, parabolas, and other curves are expressed algebraically? Yes, although the equation involved is very complicated and is not ordinarily studied until a senior year mathematics class. The complexity of the cycloid's equation, however, need not prevent you from appreciating its <u>aesthetic</u> appeal nor perhaps reading more about the role it played in the history of mathematics.

Main Idea	1	Answer	Score
	Mark the *main idea*	M	15
	Mark the statement that is *too broad*	B	5
	Mark the statement that is *too narrow*	N	5

a. Many mathematical curves are attractive in appearance. ☐ _____

b. The cycloid can be used as the shape of an arch. ☐ _____

c. The cycloid, generated by a point on a rolling circle, has a variety of properties. ☐ _____

Subject Matter　**2**　This passage is mostly concerned with
- [ ] a. the properties of all algebraic curves.
- [ ] b. the properties of a certain type of mathematical curve.
- [ ] c. geometrical oddities shown by curves.
- [ ] d. figuring out the equation of the cycloid.

　　　　　　　　　　　　　　　　　　　　　　　_____

Supporting
Details　　　**3**　The black dots in the illustration show
- [ ] a. two points on a wheel as it turns.
- [ ] b. the path of a bouncing ball.
- [ ] c. two bicycle wheels.
- [ ] d. two solutions to a cycloid equation.

　　　　　　　　　　　　　　　　　　　　　　　_____

Conclusion　　**4**　It is reasonable to assume from the passage that
- [ ] a. cycloids were discovered only recently .
- [ ] b. you cannot construct an arch unless you use a cycloid.
- [ ] c. many curves can be generated by points that move in different ways.
- [ ] d. the cycloid can only be drawn with a bicycle wheel.

　　　　　　　　　　　　　　　　　　　　　　　_____

Clarifying
Devices　　　**5**　The passage shows how a cycloid is formed by
- [ ] a. using an illustration.
- [ ] b. giving a verbal description.
- [ ] c. using an illustration and a verbal description.
- [ ] d. comparing it to more familiar kinds of curves.　_____

Vocabulary
in Context　　**6**　In this passage the word <u>aesthetic</u> means
- [ ] a. practical or down to earth.
- [ ] b. emotional.
- [ ] c. intellectual.
- [ ] d. artistic or beautiful.

　　　　　　　　　　　　　　　　　　　　　　　_____

Add your scores for questions 1–6. Enter the total here　Total
and on the graph on page 217.　　　　　　　　Score　_____

97 Keep Those Teeth Clean!

You probably are aware of proper dental hygiene practices such as those taught to children: to brush the teeth at least twice daily, to floss every day, to eat nutritious foods, and to have teeth professionally cleaned twice a year. Proper oral hygiene is important to prevent periodontal disease, or gum disease, caused by different types of bacteria that reside in the mouth. When bacteria are allowed to develop and strengthen, high levels of toxins are produced and infection and <u>inflammation</u> of the gums follows. This inflammation of the gums, marked by redness and bleeding, is called gingivitis and is the first stage of periodontal disease. If not properly treated, gingivitis can progress to a more advanced gum disease known as periodontitis, or pyorrhea, in which the gum tissues and bone that support the teeth dissolve, eventually leading to tooth loss.

Proper brushing and flossing remove some bacteria from the mouth and ensure that the remaining bacteria cannot progress to dangerous levels. When brushing and flossing are absent from daily dental care, plaque—a sticky yellow-white film consisting of bacteria, small particles, proteins, and mucus—accumulates on the gums and teeth. Over time, plaque mineralizes and calcifies, or hardens, into tartar, and then it cannot be removed by brushing or flossing.

Prevention of and treatments for periodontal disease range from simple cleaning and scaling to painful and expensive surgical procedures that involve cutting the gums away from the teeth to remove deeply imbedded bacteria, to replace lost bone tissue, to perform gum grafts, and in some instances, to bond the teeth together for increased stability. So which situation does it make more sense to choose— prevention now or treatment later?

Main Idea	1		
		Answer	**Score**
	Mark the *main idea*	M	15
	Mark the statement that is *too broad*	B	5
	Mark the statement that is *too narrow*	N	5

a. Proper oral hygiene includes brushing, flossing, and professional teeth cleaning. ☐ _____

b. Periodontal disease is often a serious problem. ☐ _____

c. Periodontal disease occurs in different stages and has varying treatments. ☐ _____

Score 15 points for each correct answer.   **Score**

Subject Matter   **2**   The purpose of this passage is to
- ☐ a. describe types of bacteria in the mouth.
- ☐ b. discuss the causes and treatment of periodontal disease.
- ☐ c. explain plaque and tartar.
- ☐ d. compare gingivitis with periodontitis.   _____

Supporting Details   **3**   The early stage of periodontal disease is called
- ☐ a. gingivitis.
- ☐ b. plaque.
- ☐ c. periodontitis.
- ☐ d. tartar.   _____

Conclusion   **4**   In the last sentence of the passage, the author suggests that if you suffer from periodontal disease,
- ☐ a. the cost and pain involved will be great.
- ☐ b. you have no one to blame but yourself.
- ☐ c. the gums will become inflamed and reddened.
- ☐ d. your teeth will loosen due to bone loss.   _____

Clarifying Devices   **5**   The first two paragraphs are developed primarily through
- ☐ a. defining terms in order of importance.
- ☐ b. using various persuasive techniques.
- ☐ c. describing the stages in a process.
- ☐ d. presenting questions and answers.   _____

Vocabulary in Context   **6**   In this passage <u>inflammation</u> means
- ☐ a. a reddened, diseased condition.
- ☐ b. the state of bursting into flames.
- ☐ c. a lessening of infection.
- ☐ d. a treatment for disease.   _____

Add your scores for questions 1–6. Enter the total here and on the graph on page 217.   **Total Score**   _____

98 The City on the Rise

Although many North American cities can boast of falling crime rates and balanced municipal budgets, the U.S. Department of Housing and Urban Development reports that middle-class families continue to move to the suburbs. In the 1990s suburbs contained 75 percent more families than did cities, compared with 25 percent more in 1970. Though salvaging the North American city as a place to live may seem impossible, many experts believe that <u>rejuvenated</u> cities can alleviate problems created by the vast suburban communities and could become attractive places to live for many types of people.

Some theorists say that the information age is giving cities this opportunity to grow. As e-mail and the Internet eliminate commuting to a corporate headquarters, a new generation of teleworkers, Web entrepreneurs, and knowledge-based professionals will have the freedom to live where they choose. This opportunity was once seen as the death knell for cities, as it was thought that people would move away from the cities to live in small towns, mountain villages, or remote getaways. But the exact opposite may prove true. Locational freedom means people can choose to live where it is pleasant, and for some or even many, that place is the city. A city with advanced telecommunications services, proximity to universities and libraries, neighborhoods that can be navigated on foot, concert halls, museums, and restaurants that are still open at 3 A.M. will be able to compete with the sprawling suburbs. Some experts say that the demand for an intense, active, vibrant, diverse atmosphere will increase as information technology spreads. And this sort of atmosphere is exactly what healthy cities will be ready to provide.

Main Idea	1		Answer	Score
	Mark the *main idea*		M	15
	Mark the statement that is *too broad*		B	5
	Mark the statement that is *too narrow*		N	5

a. The North American city can be a nice place to live. ☐ ____

b. More families live in the suburbs than in the cities. ☐ ____

c. The information age may provide the opportunity for cities to grow. ☐ ____

Score 15 points for each correct answer.   **Score**

Subject Matter   **2**   This passage is mainly concerned with
- ☐ a. why city schools are a problem to population growth.
- ☐ b. cities of the present.
- ☐ c. cities of the future.
- ☐ d. lowering city taxes.   _____

Supporting Details   **3**   Between the 1970s and 1990s the number of families living in cities
- ☐ a. declined.
- ☐ b. increased.
- ☐ c. did not change.
- ☐ d. was never specifically counted.   _____

Conclusion   **4**   This passage leads the reader to believe that
- ☐ a. the death knell has rung for cities.
- ☐ b. restaurants will be open all night.
- ☐ c. cities will turn into sprawling suburbs.
- ☐ d. cities may experience an increase in middle-class population.   _____

Clarifying Devices   **5**   The information in the first paragraph of this passage is expressed through
- ☐ a. a list of facts only.
- ☐ b. an anecdote about a personal experience.
- ☐ c. a series of steps in a process.
- ☐ d. a mix of fact and opinion.   _____

Vocabulary in Context   **6**   In this passage <u>rejuvenated</u> means
- ☐ a. rebuilt from scratch.
- ☐ b. made young again.
- ☐ c. made vigorous again.
- ☐ d. improved by planting trees.   _____

Add your scores for questions 1–6. Enter the total here and on the graph on page 217.   Total Score _____

99 The Challenge of Fitting In

Vienna at the end of the 18th century was a city of great musical importance. In addition to orchestras that performed in public capacities, many nobles also maintained their own private orchestras for which they constantly sought new supplies of music, generally commissioning local talented artists to supply it. This should have been an ideal climate for geniuses such as Mozart and Beethoven to thrive in, but for different reasons both had trouble fitting into the Viennese musical community.

Mozart was a true musical prodigy, playing the harpsichord by age three and composing his first minuet at six. In 1763, when the boy was only seven, his ambitious father began touring with him to musical capitals across Europe, where he performed—often his original compositions—to great acclaim. But Mozart was never regarded as highly in his native Austria, where Italian musicians were often given preference, and never received commissions <u>commensurate</u> with his talents. He lived in Vienna from 1781 to his death in 1791, composing symphonies, concertos, and operas in remarkable quantities, but kept by internal intrigues from significant commissions at the Viennese court. Profligate with money as well, Mozart was a pauper when he died at age 36.

Beethoven, who was 14 years younger than Mozart, also exhibited great musical talent at an early age, and he was able to study piano and music theory in Vienna as a young man. But many of his compositions, including several symphonies, were so daring and original that they were not initially critical successes there; and though popular with the music public, Beethoven never entered into a nobleman's service. His real tragedy, however, was his deafness, which began to manifest itself before he was 30 and soon became total. This affliction, together with his often gloomy personality, eventually isolated him from the active musical life of Vienna.

Main Idea   1

	Answer	Score
Mark the *main idea*	M	15
Mark the statement that is *too broad*	B	5
Mark the statement that is *too narrow*	N	5

a. Vienna was a great musical capital. ☐ _____

b. Mozart and Beethoven both showed early talent. ☐ _____

c. Mozart and Beethoven had troubles fitting in to Vienna's musical life. ☐ _____

Subject Matter   2   This passage mostly focuses on
- ☐ a. the musical community in Vienna.
- ☐ b. Mozart's and Beethoven's early childhood successes.
- ☐ c. Mozart's and Beethoven's experiences in Vienna.
- ☐ d. Mozart's and Beethoven's compositions.   _____

Supporting Details   3   Mozart and Beethoven were both composing in the
- ☐ a. second half of the 17th century.
- ☐ b. first half of the 18th century.
- ☐ c. second half of the 18th century.
- ☐ d. first half of the 19th century.   _____

Conclusion   4   A good way to succeed in Vienna was to
- ☐ a. be a child star.
- ☐ b. write works commissioned by a patron.
- ☐ c. teach piano.
- ☐ d. compose symphonies.   _____

Clarifying Devices   5   The events in paragraphs two and three are mostly presented
- ☐ a. in spatial order.
- ☐ b. in time order.
- ☐ c. from least to most important.
- ☐ d. from most to least important.   _____

Vocabulary in Context   6   <u>Commensurate</u> means
- ☐ a. carefully measuring.
- ☐ b. less than.
- ☐ c. more than.
- ☐ d. equal to.   _____

Add your scores for questions 1–6. Enter the total here and on the graph on page 217.   Total Score   _____

100 Putting the Pieces Together

An entire category of mathematical recreations involves dissection puzzles, those tantalizing and sometimes infuriating activities in which you must cut one figure into pieces in order to transform it into something else. As a very simple example, a puzzle might involve transforming a square into a triangle by cutting the square into two pieces along the diagonal. In most dissection puzzles, the number of cuts is specified but determining their location is part of the problem left to the puzzler.

In the illustration is a Greek cross with a shaded "hole" the same size as one of the five squares that, taken together, create this type of cross. The dissection puzzle is to cut the cross into four parts so that the parts can be reassembled into a square. The solution shown is fairly simple once you know it—extend each side of the shaded square until you meet a vertex, or corner, of the cross, and then arrange the four pieces as shown in the final diagram of the illustration. The solution reveals the fact that the location of the square hole in the cross is by no means random, as its position and <u>orientation</u> must be such that the extensions of its sides meet the appropriate vertices.

Dissection puzzles similar to this one can be found in books of mathematical recreations and provide people with hours of enjoyment in addition to sharpening visual thinking skills. If this small taste of dissecting intrigues you, you may well become quite addicted to solving and perhaps even creating puzzles of this type.

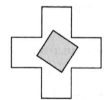

Main Idea 1 ────────────────────────────────

	Answer	Score
Mark the *main idea*	M	15
Mark the statement that is *too broad*	B	5
Mark the statement that is *too narrow*	N	5

a. A dissection puzzle involves cutting something into parts and then reassembling the parts. ☐ ____

b. Squares can be reassembled as triangles. ☐ ____

c. Solving geometrical puzzles can be quite addictive. ☐ ____

Score 15 points for each correct answer.   Score

Subject Matter   **2**   Another good title for this passage would be
     ☐ a. Cutting Shapes into Four Parts.
     ☐ b. Transforming a Cross.
     ☐ c. Properties of Cross-Shaped Figures.
     ☐ d. Creating Your Own Dissection Puzzles.   _____

Supporting   **3**   The solution to the Greek cross puzzle is a
Details   ☐ a. square made of four pieces.
     ☐ b. square made of two triangles.
     ☐ c. Greek cross without a hole in it.
     ☐ d. Greek cross with four numbered sections.   _____

Conclusion   **4**   Solving dissection puzzles like those described in
the passage requires a high degree of
     ☐ a. manual dexterity.
     ☐ b. algebraic thinking.
     ☐ c. visual thinking.
     ☐ d. ability to follow the steps in a process.   _____

Clarifying   **5**   A good way to better understand the first
Devices   dissection puzzle described in the passage is to
     ☐ a. look up the definitions of some words.
     ☐ b. ask someone to solve the puzzle for you.
     ☐ c. skim the remaining part of the passage.
     ☐ d. make a drawing or sketch of the puzzle.   _____

Vocabulary   **6**   In this passage <u>orientation</u> means
in Context   ☐ a. side length.
     ☐ b. area.
     ☐ c. angle.
     ☐ d. perimeter.   _____

Add your scores for questions 1–6. Enter the total here   Total
and on the graph on page 217.   Score   _____

Answer Keys

Answer Key: Passages 1–25

Passage 1:	1a. **N**	1b. **M**	1c. **B**	2. **a**	3. **c**	4. **b**	5. **d**	6. **b**
Passage 2:	1a. **M**	1b. **B**	1c. **N**	2. **c**	3. **d**	4. **b**	5. **a**	6. **b**
Passage 3:	1a. **M**	1b. **N**	1c. **B**	2. **d**	3. **c**	4. **a**	5. **a**	6. **b**
Passage 4:	1a. **N**	1b. **M**	1c. **B**	2. **b**	3. **c**	4. **a**	5. **d**	6. **c**
Passage 5:	1a. **N**	1b. **B**	1c. **M**	2. **c**	3. **d**	4. **b**	5. **a**	6. **b**
Passage 6:	1a. **B**	1b. **M**	1c. **N**	2. **b**	3. **d**	4. **a**	5. **b**	6. **d**
Passage 7:	1a. **N**	1b. **M**	1c. **B**	2. **d**	3. **b**	4. **d**	5. **b**	6. **c**
Passage 8:	1a. **B**	1b. **N**	1c. **M**	2. **c**	3. **c**	4. **a**	5. **b**	6. **b**
Passage 9:	1a. **M**	1b. **B**	1c. **N**	2. **b**	3. **a**	4. **b**	5. **d**	6. **b**
Passage 10:	1a. **M**	1b. **B**	1c. **N**	2. **d**	3. **a**	4. **c**	5. **a**	6. **b**
Passage 11:	1a. **M**	1b. **B**	1c. **N**	2. **c**	3. **a**	4. **c**	5. **d**	6. **b**
Passage 12:	1a. **B**	1b. **N**	1c. **M**	2. **b**	3. **d**	4. **a**	5. **b**	6. **c**
Passage 13:	1a. **M**	1b. **B**	1c. **N**	2. **b**	3. **d**	4. **b**	5. **b**	6. **a**
Passage 14:	1a. **N**	1b. **B**	1c. **M**	2. **d**	3. **c**	4. **b**	5. **a**	6. **d**
Passage 15:	1a. **B**	1b. **N**	1c. **M**	2. **c**	3. **d**	4. **c**	5. **a**	6. **b**
Passage 16:	1a. **B**	1b. **N**	1c. **M**	2. **c**	3. **a**	4. **c**	5. **d**	6. **d**
Passage 17:	1a. **M**	1b. **B**	1c. **N**	2. **d**	3. **c**	4. **a**	5. **b**	6. **c**
Passage 18:	1a. **B**	1b. **N**	1c. **M**	2. **b**	3. **d**	4. **a**	5. **c**	6. **a**
Passage 19:	1a. **N**	1b. **B**	1c. **M**	2. **d**	3. **b**	4. **b**	5. **a**	6. **d**
Passage 20:	1a. **N**	1b. **B**	1c. **M**	2. **c**	3. **d**	4. **d**	5. **a**	6. **b**
Passage 21:	1a. **N**	1b. **M**	1c. **B**	2. **a**	3. **c**	4. **b**	5. **c**	6. **b**
Passage 22:	1a. **N**	1b. **B**	1c. **M**	2. **a**	3. **c**	4. **a**	5. **b**	6. **b**
Passage 23:	1a. **M**	1b. **N**	1c. **B**	2. **a**	3. **a**	4. **a**	5. **c**	6. **b**
Passage 24:	1a. **M**	1b. **B**	1c. **N**	2. **d**	3. **c**	4. **c**	5. **b**	6. **a**
Passage 25:	1a. **M**	1b. **N**	1c. **B**	2. **a**	3. **d**	4. **b**	5. **c**	6. **a**

Answer Key: Passages 26–50

Passage 26:	1a. **M**	1b. **B**	1c. **N**	2. **b**	3. **a**	4. **a**	5. **c**	6. **a**
Passage 27:	1a. **M**	1b. **B**	1c. **N**	2. **c**	3. **c**	4. **b**	5. **b**	6. **c**
Passage 28:	1a. **B**	1b. **M**	1c. **N**	2. **b**	3. **d**	4. **a**	5. **c**	6. **b**
Passage 29:	1a. **B**	1b. **M**	1c. **N**	2. **a**	3. **d**	4. **d**	5. **a**	6. **a**
Passage 30:	1a. **N**	1b. **B**	1c. **M**	2. **a**	3. **c**	4. **b**	5. **a**	6. **c**
Passage 31:	1a. **M**	1b. **N**	1c. **B**	2. **c**	3. **d**	4. **a**	5. **a**	6. **c**
Passage 32:	1a. **B**	1b. **N**	1c. **M**	2. **d**	3. **c**	4. **d**	5. **c**	6. **c**
Passage 33:	1a. **B**	1b. **M**	1c. **N**	2. **b**	3. **d**	4. **a**	5. **a**	6. **c**
Passage 34:	1a. **M**	1b. **N**	1c. **B**	2. **b**	3. **d**	4. **d**	5. **a**	6. **d**
Passage 35:	1a. **M**	1b. **B**	1c. **N**	2. **b**	3. **b**	4. **d**	5. **b**	6. **a**
Passage 36:	1a. **M**	1b. **B**	1c. **N**	2. **c**	3. **d**	4. **a**	5. **b**	6. **a**
Passage 37:	1a. **B**	1b. **M**	1c. **N**	2. **d**	3. **c**	4. **a**	5. **b**	6. **b**
Passage 38:	1a. **B**	1b. **M**	1c. **N**	2. **d**	3. **a**	4. **b**	5. **d**	6. **c**
Passage 39:	1a. **M**	1b. **N**	1c. **B**	2. **c**	3. **b**	4. **a**	5. **d**	6. **b**
Passage 40:	1a. **B**	1b. **M**	1c. **N**	2. **c**	3. **d**	4. **a**	5. **c**	6. **a**
Passage 41:	1a. **N**	1b. **B**	1c. **M**	2. **c**	3. **b**	4. **b**	5. **d**	6. **c**
Passage 42:	1a. **N**	1b. **M**	1c. **B**	2. **d**	3. **a**	4. **b**	5. **a**	6. **b**
Passage 43:	1a. **N**	1b. **B**	1c. **M**	2. **b**	3. **b**	4. **d**	5. **b**	6. **a**
Passage 44:	1a. **M**	1b. **B**	1c. **N**	2. **b**	3. **b**	4. **d**	5. **c**	6. **d**
Passage 45:	1a. **B**	1b. **N**	1c. **M**	2. **c**	3. **b**	4. **d**	5. **a**	6. **b**
Passage 46:	1a. **M**	1b. **B**	1c. **N**	2. **c**	3. **c**	4. **a**	5. **a**	6. **c**
Passage 47:	1a. **B**	1b. **N**	1c. **M**	2. **c**	3. **b**	4. **c**	5. **a**	6. **d**
Passage 48:	1a. **B**	1b. **M**	1c. **N**	2. **b**	3. **b**	4. **b**	5. **d**	6. **c**
Passage 49:	1a. **M**	1b. **B**	1c. **N**	2. **c**	3. **d**	4. **a**	5. **d**	6. **b**
Passage 50:	1a. **N**	1b. **B**	1c. **M**	2. **a**	3. **d**	4. **a**	5. **c**	6. **a**

Answer Key: Passages 51–75

Passage 51:	1a. **M**	1b. **B**	1c. **N**	2. **b**	3. **b**	4. **b**	5. **a**	6. **c**
Passage 52:	1a. **B**	1b. **N**	1c. **M**	2. **b**	3. **c**	4. **a**	5. **b**	6. **d**
Passage 53:	1a. **B**	1b. **N**	1c. **M**	2. **b**	3. **b**	4. **a**	5. **a**	6. **a**
Passage 54:	1a. **M**	1b. **B**	1c. **N**	2. **d**	3. **a**	4. **b**	5. **c**	6. **b**
Passage 55:	1a. **B**	1b. **N**	1c. **M**	2. **b**	3. **a**	4. **c**	5. **a**	6. **d**
Passage 56:	1a. **B**	1b. **N**	1c. **M**	2. **d**	3. **c**	4. **b**	5. **d**	6. **a**
Passage 57:	1a. **M**	1b. **N**	1c. **B**	2. **c**	3. **b**	4. **a**	5. **d**	6. **c**
Passage 58:	1a. **M**	1b. **B**	1c. **N**	2. **d**	3. **c**	4. **c**	5. **b**	6. **a**
Passage 59:	1a. **N**	1b. **B**	1c. **M**	2. **d**	3. **c**	4. **b**	5. **b**	6. **a**
Passage 60:	1a. **B**	1b. **M**	1c. **N**	2. **a**	3. **b**	4. **c**	5. **c**	6. **d**
Passage 61:	1a. **B**	1b. **N**	1c. **M**	2. **b**	3. **c**	4. **a**	5. **d**	6. **c**
Passage 62:	1a. **N**	1b. **B**	1c. **M**	2. **c**	3. **c**	4. **a**	5. **b**	6. **d**
Passage 63:	1a. **M**	1b. **B**	1c. **N**	2. **c**	3. **c**	4. **b**	5. **d**	6. **a**
Passage 64:	1a. **B**	1b. **M**	1c. **N**	2. **c**	3. **d**	4. **b**	5. **a**	6. **b**
Passage 65:	1a. **N**	1b. **M**	1c. **B**	2. **c**	3. **d**	4. **a**	5. **b**	6. **b**
Passage 66:	1a. **B**	1b. **N**	1c. **M**	2. **a**	3. **b**	4. **d**	5. **c**	6. **b**
Passage 67:	1a. **B**	1b. **M**	1c. **N**	2. **d**	3. **d**	4. **a**	5. **b**	6. **b**
Passage 68:	1a. **M**	1b. **B**	1c. **N**	2. **b**	3. **d**	4. **c**	5. **a**	6. **d**
Passage 69:	1a. **M**	1b. **N**	1c. **B**	2. **b**	3. **b**	4. **b**	5. **b**	6. **d**
Passage 70:	1a. **B**	1b. **M**	1c. **N**	2. **c**	3. **a**	4. **b**	5. **d**	6. **c**
Passage 71:	1a. **N**	1b. **M**	1c. **B**	2. **b**	3. **a**	4. **d**	5. **c**	6. **b**
Passage 72:	1a. **B**	1b. **M**	1c. **N**	2. **b**	3. **c**	4. **b**	5. **b**	6. **d**
Passage 73:	1a. **M**	1b. **N**	1c. **B**	2. **c**	3. **a**	4. **d**	5. **b**	6. **a**
Passage 74:	1a. **M**	1b. **B**	1c. **N**	2. **d**	3. **a**	4. **b**	5. **c**	6. **a**
Passage 75:	1a. **N**	1b. **B**	1c. **M**	2. **d**	3. **c**	4. **a**	5. **b**	6. **c**

Passage 76:	1a. N	1b. B	1c. M	2. b	3. d	4. a	5. c	6. c
Passage 77:	1a. B	1b. M	1c. N	2. c	3. c	4. b	5. b	6. b
Passage 78:	1a. M	1b. N	1c. B	2. c	3. d	4. a	5. b	6. d
Passage 79:	1a. B	1b. N	1c. M	2. b	3. c	4. d	5. c	6. b
Passage 80:	1a. N	1b. B	1c. M	2. d	3. d	4. a	5. a	6. b
Passage 81:	1a. M	1b. N	1c. B	2. c	3. d	4. a	5. c	6. b
Passage 82:	1a. B	1b. M	1c. N	2. b	3. c	4. b	5. d	6. c
Passage 83:	1a. M	1b. N	1c. B	2. c	3. a	4. d	5. c	6. b
Passage 84:	1a. M	1b. N	1c. B	2. b	3. c	4. d	5. a	6. c
Passage 85:	1a. N	1b. B	1c. M	2. d	3. a	4. c	5. d	6. d
Passage 86:	1a. N	1b. B	1c. M	2. b	3. a	4. d	5. a	6. b
Passage 87:	1a. M	1b. B	1c. N	2. a	3. c	4. b	5. b	6. c
Passage 88:	1a. B	1b. M	1c. N	2. d	3. b	4. b	5. c	6. a
Passage 89:	1a. M	1b. N	1c. B	2. b	3. b	4. a	5. d	6. c
Passage 90:	1a. N	1b. M	1c. B	2. c	3. c	4. b	5. a	6. d
Passage 91:	1a. M	1b. B	1c. N	2. b	3. c	4. c	5. a	6. d
Passage 92:	1a. B	1b. N	1c. M	2. b	3. a	4. a	5. b	6. c
Passage 93:	1a. B	1b. M	1c. N	2. d	3. c	4. a	5. b	6. b
Passage 94:	1a. M	1b. B	1c. N	2. a	3. d	4. d	5. b	6. a
Passage 95:	1a. N	1b. B	1c. M	2. d	3. c	4. c	5. b	6. a
Passage 96:	1a. B	1b. N	1c. M	2. b	3. a	4. c	5. c	6. d
Passage 97:	1a. N	1b. B	1c. M	2. b	3. a	4. b	5. c	6. a
Passage 98:	1a. B	1b. N	1c. M	2. c	3. a	4. d	5. d	6. c
Passage 99:	1a. N	1b. M	1c. B	2. c	3. c	4. b	5. b	6. d
Passage 100:	1a. M	1b. N	1c. B	2. b	3. a	4. c	5. d	6. c

Diagnostic Charts
For Student Correction

Diagnostic Chart: Passages 1–25

Directions: For each passage, write your answers to the left of the dotted line in the blocks for each skill category. Then correct your answers using the Answer Key on page 204. If your answer is correct, do not make any more marks in the block. If your answer is incorrect, write the letter of the correct answer to the right of the dotted line.

	Categories of Comprehension Skills								
	1 Main Idea			**2**	**3**		**4**	**5**	**6**
	Statement a	Statement b	Statement c	Subject Matter	Supporting Details	Conclusion	Clarifying Devices	Vocabulary in Context	
Passage 1									
Passage 2									
Passage 3									
Passage 4									
Passage 5									
Passage 6									
Passage 7									
Passage 8									
Passage 9									
Passage 10									
Passage 11									
Passage 12									
Passage 13									
Passage 14									
Passage 15									
Passage 16									
Passage 17									
Passage 18									
Passage 19									
Passage 20									
Passage 21									
Passage 22									
Passage 23									
Passage 24									
Passage 25									

Diagnostic Chart: Passages 26–50

Directions: For each passage, write your answers to the left of the dotted line in the blocks for each skill category. Then correct your answers using the Answer Key on page 205. If your answer is correct, do not make any more marks in the block. If your answer is incorrect, write the letter of the correct answer to the right of the dotted line.

| | Categories of Comprehension Skills | | | | | | | | |
| | 1 Main Idea | | | 2 | 3 | 4 | 5 | 6 | |
	Statement a	Statement b	Statement c	Subject Matter	Supporting Details	Conclusion	Clarifying Devices	Vocabulary in Context	
Passage 26									
Passage 27									
Passage 28									
Passage 29									
Passage 30									
Passage 31									
Passage 32									
Passage 33									
Passage 34									
Passage 35									
Passage 36									
Passage 37									
Passage 38									
Passage 39									
Passage 40									
Passage 41									
Passage 42									
Passage 43									
Passage 44									
Passage 45									
Passage 46									
Passage 47									
Passage 48									
Passage 49									
Passage 50									

Diagnostic Chart: Passages 51–75

Directions: For each passage, write your answers to the left of the dotted line in the blocks for each skill category. Then correct your answers using the Answer Key on page 206. If your answer is correct, do not make any more marks in the block. If your answer is incorrect, write the letter of the correct answer to the right of the dotted line.

	Categories of Comprehension Skills							
	1 Main Idea			**2**	**3**	**4**	**5**	**6**
	Statement a	Statement b	Statement c	Subject Matter	Supporting Details	Conclusion	Clarifying Devices	Vocabulary in Context
Passage 51								
Passage 52								
Passage 53								
Passage 54								
Passage 55								
Passage 56								
Passage 57								
Passage 58								
Passage 59								
Passage 60								
Passage 61								
Passage 62								
Passage 63								
Passage 64								
Passage 65								
Passage 66								
Passage 67								
Passage 68								
Passage 69								
Passage 70								
Passage 71								
Passage 72								
Passage 73								
Passage 74								
Passage 75								

Diagnostic Chart: Passages 76–100

Directions: For each passage, write your answers to the left of the dotted line in the blocks for each skill category. Then correct your answers using the Answer Key on page 207. If your answer is correct, do not make any more marks in the block. If your answer is incorrect, write the letter of the correct answer to the right of the dotted line.

	Categories of Comprehension Skills								
	1 Main Idea			2	3	4	5	6	
	Statement a	Statement b	Statement c	Subject Matter	Supporting Details	Conclusion	Clarifying Devices	Vocabulary in Context	
Passage 76									
Passage 77									
Passage 78									
Passage 79									
Passage 80									
Passage 81									
Passage 82									
Passage 83									
Passage 84									
Passage 85									
Passage 86									
Passage 87									
Passage 88									
Passage 89									
Passage 90									
Passage 91									
Passage 92									
Passage 93									
Passage 94									
Passage 95									
Passage 96									
Passage 97									
Passage 98									
Passage 99									
Passage 100									

Progress Graphs

Progress Graph: Passages 1–25

Directions: Write your Total Score for each passage in the comprehension score box under the number of the passage. Then plot your score on the graph itself by putting a small *x* on the line directly above the number of the passage, across from the score you got for that passage. As you mark your score for each passage, graph your progress by drawing a line to connect the *x*'s.

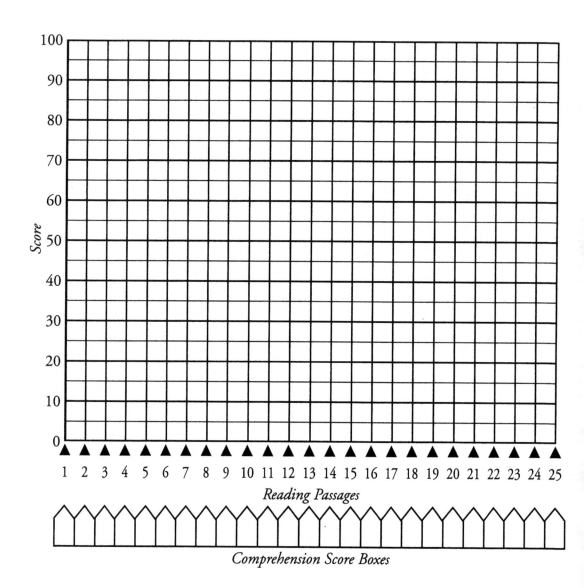

Reading Passages

Comprehension Score Boxes

Progress Graph: Passages 26–50

Directions: Write your Total Score for each passage in the comprehension score box under the number of the passage. Then plot your score on the graph itself by putting a small *x* on the line directly above the number of the passage, across from the score you got for that passage. As you mark your score for each passage, graph your progress by drawing a line to connect the *x*'s.

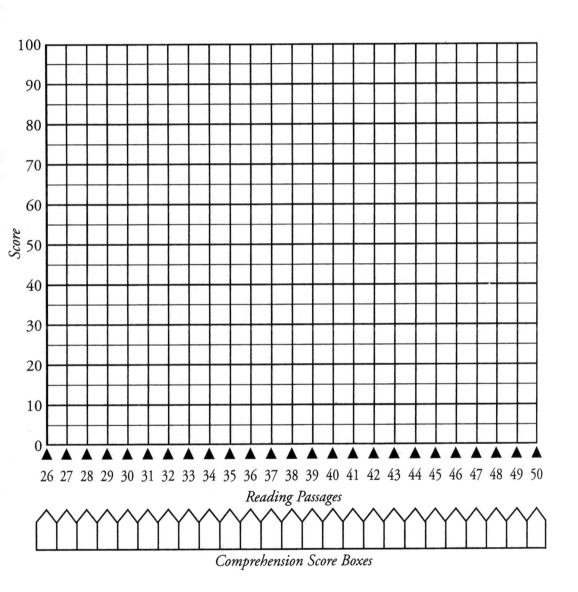

Reading Passages

Comprehension Score Boxes

Progress Graph: Passages 51–75

Directions: Write your Total Score for each passage in the comprehension score box under the number of the passage. Then plot your score on the graph itself by putting a small *x* on the line directly above the number of the passage, across from the score you got for that passage. As you mark your score for each passage, graph your progress by drawing a line to connect the *x*'s.

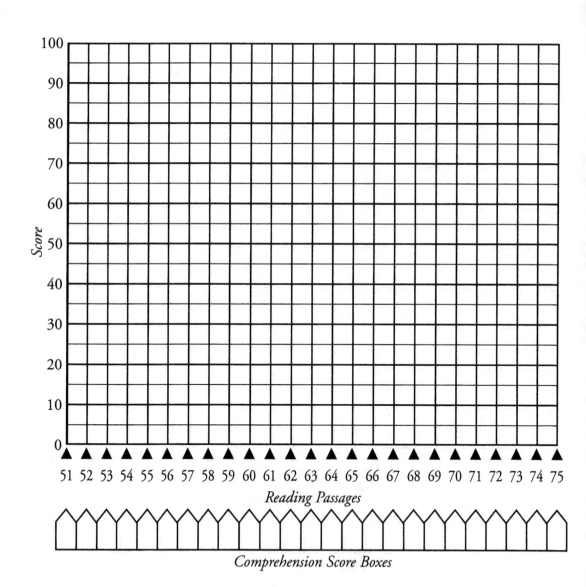

Reading Passages

Comprehension Score Boxes

Progress Graph: Passages 76–100

Directions: Write your Total Score for each passage in the comprehension score box under the number of the passage. Then plot your score on the graph itself by putting a small *x* on the line directly above the number of the passage, across from the score you got for that passage. As you mark your score for each passage, graph your progress by drawing a line to connect the *x*'s.

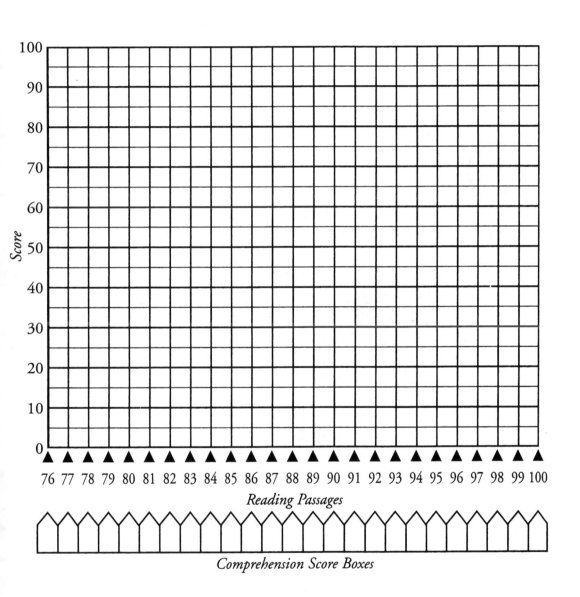